THE AMERICAN PRINTER
1787–1825

Rollo G. Silver

THE AMERICAN PRINTER
1787–1825

Published for the Bibliographical Society of the
University of Virginia

The University Press of Virginia
Charlottesville

TO ALICE

PREFACE

THIS volume describes the condition of the American printer during the years 1787 to 1825, his methods of work, the equipment he used, and the policies by which he conducted his business. He lived in a hard and critical time which demanded of him extraordinary stamina and versatility for survival; and he insisted on surviving. A practical realist, he saw the output of his printing press as a primary tool in the building of a new country. The fact that he had under his control the chief means of communication brought him pride in his craft, and he regarded his craft as a high profession. He was a formidable man; he loved his country simply and openly and believed that he was the equal of anyone. He knew the distress of the small businessman; often he did not make expenses, but he managed to bring the printing press into every part of an expanding society.

This is not a history of printing in America during the period, nor does the scope include the occupation of publishing. Here is a picture of the craft of printing between the colonial period and the arrival of mechanization. After 1825 the cylinder press and the use of power radically altered printing practices, though not as much, it should be understood, as do the electronic devices of today.

More people than one would have suspected have already contributed to our knowledge of American printing between 1787 and 1825. My debt to them is acknowledged, but not adequately, in the footnotes. As usual, those two great aids to bibliographical knowledge, the catalogues of antiquarian booksellers and the Photographic Service of the New York Public Library, have been most helpful. Particular thanks are also due to Mr. John Alden of the Boston Public Library, Dr. H. Richard Archer of the Chapin Library, Miss Margaret Hackett of the Boston Athenaeum, Mr. Thompson R. Harlow of the Connecticut Historical Society, Dr. Stephen T. Riley of the Massachusetts Historical Society, Dr. Clifford K. Shipton of the American Antiquarian Society, Mr. Roger E. Stoddard of the Houghton Library, Mr. Edwin Wolf, 2nd, of the Library Company of Philadelphia, and Mr. John Cook Wyllie of the University of Virginia Library.

I thank the Harvard University Press for permission to quote from Thomas W. Streeter's *Bibliography of Texas, 1795–1845* (copyright 1955 by Thomas W. Streeter), the firm of Harper & Row, Inc., for permission to quote from J. Henry Harper's *The House of Harper*, and the Bibliographical Society of America for permission to quote from Samuel M. Wilson's paper, "The 'Kentucky Gazette' and John Bradford," *Papers of the Bibliographical Society of America*, XXXI (1937), 110–14.

ROLLO G. SILVER

December 27, 1966
Boston, Massachusetts

CONTENTS

PLATES

The printers whose marks appear at the chapter openings are: Chapter 1, Samuel Green, New London, Connecticut; Chapter 2, Thomas Dickman, Greenfield, Massachusetts; Chapter 3, Belknap and Hall, Boston, Massachusetts; Chapter 4, Hosea Sprague, Boston, Massachusetts; Chapter 5, John Russell, Boston, Massachusetts; Chapter 6, Enoch Story, Philadelphia, Pennsylvania.

THE AMERICAN PRINTER
1787–1825

umble and trembling on his first
e victim of a rude initiation. Be-
ut, to look docile while emptying
: fellow apprentices and journey-
the customary "treat." Joseph T.
oole, New Hampshire, in 1796,

ly entrance into the office, before
ted the call for several days, but
ly and almost hourly annoyance,
mount of money I possessed was
eggs, crackers, cheese, &c. &c.[7]

ing Buckingham who had never
lly *compelled* to swallow them,
they were."[8] Initiation was not
op, but the duties of the appren-
ere were few boys who did not
terate, ragged, fatigued, the ap-
d the master's wife, swept floors,
ted pi, carded wool for ink balls,
as for wetting paper, and, as the
pelts used for ink balls.[9] These
the pressroom a characteristic
s expressed their bitterness and
r reminiscences, among them
f treading pelts is most realistic:

ested of the wool, immersed in
hen taken out, rinsed [wrung]
far as practicable, for *treading*.
apers and rolled under the foot,
d until every particle of moisture
dered the skin as pliable and
as in order for a Printer's ball.
n epoch in a printers devil's life
til *odor* is lost in forgetfulness.[11]

5.   [8] *Ibid.*
meon Ide (Rutland, Vt., 1931), p. 26.
Bookmaking (New York, 1894), p. 35.

CHAPTER 1

APPRENTICE, JOURNEYMAN, AND MASTER

AMERICAN businessmen of the late eighteenth century and early nineteenth century, consciously or unconsciously, conducted their business operations in the manner inherited from Europe. They adopted the European apprentice system, already hundreds of years old, and did little to change it, disregarding their modern experiences in a free world. Indentureship, despite its frequent inconvenience to masters and the possibility of brutal treatment and corruption of apprentices, survived. Beneath the surface of a pious society enslavement of young boys of the poorer classes took place in an environment that, at times, was sinister and immoral and, at best, totally unsuited to a new country that prided itself on the betterment of mankind. Its justification was the unique advantage to the master, who had a constant supply of labor, to many parents who could not support their sons, and to the boy who had no means of making a living except by learning a craft.

It was well understood: to become a craftsman was to endure the severe, long European discipline, to leave home early—in printing, for example, at the fourteenth year or even earlier. Occasionally, when opportunities were few or family troubles intervened, apprenticeship was postponed until the late teens. Nine indentures recorded for Baltimore printers between 1794 and 1799 show one boy beginning service at twelve years, one at thirteen, three at fourteen, one at fifteen, one at sixteen, one at seventeen, and one at eighteen.[1] Of ten known Boston apprenticeships between 1800 and 1825, one started at twelve, three at fourteen, four at fifteen, one at sixteen, and one at seventeen.[2] The figures were alike in large cities and small towns. Hamilton, in his fine study of the New York country printer, 1785–1830, found one apprenticeship beginning at seven, another at eighteen, but "the greatest number of cases fall between the ages of thirteen and fifteen," with the higher age "more frequently the case in the second half of the period."[3] Throughout the period covered by the present study most apprenticeships, following the limits set in the colonies, expired when the boy became twenty-one.

When a boy was apprenticed, his family usually received an indenture from his master. This contract, sometimes registered by the local authorities, was in reality a set of restrictions and controls according to approved ideas of behavior by which a boy was made a prisoner of the master. The indenture might be a brief, handwritten note of solace such as that given by Isaac Hill of the *New Hampshire Patriot*:

Concord, March 5, 1814.

Mr. Hill's respects to Mrs. ——, and would inform her that he will take her son, and instruct him in the art of printing, finding him food and clothing for his services; that, as he is left without a father, he will, as far as is in his power, endeavor to supply the place of a father, and interest himself in her son's favor whenever his aid can be of service or advantage; that, in his turn, he shall expect the faithful services of her son, who will make his master's interest his own; and so long as he does this, he shall never want for a protector and friend. Mr. Hill cannot conclude this without expressing his high sense of the worth and inflexible patriotism of her departed husband; and ardently prays that the virtues of the father may descend to the son.[4]

Or it might be a printed legal blank with the spaces for a particular trade to be filled in. The following example, besides showing a thoroughgoing belief in original sin in young boys, declares the

[1] Information in a letter from Professor Louise Hall of Duke University, Dec. 10, 1950.
[2] Rollo G. Silver, *The Boston Book Trade, 1800–1825* (New York, 1949), p. 4.
[3] Milton W. Hamilton, *The Country Printer* (New York, 1936), p. 30.
[4] *Moore's Historical, Biographical, and Miscellaneous Gatherings*, comp. John W. Moore (Concord, N.H., 1886), p. 110.

The apple-cheeked apprentice, [...] day at work, sometimes became t[...] sides learning to keep his mouth s[...] the slops, and to accept the jibes [...] men, he would be called upon for [...] Buckingham, apprenticed in Wa[...] described the indignity of his trial:

Two hours had not elapsed after [...] I was called upon "to treat." I resi[...] was at length overcome by the da[...] and more than half of the small a[...] expended for brandy, wine, sugar [...]

Then humiliated and defeated, yo[...] tasted brandy or wine "was liter[...] distasteful and nauseous though [...] always as coarse as this in every s[...] tice were always the same, and t[...] live in terror of their days. Semil[...] prentice ran errands for the shop a[...] kindled fires, washed type, distribu[...] carried water for cleaning as well [...] most degrading task of all, trod th[...] pelts, soaked in chamber lye, gav[...] reeking smell.[10] Former apprentice[...] described their miseries in the [...] Lewis G. Hoffman, whose account [...]

A Pelt was a dried sheepskin, di[...] the *slop pail* until well soaked, [...] by hand of the surface water, as [...] It was then rolled up in old news[...] changing the papers as was require[...] was expunged from it, which re[...] soft as a lady's glove. Then it w[...] Treading out a pair of skins was [...] which he will always remember u[...]

[7] *Personal Memoirs* (Boston, 1852), I, [...]
[9] Hamilton, p. 31; Louis W. Flanders, S[...]
[10] *American Dictionary of Printing and* [...]
[11] Hamilton, pp. 32–33.

Sections of these skins, stuffed with wool ("knocked up") and mounted on wood stocks, served to ink the type. About 1814 dressed deerskin began to replace pelts, thereby eliminating the necessity of treading.[12]

If an apprentice had patience, showed no fear, and had the mixture of compliance and tenacity his lot in life demanded, he could survive the first period of his indenture and begin to learn how to set type, ink type, and work the press. When he had still further adapted himself, he could become skillful enough to handle full-time jobs at case or at press. If a shop expanded and business grew, a capable boy could make headway rapidly. Uriel Crocker in 1811, two months after his apprenticeship began in Boston at the age of fifteen, became a full-time compositor when a new apprentice entered the shop. For his work at the case Crocker received twenty-five cents a thousand ems for all above four thousand set in a day. Since his daily rate ranged between six and seven thousand, he earned $180.02 for extra typesetting during the first four years of his apprenticeship. In 1817 Crocker, still an apprentice, became the shop foreman, supervising twenty compositors and pressmen as well as seven apprentices. For managing the seven-press printing office, he received two dollars a week. His ambitions were finally satisfied and he evidently achieved his goal, for when his term expired he became a partner in the firm.[13]

For an apprentice in a failing shop, there was another fate. Seven months after he started a Boston apprenticeship in 1822 at the age of sixteen David Clapp recorded his situation in his journal: "Mr. Cotton has dismissed his other apprentice, and I am now left alone, with neither master, journeyman, nor apprentice to work with." Later he wrote: "I still continue to work alone, with nobody but the mice, who scamper around the silent office as if they thought it had been deserted on purpose to oblige them."[14]

In general, the apprentice completed his term despite all manner of obstacles, but occasionally the bond was terminated before expiration: by agreement, by purchase of the bond, by violation of the

[12] *Autobiography of Thurlow Weed*, ed. Harriet A. Weed (Boston, 1884), I, 22.

[13] *Memorial of Uriel Crocker* [Boston, 1891], pp. 28–32, 37.

[14] William B. Trask, "Memoir of David Clapp," *New Eng. Hist. Gen. Reg.*, XLVIII (1894), 148.

bond by one of the parties, by the printer's removal or failure, or by the escape of the apprentice. Sometimes, as in the example of Simeon Ide, the apprentice who wished to become independent would buy his time from his own father.[15] A few boys, such as Joseph T. Buckingham, were not indented and therefore free.[16] The rest were obliged to stay in the same shop even if it was sold to another master or if they were mistreated, and, worse still, if they were constitutionally unfit for their tasks. Some masters made every effort to provide good training in a reasonably good environment, but often the system itself promoted waywardness and immorality. When runaway apprentices were sought by newspaper advertisments offering rewards, the rewards were so low that it may be inferred that the advertisements were warnings to prospective employers rather than honest efforts to secure return. The unfaithful apprentice was forced to seek employment in a distant town or city, at less than journeyman's wages, in a shop sometimes in poorer repute than his own.

Many printers hiring runaways also got help at minimum wages by hiring full-grown men (usually foreigners) as apprentices for short terms of twelve or fifteen months. The success of the runaways in obtaining work had a haphazard result: printers, aware that apprentices would leave, took on more than necessary, and soon the number of runaways increased enough to affect business competition. In 1803 the Baltimore Typographical Society unsuccessfully attempted to persuade the Philadelphia Typographical Society to concur in an address to parents and guardians "to prevent their placing so many boys as apprentices to the printing business." Thirteen years later the New York Typographical Society ordered a committee to "draft a pathetic address on the state of the business in which they shall persuade guardians and parents not to put their children to it." But apprenticeships did not decrease. The typographical societies, well cognizant of the unfair competition, frequently discussed the violation of the rules in hiring young men with incomplete apprenticeships ("half-way journeymen"). In 1810 a committee of the New York Typographical Society reported a considerable number of persons "working at the printing business in the capacity of journeymen" but "not considered as such by this

[15] Flanders, p. 31.   [16] I, 30.

society."[17] In the following year the society issued an address to the master printers declaring:

The practice of employing what is termed half-way journeymen in preference to those who have served their time, while it holds out encouragement to boys to elope from their masters as soon as they acquire a sufficient knowledge of the art to be enabled to earn their bread, is a great grievance to journeymen and almost certain ruin to the boys themselves. . . . It is an incontrovertible fact that nearly one-half who learn the trade are obliged to relinquish it and follow some other calling for support. Under the direct influence of these unwarranted practices, the professors of the noblest art with which this earth is blest have become *birds of passage* seeking a livelihood from Georgia to Maine.[18]

The Philadelphia Typographical Society, too, protested, but it was not until the 1830's that apprentices were required to serve out their terms before they were hired as journeymen.[19]

A resolute apprentice who fulfilled his obligations became a journeyman at the age of twenty-one or at the expiration of his indenture, an event celebrated by a "freedom treat":

When I was free, the journeymen claimed that I must give them a treat. I told them I would do so, but that it must be postponed until Saturday. We fixed up some tables in the attic of the printing-office, and I sent out and got some ham, corned beef, etc., etc. I also had lemonade, punch, and Jamaica rum. I bought a dozen bottles of Madeira wine and paid a dollar a bottle for it. The men, however, did not take kindly to the Madeira, but preferred the lemonade and the rum.[20]

This treat, it must be noted, may have been more elaborate than most because Uriel Crocker, the apprentice who was host in 1817, supervised the shop.

As a journeyman a printer was free to work where he wished or, if he possessed funds, to set up his own shop as a master. His passport to independence was his indenture, sometimes accompanied by a letter of recommendation such as this:

I hereby certify that the within named David Graham served the term of six years as an apprentice to the printing business, with me, and conducted himself decently, soberly, and honestly. He was with me five months previous to the date of his indenture, upon

---

[17] George E. Barnett, "The Printers," *Am. Ec. Assn. Quart.*, 3rd ser., X, No. 3 (1909), 160n.–62.

[18] *Ibid.*, pp. 162–63.   [19] *Ibid.*, p. 163.   [20] *Mem. U. Crocker*, p. 35.

trial, during which, and the whole time of his apprenticeship, he behaved in such manner as to gain the esteem of myself and family. I am of the opinion that he will give satisfaction to any person, in the printing line, who may think proper to employ him.

William Hall

August 21, 1790.

I certify that David Graham served the time above mentioned, in the printing office under the name of Hall and Sellers, and I think he justly deserves the recommendation given by Mr. Hall.

William Sellers

Philadelphia, August 21, 1790.[21]

The long hours of labor for apprentices and journeymen usually began at six o'clock, with one hour (seven to eight) for breakfast and another for dinner. During the summer, work continued until dark, and after September 20 the men returned after tea and worked until eight by candlelight.[22] Almost a half-century later Joseph T. Buckingham had not forgotten the severity of the regime:

From the spring of 1800 to that of 1804, I was employed, with the exception of a few months, in the office of Messrs. Thomas & Andrews. The wages of a journeyman were then not more than six or seven dollars a week. I am confident that I then worked harder and more hours in a week to secure the sum of seven dollars, than any one does, at this time, for twice that sum. For piece-work, *six-pence a token* at press, and *a shilling for composing a thousand ems*, was the highest price paid in Boston.[23]

In the course of the day there were, for one reason or another, breaks in the monotony: perhaps a treat by a new apprentice, perhaps a treat ("footing") by a new journeyman, perhaps a treat by journeymen and master when the middle signature "O" was put to press, and every day at eleven, as well as at other times, journeymen "jeffed" for beer.[24] These customs certainly inspired the notoriety of journeymen printers as unseemly imbibers. The temptation, moreover, affected the lives of the journeymen. "The number of those who were in my employment from 1804 to 1820," said Buckingham, "who have fallen victims to diseases produced by irregular habits and vicious indulgences, I find, very much exceeds the number of those who 'defied the foul fiend,' and studied how 'to prevent

---

[21] A. Rachel Minick, *A History of Printing in Maryland, 1791–1800* (Baltimore, 1949), p. 28.

[22] *Mem. U. Crocker*, pp. 35–36.

[23] [Buckingham], "Croaker, No. XXVI," Boston *Courier*, Sept. 22, 1849.

[24] *Autobiog. T. Weed*, I, 58.

wine,' and thus become masters of their own destiny."[25] Thurlow Weed recalled that at least one-quarter of the journeymen he knew were habitually intemperate and more than another quarter drank enough to remain impoverished. He did point out, however, that those from New England towns were mostly temperate and frugal while most of those from Baltimore, Philadelphia, "etc., etc.," were thriftless or dissipated.[26] Buckingham viewed this subject calmly:

It was not then discreditable,—even to men of much higher pretensions to notoriety than journeymen printers,—to be a little *mellow;* and they were known to take bitters in the morning before breakfast, flip or punch at eleven o'clock, brandy before dinner, and wine after it, and repeated till bed time, as taste, habit, or opportunity could authorize. Such *liberality* no printer, especially no journeyman, could afford to practise.[27]

Buckingham's final point is apt. Furthermore, it would be difficult for a journeyman to cope with a case or a press when intoxicated, for the skill and dexterity required to follow copy, pick up sorts, space words and justify lines would have decreased with unsteady hands or blurred vision. Also, it must not be forgotten that the compositor worked from manuscript copy which in itself probably contained false grammar, bad orthography, poor punctuation—all of which called for correction by the compositor. Nor was this limited to the manuscripts of nonprofessional people:

I have seen the arguments of lawyers, who stood in high repute as scholars, sent to the printer in their own hand-writing,—chirography which would defy the sagacity of the most inveterate investigator of ancient hieroglyphics,—abounding with technical and foreign terms abbreviated, words misspelled, and few (or no) points, and those few entirely misplaced. I have seen sermons of eminent scholars and "divines" sent to press without points or capitals to designate the division of sentences,—sermons which, if published with the imperfections of the manuscript, would be a disgrace to any apprentice if he were the author. Some writers use no points whatever; some use a comma for all occasions; some prefer the dash, and use it in place of all other points. . . . Suppose these productions had been printed as they were written. The disgrace would have fallen upon the printer.[28]

Journeymen working at press needed strength of muscle besides steady hands and eyes. Two "partners" worked the press, one ink-

[25] [Buckingham], "Croaker—No. XLI," Boston *Courier*, Feb. 2, 1850.
[26] *Autobiog. T. Weed*, I, 44, 58.   [27] *Pers. Mem.*, I, 33.
[28] *Ibid.*, pp. 31–32.

ing, the other pulling, with the partners changing work at intervals.[29] The cumbersome presses demanded so much brawn to pull that the right shoulder and foot of men who constantly worked at press became enlarged, causing them to walk in a sidewise manner.[30] Aside from actual labor the pressman supervised the wetting of the paper, the condition of the ink balls, and the impressions as they were pulled. It is no wonder, then, that journeymen preferred composition to presswork.

Letters from Ebenezer T. Andrews of Boston to his Worcester partner, Isaiah Thomas, show the quandary of the master when faced with more presswork than composition. In the discussion of one project Andrews wrote, on January 29, 1791: "If the Journeymen did not object to so much presswork, we might set 4 hands upon it. . . . I will consult the journeymen. . . . Do you know of one or two good Pressmen? I should like to have one or two in case our Journeymen should refuse doing so much presswork as we are like to have." On January 18, 1792, Andrews again commented: "The devil seems to have got into Journeymen—they want now more than *one shilling* per token—and I expect the next thing will be more than *one shilling* per thousand m's. They say press work is not in proportion to composing, and that we have a great proportion of it." Less than a month later, on February 12, Andrews informed Thomas that he wanted "2 Pressmen very much to do Spelling Book—our Journeymen will not work all the time at Press without extra price." Unable to discipline his rebellious journeymen, he drew upon the skills of his apprentices. On May 5, 1793, Andrews told Thomas that "many of our lads are better than most Journeymen and we shall be able to do considerable work this summer without hiring much help." One week later he emphasized this: "I am almost sick of Journeymen, they are in general so poor workmen. We have got a very good set of lads, and I think I shall be able to do all our work without any, or with very few Journeymen—we have 12 lads in the office."[31] With this correspondence in mind, it is easy to understand how Uriel Crocker became a foreman while still an apprentice.

[29] J. Henry Harper, *The House of Harper* (New York, 1912), p. 15.
[30] Hamilton, p. 45.
[31] American Antiquarian Society, Isaiah Thomas Papers; hereafter cited as Thomas Papers.

Whether because of the ability of the master to recruit good journeymen or because of sheer luck, some shops enjoyed a congenial atmosphere. Thurlow Weed worked in one as a journeyman in New York about 1816:

My situation at the office of Mr. [Jonathan] Seymour was a very pleasant one. My press partner was James Harper, the senior of the great publishing house of Harper & Brothers, who was subsequently elected mayor of the city. We were employed upon a quarto edition of "Scott's Family Bible," and worked with a will, earning from twelve to thirteen dollars a week. We were at the office in the morning as soon as it was light, doing, in the summer months, a third of our day's work before breakfast. It was a well-regulated office and most of the journeymen were intelligent and temperate. Mr. Seymour himself was a kind-hearted man, who had an encouraging word for us all, and it afforded him evident pleasure to find his journeymen coming to him on Saturday nights to receive their wages, especially if their bills were large ones.[32]

Seymour, who obviously understood human nature as well as how to make money, kept his good people by supplying them with steady work. But the fluctuating business of many shops plus competition from "half-way journeymen" increased the erratic inclinations of many men, sending them on the move from shop to shop and from town to town. They called themselves euphemistically "birds of passage." This roving labor force, the "tramp printers" of the nineteenth century, may have been unfortunate, rebellious, and certainly freakish, but, as Hamilton has stated, their fund of information and their assortment of experiences were real assets to a shop.[33] In a rapidly growing nation they were part of the new mobility; they went where there was work to be done.

Now and then a master contrived to retain satisfactory employees by barter or by legal action. James Adams, in 1788, wrote to Mathew Carey saying that because of slackening business he could provide Carey with a good compositor: "His weekly wages, except for his boarding and washing, and a triffle for pocket-money, I shall take in such books as I will notify . . . in case you employ and allow him common wages." After Carey accepted the proposal, Adams specified some of the terms: "His constitution is not of the strongest, therefore hope you'll employ him as little as possible at press.—

[32] *Autobiog. T. Weed*, I, 57.   [33] P. 43.

You'll please to let him have two shillings & six-pence each week for pocket-money"; and, in a postscript, added: "I expect his washing with boarding, which will be but one shirt, &c. a week."[34] Undoubtedly other printers also sent out their men on temporary assignments. An instance of legal action occurred in New York in 1818. In that case a master printer sued a journeyman for damages because the journeyman left without notice. According to Munsell, "judgment was given for the plaintiff, upon the ground, that when a journeyman is engaged, an implied contract is entered into to finish the work he begins; and if he leaves it unfinished, he forfeits what he has earned on that form; and further, if he leaves without due notice, he is liable to pay damages sustained."[35]

A master more interested in publishing and business ventures than in managing a printing shop engaged a foreman to supervise the journeymen and apprentices. The foreman usually worked at case or press when not occupied with his primary responsibility—the day-by-day operation of the shop. It was the foreman's job to assign work to compositors, pressmen, and apprentices. He purchased the minor supplies needed: pelts, wool, oil for lamps and presses, candles, potash for cleaning type, skins for the tympans.[36] As has been noted, sometimes an able apprentice became a foreman. In 1816 Joseph T. Buckingham, then a journeyman, became overseer in the Boston shop of West & Richardson, where he was "nothing more than a journeyman, except in responsibility, and with a compensation that never exceeded twelve dollars a week, and often fell below ten."[37] Apparently a foreman's wage was not much greater than that of an ordinary journeyman. Support for this assumption may be found in some correspondence of a period when wages were lower. Writing on July 24, 1792, Ebenezer T. Andrews told Isaiah Thomas that

Etheridge mentioned to me that he had received a letter from Mycall, wishing him to become his foreman, &c. and that he had offered him 5½ dols. per week, but that he would not go under six. He at the same time intimated a wish to become foreman to us. . . .

[34] Dorothy L. Hawkins, "James Adams: The First Printer of Delaware," *PBSA*, XXVIII (1934), 55–56.

[35] J. Munsell, *The Typographical Miscellany* (Albany, 1850), p. 136.

[36] Rollo G. Silver, "The Costs of Mathew Carey's Printing Equipment," *SB*, XIX (1966), 103–22.

[37] *Pers. Mem.*, I, 63.

At any rate, we cannot if we would, engage him until we hear from Hoyt. . . . I offered Hoyt 100 £ per annum, provided, after trial, we should mutually like.[38]

Hoyt's proposed annual salary, approximately two pounds a week, may be compared with the journeyman's piecework rate of about one shilling a token mentioned by Andrews in the letter of January 18, 1792, quoted above. Eight tokens a day were considered normal production, although an unusually able pressman such as Hosea Sprague "would work off his *twelve tokens* a day at press with perfect ease."[39]

The recompense of a journeyman at the end of the eighteenth century was very flexible, depending upon supply and demand in his locality. In an anonymous comment on the American book trade printed in London in 1789 there appears a discussion of the geographical differences:

The wages of printers are very great; and progressively so from the extreme parts of the northern to the southern state[s]. In New Hampshire, Massachusetts, Connecticut, and Rhode Island, journeymen printers have from three to eight dollars per week. In New York, Philadelphia, and Maryland, from five to ten per week; and in Virginia, North and South Carolina, and Georgia, from eight to twenty and twenty-five, according to their merit and ability. Printers are very scarce in the southern states.[40]

This statement, however, must be regarded as a very rough generalization because the value of the dollar also differed. In 1790, for example, a dollar passed at 8*s* in New York and North Carolina; at 7/6 in New Jersey, Pennsylvania, Maryland, Delaware; at 6*s* in New Hampshire, Massachusetts, Rhode Island, Connecticut, and Virginia; at 4/8 in South Carolina and Georgia.[41] The new monetary system was established by Congress in 1792, but about a decade passed before tradesmen conducted transactions in dollars, cents, and mills rather than in pounds, shillings, and pence.

Of all American craftsmen journeymen printers were among the first to organize for higher wages. Beginning with a strike threat

[38] Thomas Papers.
[39] George A. Stevens, *New York Typographical Union No. 6* (Albany, 1913), p. 49; Buckingham, *Pers. Mem.*, I, 41.
[40] *Bibliotheca Americana* (London, 1789), p. 15.
[41] [Ezra Gleason], *Thomas's . . . Almanack . . . for . . . 1791* (Worcester, Mass., [1790]), p. 41.

here and there, the pressures of this labor movement quickly increased as local typographical societies sprang up throughout the nation. As early as 1778 the journeymen of New York, requesting an additional three dollars weekly, had informed the master printers that they would not work without a raise in the face of rising prices. One master, James Rivington, printed his consent to the raise in the columns of his newspaper.[42] Eight years later twenty-six Philadelphia journeymen signed a statement in which they agreed to counter a reduction in wages by refusing to work for less than six dollars weekly. They also agreed to contribute to the support of any journeyman thrown out of a job because he refused to work for less than six dollars.[43] This, Morris points out, is probably the first recorded provision for a union strike-benefit fund in the country.[44] According to Stewart, the conflict lasted for some time before terms were finally accepted.[45] But once, at least, journeymen lost at the bargaining table. In 1799 the compositors and pressmen of the Philadelphia *Aurora* petitioned the editor, Margaret H. Bache, when they heard of her plans to reduce compositors to seven dollars weekly and her refusal to hire another pressman. "*We must persist in our demands*," the petition read, but Mrs. Bache gave them an irrefutable answer: "She cannot give more than what is given to compositors in the Printing offices whose papers are more profitable from advertisements. . . . The Editor must however determine . . . how many Pressmen are absolutely necessary."[46]

In New York journeymen printers dissatisfied with working conditions had for some time used their understanding of the power of communication to organize their fellows. Their respect for printed words, far beyond that of artisans in other trades, taught them to use words as a device to hold their members together. They printed announcements of proposals for mutual action, kept proper records, sent out notices of meetings, and maintained the procedures necessary to build a solid fraternal structure. Between 1794 and 1825 the

---

[42] New York *Royal Gazette*, Nov. 14, 1778.

[43] Ethelbert Stewart, "A Documentary History of the Early Organizations of Printers," *Bull. Bureau of Labor*, No. 61 (1905), p. 860.

[44] Richard B. Morris, *Government and Labor in Early America* (New York, 1946), p. 201.

[45] P. 860.

[46] Bernard Faÿ, "Benjamin Franklin Bache, A Democratic Leader of the Eighteenth Century," *Proc. Am. Ant. Soc.*, XL (1930), 300–302.

quickening of organizational techniques had fostered more than a dozen typographical societies in seven cities extending from Boston to New Orleans. From their beginnings as defensive wage regulatory societies they changed until at the end of the period they were primarily concerned with beneficiary functions.

The first known society was organized in New York City in the spring of 1794. Under the name of the Typographical Society the membership, which included most of the printers working in New York at that time, adopted a constitution, now unlocated. In the three and one-half years of its existence, the Typographical Society obtained an increase in wages to one dollar a day for the New York printers and probably maintained a price list.[47]

Subsequent to dissolution New York journeymen realized that they could not afford to be without unified representation. They then founded the Franklin Typographical Association in 1799 after a preliminary meeting had been held on November 24, 1798. Although the constitution, signed by fifty members, has been said to define the objectives as "the promotion of harmony among journeymen and for philanthropic purposes," activities centered on fixing a scale of prices. In 1800 the association set its demands: twenty-five cents a thousand ems for pieceworkers, at least seven dollars a week in book and job offices, and eight dollars a week on newspapers. To secure these prices, the journeymen went on strike and won the first complete wage scale ever adopted by New York City printers.[48] This scale became so effective that it remained for at least five years after the association disbanded in 1804. By 1803, when the association grew large enough to have rooms of its own, its activities ranged from petitioning Congress about tariffs on type and books to obtaining relief for its own members.[49] During the yellow fever epidemic of that year the association received $83.60 from the Philadelphia Typographical Society, for "journeymen printers distressed by the calamity," as well as a sum from the Baltimore Typographical Society.[50] Undoubtedly the corrosion of membership after the epidemic was one of the major reasons for dissolving the association.

[47] Stevens, p. 36; Barnett, p. 3; Stewart, p. 863.   [48] Stevens, pp. 37–39.

[49] Stewart, p. 864; Rollo G. Silver, "Printers' Lobby: Model 1802," *SB*, III (1950–51), 217–19.

[50] Rollo G. Silver, *The Baltimore Book Trade, 1800–1825* (New York, 1953), p. 15; Barnett, p. 4.

In the absence of enforcement the wage scale eventually decayed, and by June, 1809, anarchy in working conditions drove some journeymen to hold a meeting to discuss the formation of a protective and benevolent society. This preliminary session selected a committee on the constitution, instructing it to report on the first of July. On that evening the forty-nine printers present adopted the constitution of the New York Typographical Society. It is a rather lengthy instrument in which many parts of the text closely follow the wording of the 1802 constitution of the Philadelphia Typographical Society. One important alteration relates to the right to membership: the Philadelphia society denied any person who had not served an apprenticeship satisfactory to the board; New York omitted any reference to apprenticeship. Both constitutions provided for beneficiary functions, but the New York constitution also instructed the board of directors to "keep a list of the prices of work."[51]

The New Yorkers went into action at once. Within a month the Board resolved to ask every member to obtain more members "to the end that we may effect our grand purpose—the raising and establishing of our prices." An investigation of printers' claims which accused a master of paying less than the scale of 1800 was begun. In September the society sent letters to all the other typographical societies proposing an exchange of information about journeymen who worked for less than scale, who refused to strike, or who worked in shops on strike.[52] These men were called, in later years, "rats."[53] The board also constructed a new scale, having appointed a committee late in August to draw up a list of prices. The list was prepared, thoroughly discussed, and submitted to the master printers in the middle of October. The masters introduced a counterproposal, but the delay before a compromise was reached caused the society to fear that the masters would bring journeymen in from other towns to work at lower prices. To hasten a settlement, the society called a strike on October 30. Most of the masters soon accepted the scale, but a few held out and strike benefits were paid until the middle of December. The appearance of strikebreakers in some of the shops called attention to one weakness in the constitution which the society

[51] Stevens, pp. 41–45; Stewart, pp. 942–45.   [52] Stevens, pp. 48–51.
[53] Barnett, p. 23n.

quickly excluded: on December 23 an amendment limited membership to those who had served "three years as an apprentice to one branch, namely, either as a compositor or as a pressman."[54]

The wage scale of 1809, as finally established, specified prices for all kinds of work. Charges for composition included such items as common matter ("on minion or larger type, 25 cents; nonpareil, 27 cents; pearl, 30 cents per 1,000 ems. Above English to be counted as English"), work in foreign languages, imposition, arithmetical works, newspaper work, and distribution. Charges for presswork included such items as bookwork ("on minion or larger type, on medium or smaller paper, 30 cents per token; on smaller type, 33 cents"), cards, broadsides, forms containing wood engravings, and newspaper work.[55] With the exception of one incident in 1810 when the pressmen unsuccessfully badgered the society to change the prices for presswork, revision of the wage scale was not considered for a period of six years.

The society with a membership of 120 in 1810, vigilantly protected the wage scale to the best of its ability. It protested the use of "half-way journeymen" and it set age limits for beginning apprenticeships, thereby closing the trade to adult men. It warned other societies when a New York printer who refused to pay the scale advertised for out-of-town help, and it aided the unemployed to secure work. Its powers waned when the War of 1812 pulverized business so badly that more than two-thirds of the members left New York, and only in the following peaceful years did the society begin to debate a revised scale.[56] The new scale adopted on October 7, 1815, called for compositors to be raised two cents a thousand ems and their weekly wages one dollar. Some compositors' prices for other work were also altered up or down and an interesting clause was added: "All works composed from manuscript copy, 2 cents extra." Presswork increases included books, two to three cents a token, newspapers about seven or eight cents a token, and weekly wages one dollar. Here, too, a significant clause was added: "A pressman shall receive for teaching an apprentice presswork for the first three months 5 cents per token, and for the three months

[54] Stevens, pp. 51–57; Stewart, pp. 873–74; Barnett, pp. 363–66.
[55] Stevens, pp. 57–58.   [56] Stewart, p. 876: Stevens, pp. 42–70.

following 3 cents per token."[57] Most employers accepted these demands at once; the few hesitant minor offices capitulated after a strike.[58]

After this triumph the New York journeymen were confronted with the possibility of pricing themselves out of the market. Soon the masters contended that unless prices were stabilized throughout the country, New York would lose work. The new idea of a national scale led to a call for a meeting. The New York Typographical Society voted, on November 4, 1815, to confer with other societies for the purpose of persuading them to raise prices. Albany replied that they had raised their prices; Boston said that they would introduce a new scale; Philadelphia did not answer. Three months later the New York society proposed another national scheme: traveling cards enabling members to join the local society whenever they moved to another city.[59] This plan, too, foundered; the residency requirements of its constitution prevented the participation of the Philadelphia Typographical society.

Internal problems began to warp the New York Typographical Society. A threat to its existence arose when a member who had become an employing printer refused to resign. To restore the faith of the membership, a resolution was passed in 1817 declaring any employing printer to be "without the limits of this society." The restriction had little moral effect; by that time 101 of the 120 members were in arrears. This general indifference may be attributed to widespread suspicion about the legality and efficacy of the society's protective maneuvers. This was foreshadowed in 1816 when the society asked the New York Legislature to incorporate it as a protective and benevolent institution. Although the Assembly passed the bill, the Senate rejected it because of a clause permitting regulation of trade matters. For two years the society unsuccessfully appealed for legislation, finally accepting an act of incorporation, February 27, 1818, which permitted it to function as a benevolent institution but prohibited it from at any time passing "any law or regulation respecting the price or wages of labor or workmen or any other articles, or relating to the business which the members thereof

---

[57] Stevens, pp. 62–63.   [58] Stewart, p. 877.   [59] Stevens, pp. 64, 72–73.

practice or follow for a livelihood."[60] The experiment in trade union-
ism ended as the odds piled up; henceforth the society shrank into a
high-grade mutual aid and burial society with a complete system of
visiting committees and paid watchers for the sick.[61] The problems
of inadequate pay, primitive working conditions, violation of contract awaited a later day.

Aside from the fact that it existed, little is known about the first
society of journeymen printers in Philadelphia. On December 6,
1800, the Asylum Company of Journeymen Printers advertised an
open meeting called to sign a memorial to Congress asking an
additional duty on books.[62] Another reference appears in the records
of the Philadelphia Typographical Society when, at the time of its
organization in 1802, the directors appointed a committee to obtain
the books and papers of "the former Asylum Company" and ordered
the constitution left open for the signatures of "former members."[63]
The Philadelphia Typographical Society lost no time in setting
prices; it issued a price list eight months before the constitution was
adopted. The list, dated February 22, 1802, began with a tactful
address to the employers, stating in part:

We would wish to be placed on a footing, at least, with mechanics. . . . our wages have, in no instance, kept pace with them. We
have the merit of not being the most dissatisfied, and in no one
instance of demanding any thing unjust. We have, in the following
statement, confined ourselves to what a majority of the employers
in this city give. Our object is, to have one uniform price established.
In doing this, we shall act as men towards men. . . . no person
will leave his employ until he has given a reasonable notice. . . .
in return, we expect that your conduct towards us will be equally
candid. Indeed, we cherish a hope, that the time is not far distant,
when the *employer* and the *employed* will vie with each other, the
one, in *allowing* a competent salary, the other, in *deserving* it.[64]

Composition prices were twenty-five cents per thousand ems from
brevier to English, inclusive; fifty cents for rule or figure work; not
less than eight dollars per week. Presswork prices included paper
below medium, thirty cents per token; above medium, thirty-seven

---

[60] *Ibid.*, pp. 76–80.   [61] Stewart, p. 880.
[62] Rollo G. Silver, "The Book Trade and the Protective Tariff: 1800–1804,"
PBSA, XLVI (1952), 34.
[63] Barnett, pp. 4–5.   [64] Stewart, p. 865.

and a half cents; broadsides, seventy-five cents; all small jobs, thirty cents; not less than eight dollars per week.[65]

After the employing printers accepted these prices, the society, with "a desire to consolidate the present good understanding and harmony which now happily subsists among the brethren of our profession," adopted a constitution on November 6, 1802. As previously mentioned, it limited membership to those who served an apprenticeship satisfactory to the board of directors. While emphasizing the beneficiary functions of the society, it also provided for advance payments to any member, on his own security, who "may be thrown out of employ, by reason of his refusing to take less than the established prices." Furthermore, the oath of officers included a declaration that the officer would, to the utmost of his power, "procure employment, for any member or members of this society, in preference to any other, when occasion requires." In this, one of the oldest constitutions of a labor organization in the United States, a precursor of the union label appears: Article 21 described the badge of the society, "when such a distinction shall be necessary"—a silver rule with the member's name engraved on one side and a press on the other.[66] Members met monthly, but the major work was done at the weekly meetings of the sixteen directors, who dealt with admission and expulsion, benefits, and work regulation. The membership heard, but could not reverse, these actions.

The Philadelphia Typographical Society also contained opposing factions in its membership: those primarily interested in benefits and those whose aims were trade regulation. Evidently the directors disciplined them both into a workable unit. In addition to regular business, the minutes record such activities as sending a petition to Congress for a higher duty on imported books (1802), raising composition on daily newspapers to thirty cents per thousand ems, prohibiting members from working at presswork "with any person who is not regularly bred, bound apprentice till 21 years of age," as well as voting the money sent to New York printers (1803).[67] In the same year an advertisement placed by five Philadelphia printers in the *Gazette of the United States* for sober young men from the country was immediately followed by an assurance signed by the officers and directors of the Philadelphia Typographical Society that

[65] *Ibid.*   [66] *Ibid.*, pp. 942–44.   [67] *Ibid.*, pp. 866–67; Barnett, p. 55.

plenty of workmen were already in the city.[68] During the next four years the society expelled members for working below scale and passed a resolution to fine or expel members who secured employment for nonmembers with the sympatric proviso that "this resolution shall not be construed to the prejudice of members interesting themselves in behalf of strangers in distress or emigrants from Europe."[69]

The two rival groups mentioned earlier continued to press for their objectives; in 1807 the initiation fee and funeral benefit were increased at the same time that a committee was appointed to investigate abuses. Soon "working cards" were printed, but this, of course, could not prevent violations of the apprenticeship system. In December, 1808, the society not only forbade any member to teach any apprentice not bound before his eighteenth year but also resolved to send the other typographical societies names of members expelled for this reason. As Stewart pointed out, this marks the beginning of the "unfair list."[70]

After the society incorporated in 1810, the pressures exerted by the two factions mounted. In order to placate those who were greedy for benefits, a clause was added to the constitution in 1810 denoting members who paid dues for twenty years "free members." This eventually brought on a reorganization in 1831 when "free members" began to get most of the benefits. For the champions of trade regulation, a new wage scale was presented to employers three months after the constitution was amended. The new scale provoked a strike, apparently unsuccessful, which reduced the society from 119 members to 55 and almost depleted the treasury. With one disaster begetting another, the society took the easiest way out, continuing its welfare aid but giving up the fight for higher wages, except to endorse a compositors' scale in 1816. At that time the pressmen, probably in a mass meeting, also prepared a new scale calling for, among other items, wages of not less than nine dollars a week for a ten-hour day, thirty-three and one-third cents a token for medium or below, thirty-seven and a half cents a token above medium, and thirty-five cents for stereotype editions.[71] Evidently the

---

[68] H. Glenn Brown, "Philadelphia Contributions to the Book Arts and Book Trade, 1796–1810," *PBSA*, XXXVII (1943), 287–88.
[69] Stewart, p. 867.   [70] *Ibid.*, pp. 867–69.   [71] *Ibid.*, pp. 881–83.

society did not directly participate in setting the scale. Thus the date when the Philadelphia Typographical Society became a purely beneficial organization remains unclear: Barnett stated that this occurred by 1815; Stewart said that the date was 1831.[72]

Much less is known about the early typographical societies of Boston. In March, 1802, the members of the Boston Franklin Association, "journeymen Printers of Boston," petitioned Congress against an increased duty on type, but, aside from a printed oration, neither the nature of the other activities nor the length of time the association existed have been determined.[73] Two shreds of evidence refer to a society of another name a year later: Stewart quotes a statement that the Boston Typographical Society was organized in 1803, and a society in Boston in that year is also mentioned in the minutes of the Philadelphia Typographical Society.[74] Six years later the Philadelphia society received a list of prices from the Boston Typographical Society, but whether this was the same society or a new one is still in doubt. The society of 1809, however, was probably the same society mentioned in the minutes of the New York Typographical Society for 1811.[75] It must have dissolved within the next four years because a new Boston Typographical Society was formed in 1815. In March, 1816, it grimly notified the New York society of a new scale saying that the employers "will be obstinate at first, but must eventually agree to give us the prices we ask, provided we are united and the journeymen of your city do not think proper to come to this town for work at the call of the masters." This society, according to Stewart, continued until 1826 or beyond.[76]

Meanwhile two more associations originated in Boston. One is noted in the diary of Isaiah Thomas, under date of February 27, 1822: "I see by the Newspapers, that there is a Society in Boston, called Thomas Typographical Society—I never heard of this Society, or knew there was such an one till I saw an advertisement notifying the members to meet, &c."[77] The other, the Franklin Typographical Society, "An Association of Compositors and Pressmen,"

---

[72] Barnett, p. 7; Stewart, p. 882.
[73] Silver, *SB*, III, 222–24; William Burdick, *An Oration* (Boston, 1802).
[74] Stewart, p. 869; Barnett, p. 5.   [75] Barnett, p. 6.
[76] Stewart, pp. 869, 888–89.
[77] *The Diary of Isaiah Thomas, 1805–1828*, ed. Benjamin T. Hill (Worcester, Mass., 1909), II, 108.

was instituted in 1824 and incorporated in 1825.[78] Always a strictly beneficial society, it still (1966) functions. The New England workman had learned that to fight entrenched power he must form groups of his own. The unusually large number of organizations in New England were the result of his understanding that survival depended on his alliance with men like himself against despotism in the shop.

The little information available on Baltimore societies reveals that the Baltimore Typographical Society held meetings in 1802 and sent relief money to New York printers in 1803. Newspaper notices of meetings in 1807 are found, but an 1808 meeting of journeymen printers "to vote on a constitution for the government of a typographical society" indicates a new organization or a reorganization. Under the same name they remained united for only two or three years, during which time they joined the employers in a procession (1809) and discussed cooperation with Philadelphia printers in an alteration of prices (1810). Another society, the Baltimore Typographical Association, began in 1812 and lasted at least three years.[79]

The organization of journeymen in Washington was limited by great fluctuations in the printing trade, which depended for business on the intermittent sessions of Congress. Powell mentions a call for an association in 1807, but this seems to have failed to create a permanent society.[80] At a meeting in December, 1814, a committee was asked to draft a constitution for the new Columbia Typographical Society. One month later nineteen members adopted a constitution which defined the objective as "for the mutual benefit of each." It was accepted so responsibly by the membership that Stewart could say, in 1905, that the society "was at once liberally benevolent and conservatively persistent in trade matters, being the only one of the old societies that has survived until to-day, and developed into a modern trade union, rather than a mutual benefit association." From the beginning there was solidarity, with trade regulation an objective. A letter accompanying the first price scale and circulated to other societies in July, 1815, proclaimed that they were a group

---

[78] Jefferson Clark, *Address Delivered at the Anniversary Celebration of the Franklin Typographical Society* (Boston, 1826), pp. 20–22.

[79] Silver, *Balt. Book Trade*, p. 15; Barnett, p. 5.

[80] J. H. Powell, *The Books of a New Nation* (Philadelphia, [1957]), p. 114.

"having for its object, first, benevolence, and, second, the establishment of a regular system of prices." The scale itself was revolutionary because it set two weekly prices: ten dollars per week during sessions of Congress ("journeymen are altogether employed by the week during the session of Congress") and nine dollars during the recess. Other prices included working on a Sunday, two dollars; composition, twenty-eight cents per thousand ems for brevier and above; presswork, thirty-three and one-third cents per token, but thirty-seven and a half cents on newspapers. The Baltimore Typographical Association was impressed; it expressed pleasure "in the establishment of any regulations which have the least tendency to promote the interest and happiness of our brethren in every section of the Union" and sent congratulations on success "in rebuffing the many obstacles naturally incident in the formation of such associations." In October of the same year the Columbia Typographical Society designated a committe to "draft a list of prices similar to that of Baltimore." A more detailed price scale, based on the earlier one, was prepared and approved, thereby creating a list to serve both cities. Soon after this list went into effect, the Columbia Typographical Society found enforcement more difficult than expected. Some of its members claimed that, since the constitution made no reference to wage scales, working for less than scale was not a violation of the constitution. Furthermore, some "tramp printers" arriving for sessions of Congress worked according to the lower scales of their home societies. As a reply to the members who regarded constitution and price list as entirely separate, the society printed the constitution "with the list of prices annexed thereto"—a custom later adopted by other societies for the same reason. To suppress the roving printers, the society approved a new constitution in 1818. The new version required an interrogation of applicants as well as a pledge of every member that he would procure employment for members in preference to others and that he would not divulge secret proceedings. It also provided for traveling cards. At that period the faction in favor of trade regulation dominated, but in a few years the mutual benefit faction gained control, introducing a revised constitution in 1821. For a while the "alimoners" kept the "industrialists" from taking action in trade regulation. Nevertheless, the factions continued to be almost equally divided throughout the 1820's. When, for example, the mutual benefit faction proposed incorporation of the society, the vote was a tie and incorporation was prevented by the deciding ballot of the president.[81]

Two of the smaller cities also had typographical societies: the New Orleans Typographical Society, founded in 1810, and the Albany Typographical Society, founded in 1813.[82] The latter increased a scale in 1815 in order to make it similar to the new New York scale.[83] Perhaps because of New York influence, the Albany society became very arbitrary in trade matters, probably even forbidding its members from working with men who received less than the scale. Moreover, it sent the names of these lower-wage men to other societies. In an 1816 letter from the Albany Typographical Society appears the first known American use of the term "rat."[84]

The journeymen who organized and managed all of these societies deserve admiration for their courage and perseverance in the face of many problems. At first, the unaffiliated journeymen in a town sometimes outnumbered the members of a society. Once wage scales were established, many members ceased paying dues or lost interest. It was not easy thereafter to sustain efforts in trade regulation and so the beneficiary functions gradually became paramount. These, in turn, eventually led to the termination of the societies when members who had paid dues for a certain period, or an equivalent lump sum, became "free members," collecting most of the benefits and thereby discouraging new members. The deterioration in collective fair play occurred between 1815 and 1830.[85]

Because most of them were paid on a piecework basis, members never were very interested in regulating working hours. During the first decade of the nineteenth century, when the working day varied from ten to eleven hours, the New York and Philadelphia societies wished to establish a ten-hour day, but they did not regard it seriously enough to insist that it appear in the wage scales.[86] On the other hand, they did enlarge the scales to include various classifications of composition, among them prices for different sizes of type, for foreign languages, and for rule and figure work. Additional classifications such as broadsides of various sizes, work on parch-

[81] Stewart, pp. 885–92, 948–51, 1002. [82] Barnett, p. 6; Munsell, p. 121.
[83] Stevens, p. 64. [84] Barnett, p. 23n. [85] Stewart, pp. 894–95.
[86] Barnett, p. 143.

ment, and covering the tympan were also defined for presswork.[87] In the attempts of societies to establish the same prices in more than one city, in the introduction of traveling cards, in their mutual problem of "half-way journeymen" as well as in their correspondence with each other, the trend toward one national union began.

Members of these societies who were proud of their craft would not tolerate poor workmanship. In 1817, for example, the New York Typographical Society expelled a pressman for "turning wrong a half sheet of twenty-fours, and without mentioning the circumstances to his employer, leaving the city, even neglecting to note down the signature letter in his bill."[88] The societies also took public action. They tried to help the trade by sending petitions to Congress about protective tariffs.[89] On the Fourth of July the members, wearing their badges, had their assigned places in the parade, sometimes accompanying a press on a wagon with journeymen printing and distributing an appropriate broadside.[90] That this patriotism was sincere is proved by their activities during the War of 1812. The Philadelphia Typographical Society voted a day's labor on the fortifications of the city for each member and provided benefits to the wives of members in service. In New York the secretary of the New York Typographical Society organized an artillery company of printers to defend the harbor.[91] In Boston, too, the printers volunteered for defense.[92]

The societies brought out the best in the journeymen of that period before industrialization. A journeyman printer worked hard and long, but many realized that there was something special about the craft, something which cabinetmaking or shoemaking lacked. Yet underneath this feeling lay the constant awareness that they were workingmen at the mercy of unfair practices. The characteristics of their spirit appear in two of the twenty-nine toasts at the second anniversary celebration of the Franklin Typographical Society:

By Mr. Edmands. The Members of the Franklin Typographical Society—May those who are hourly giving the world *tokens* of *good works*, and daily adding *proofs* of *correct matter*, be *justified*

[87] Stewart, pp. 1001–2.   [88] Stevens, p. 70.
[89] Silver, *SB*, III, 217–24; Silver, *PBSA*, XLVI, 38–43.
[90] Silver, *Balt. Book Trade*, pp. 15–16; Stewart, p. 893.
[91] Stewart, pp. 880–81.   [92] *Diary of I. Thomas*, I, 244n.–245n.

by the *Great Composer*, at that *period*, when he shall *make up* his last *form* of jewels.

. . . . .

By Mr. S. T. Armstrong. *Full Price*, and money every Saturday night.[93]

[93] Clark, p. 21.

CHAPTER 2

THE PRINTING OFFICE

THE printer's equipment depended on his volume of business, his access to suppliers, his motives for limiting or upgrading his facilities, and his solvency. The economy of his shop was still rudimentary, and most of its contents were traditional, soon to become part of an obsolescent world. A comparatively few inventories found in estate audits and newspaper advertisements reinforce this appraisal.

In 1798 a New York newspaper advertisement offered for sale a printing office consisting of one press, one imposing stone, composing sticks, frames, galleys, letter boards, letter cases, font cases, "and a variety of other articles that belong to an office." The type was also listed: one font each of long primer (429 lbs.), pica (388 lbs.), great primer (106 lbs.), two-line English (66 lbs.), French cannon (80 lbs.), two-line pica script (60½ lbs.).[1] This one-press shop may be compared with the two-press shop, probably Samuel Sower's, advertised in the following year:

To printers. A person wishing to decline the printing business, offers for sale a German and English Printing office. Consisting of two complete mahogany presses, one standing press, about 30 fonts of letter, 62 pair of letter cases, and three pair of fount ditto, twelve stands, thirty-two chases, 2 imposing stones, 7 composing sticks, eight double and single copperbottom galleys, and many other articles in his line of profession.[2]

Robert Aitken, who possessed the same number of presses, did not

[1] New York *Commercial Advertiser*, February 5, 1798.
[2] Minick, pp. 105–6.

specify the smaller equipment but described his building in Philadelphia in 1801:

The subscriber in the decline of life, having determined to relinquish the printing business. He therefore offers at private sale,
two excellent mahogany printing-presses, together with an extensive
assemblage of printing types, including an Hebrew and Greek font,
the whole amounting to 34 fonts well assorted, with every requisite,
in excellent order and in good condition; calculated for an extensive
book-work or a daily newspaper, including also, a general and useful assortment of flowers, cuts and ornaments, with every other
implement in the printing business. He will also dispose of, a two
story-story [*sic*] brick house, on the corner of Laetitia Court and
Black Horse Alley, which he now occupies as a printing office, 18
feet by 35—the second story has 8 large windows, 24 panes in
each—and a lofty garret for drying paper, with a cellar under the
whole.[3]

The inventory of another two-press shop appeared in the daybook of
the Rev. Dr. Samuel Williams, of Rutland, Vermont, when he
entered into partnership with William Fay, a former apprentice, on
September 1, 1802:

A printing Press bought of James Lyon—Cost	75.00
A printing Press bought of Judge Williams—Cost	95.00
Types of different kinds and sizes bought of James Lyon—500 lbs. at 2/ per lb.	166.67
A Font of Types bought of Anthony Haswell	50.00
A Font of Types bought of Chs. and George Webster of Albany—200 lb. at 2/	66.67
A Font of Types bought last year of Jesse Buel 300 lb. —Cost	75.00
An Iron Stove bought of Lewis Walker	22.50
Case and Stands for the Types—worth about	45.00
A small desk or cabinet	4.00
Shovel and tongues bought of William Smith	3.00
An Iron Pott—cost	1.25
Do. smaller	1.00
An Iron Dishkittle	1.00
4 Chairs	3.00
2 Tables	3.00
3 Composing Sticks 12/	6.00
4 Candlesticks	.75

Sundry smaller articles—Furniture for the Press—
boards for wetting paper—Galleys—Saw—2 Iron Skillets
—Screw drivers—Snuffers—wooden boxes—Twine &c &c
—worth about   25.00

                                                                                                     643.84[4]

[3] Philadelphia *Aurora*, Jan. 21, 1801.

[4] Marcus A. McCorison, "Report of the Librarian," *Proc. Am. Ant. Soc.*, LXXV
(1965), 250.

At that time a printer with two presses could prosper. Thomas and James Swords of New York, wrote John Pintard in 1800, "have risen to some degree of wealth by their industry, have two printing presses & 6 or 8 hands, with more work to execute than they can perform."[5] Of larger shops, two guided by Isaiah Thomas were the most extensive in America at the end of the eighteenth century. In the 1790's Thomas had twelve presses in his Worcester office and five in the Boston shop of Thomas & Andrews. An inventory of the Worcester plant in 1796 showed the twelve presses ("besides Six-fold") valued at $732.66⅔, type at $12,361.01, printing materials at $504.43, cuts at $525.16.[6] After that year the Worcester business declined, but the Boston shop kept its trade. Joseph T. Buckingham, in his recollections, told of working in 1800 in "the office of Thomas & Andrews, which was then supposed to be the largest printing establishment in America. Five presses were kept continually in operation, which employed ten persons, and there were several apprentices and journeymen, who worked at *case* and *press*, as circumstances might demand."[7] However, it is likely that, at the beginning of the nineteenth century, most of the printing offices in the United States owned only one or two presses.

Setting up a two-press shop was a time of stress. The presses had to be purchased, the type bought from one of the few domestic founders, imported, or acquired from fellow printers, the other equipment obtained second-hand or manufactured by craftsmen. Fortunately a record of setting up one such shop has been preserved. When Samuel T. Armstrong and Joshua Belcher entered into partnership as Belcher & Armstrong in Boston, Armstrong itemized the expenses in his journal:

Page [1]:

Belcher & Armstrong, began Oct. 21, 1805
The expense of their office is annexed, according to the bills———

1	Press of Adam Ramage	$136.00
322ʷᵗ	Brevier, a 73	235.06
330	Long Primer a 53	174.90
335	Pica a 41	137.35
68	Great Primer a 38	25.84

[5] Austin B. Keep, *History of the New York Society Library* ([New York], 1908), pp. 239–41.
[6] Clifford K. Shipton, *Isaiah Thomas* (Rochester, N.Y., 1948), pp. 66, 86.
[7] *Pers. Mem.*, I, 40.

74	Double Pica a 38	28.12
6	English Flowers a 38	2.28
2..14	Brevier two lines letters 38	1.09
3.. 8	Long Prim do do	1.33
5..	Pica do do	1.97
6	L. Prim flowers a 53	3.18
5	Brevier do 73	3.65
	Boxes	3.80
	2d Importation of imperfections &c.	
17..10	Long Primer a 53	9.33
4..13	Pica 41	1.97
47..	French Coennon 38	17.86
26.. 6	Quotations 36	9.49
30..	Scabbards 36	10.80

Page [2]:

2ᵈ	Press of A. Ramage	$135.00
41	Cases & 2 gallies	43.00
	Stands and other gallies as bills	44.50
	Cotton & Marston's bill[8]	24.00
1	Stand	5.00
	Sticks, &c.	6.00
	trough	7.00
	Stove, shovel & tongs	7.00
	Chases 5	28.00
	Sundries	25.00
		1,137.00[9]
	a bank	5.50
2	sticks & 1 royal chase	12.00
	Brev. open 2 line letters & flowers and english letters, rules, &c.	14.00
	Font of Script & Cases	42.80
	Double rule & single do for al[manac]k and other purposes	15.00
	do	5.00
	Lamps & Cord	1.25

Page [3]:

Expences of their Office (*continued*)

Imposing stone	D10.00
Duodecimo leads	15.00
Flowered Rules	1.00
Lothian's bills for large flowers for open letter & several other kinds[10]	12.00

[8] Cotton & Marston were painters (*The Boston Directory* [Boston, 1803], p. 36).

[9] This amount was originally written 1,128.00 and "corrected" to 1,137.00.

[10] Probably the Robert Lothian cited as a letter founder in the Boston *Columbian Centinel*, July 11, 1807.

	Russell & Cutler for 3 fonts Black Type viz D. P. G. P. & L. Primer & 3 pairs Cases[11]	30.50
	Charles Spear for 2 pairs old Cases[12]	3.00
2	Crown Chases	3.50
	Oliver & Monroe for royal chase[13]	5.00
	Gilbert & Dean for Pigeon Holes[14]	10.00
	Thos Foster jun for paper poles	9.50
	To Abner Wood for bill Exchange on Peter Wynne & Son for types &c &c	444.44
	18 mo leads wt a 56 cents	12.60
	Small Chase	2.33

Page [4]:

Expenses of the Office—continued

	English importation from Mess. Peter & W. Wynne amounted to	$623.69
	Duties on the same to	88.00
	Bond $1—Truckage $1	2.00
	pair Cases @ 2$	
	Shelves for Books, &c	

Oct. 8, 1807

566^{wt} Long Primer a

Ten lines Pica a

5 lines Do a

Whole amt of types of Wynne & Co.

$602.11[15]

An inventory of a one-press shop of 1805 appears in the estate papers of William Carlton of Salem, Massachusetts. This, it must be remembered, comprised used equipment tabulated for legal purposes:

Press	$100.
Brevier type, 350 lb.,	90.
Long Primer, 350 lb.	50.
Double pica, 79 lb.	25.
Great primer, black, 35 lb.,	20.
Double pica, script,	5.
Flowers,	5.
Small pica, English, Pica, Great Primer, French canon, much worn, and 60 to 100 lb. old type in "pye,"	90.
Rules, cuts,	5.
6 Composing sticks,	10.

[11] Russell & Cutler were printers in Boston (Silver, *Bost. Book Trade*, p. 41).
[12] Charles Spear was a printer in Boston (*ibid.*, p. 42).
[13] Oliver & Munroe were printers in Boston (*ibid.*, p. 38).
[14] Gilbert & Dean were printers in Boston (*ibid.*, p. 29).
[15] Rollo G. Silver, "Belcher & Armstrong Set Up Shop: 1805," *SB*, IV (1951–52), 202–3.

5 Chases,	10.
29 pair cases,	36.
6 stands and one broken imposing stone,	20.
Racks, bank and trough,	5.
Gallies and boards,	8.
Tables, desk and case of pigeons holes,	18.
2 horses for drying blankets,	3.
Two reams fine Demy paper,	8.
Dictionary and Gazetteer,	2.
Blank books and pamphlets,	12.
Four reams fine Demy paper,	16.
Blanks,	30.
Large Iron Stove and funnel,	27.[16]

The size of the shops expanded along with the growing demand for printed matter. By 1809 the largest office in New York, that of David and George Bruce, contained nine presses, while in Baltimore in the same year George Dobbin & Murphy had three.[17] As far west as Cincinnati in 1815 the two newspapers each used an extra press for book printing.[18] Four presses were in the shop which did the government printing in Washington in 1816, and by the next year Samuel T. Armstrong was using seven presses in Boston.[19] Aggressive printers were quick to enlarge their plants in an expanding economy. Within five years after they began in 1817, J. & J. Harper of New York had at least six presses.[20]

If the size of a person's estate at death indicates financial success, analysis of Boston records between 1800 and 1825 discloses that the most prosperous printers were those who owned newspapers, that book and job printers did not do as well, and that journeymen seldom left an estate at all.[21] An inventory of a successful newspaper office, the Boston *Gazette*, in 1824 is found in the estate papers of its owner, Simon Gardner:

3 printing presses	200.000
1 standing press and 1200 boards	15.00

[16] Harriet S. Tapley, *Salem Imprints, 1768–1825* (Salem, Mass., 1927), p. 298. Other inventories of printing shops appear in Carrol H. Quenzel, *Samuel Snowden, A Founding Father of Printing in Alexandria* (Charlottesville, Va., 1952), p. 10; Minick, pp. 96–97, 156; Tapley, pp. 298–99; Rollo G. Silver, "Abstracts from the Wills and Estates of Boston Printers, 1800–1825," SB, VII (1955), 213.

[17] *Am. Dict. Print.*, p. 73; Silver, *Balt. Book Trade*, p. 25.

[18] Walter Sutton, *The Western Book Trade* (Columbus, 1961), p. 10.

[19] Stevens, p. 96; *Mem. U. Crocker*, p. 32.

[20] Harper, p. 24.   [21] Silver, SB, VII, 212.

40 chases large and small	@ 3.00	120.00
150 lbs. Pearl		25.00
150 " Nonpareil	.40	60.00
242 " Brevier	.60	145.20
600 " Long Primer	.30	180.00
650 " " " old	.20	130.00
300 " Small Pica	.20	60.00
700 " Pica	.20	140.00
350 " English	.20	70.00
175 " Great Primer	.20	35.00
150 " Double Small Pica	.20	30.00
150 " Double English	.20	30.00
100 " American Canon	.20	12.00 [*sic*]
60 " 4 line Small Pica	.20	12.00
75 " 4 line Pica	.20	15.00
40 " 4 line shaded	.60	24.00
50 " 5 line Roman	.20	10.00
50 " 5 line Italic	.60	30.00
70 " 7 line Italic	.60	42.00
100 " 10 line Roman	.30	30.00
100 " 10 line Italic	.16	16.00
6 " 5, 6, 7 line alphabets		50.00
45 " Black Letter	.30	13.50
100 " Quotations	.30	30.00
100 " Leads	.50	50.00
Brass rule cuts, etc.		100.00
Galleys		10.00
Furniture and quoins		12.00
80 lbs. Minion and Pica Quadrats	.16	12.80
90 pr. Cases and 15 stands		132.50
30 lbs. Small ornamental letter	.60	18.00
3 Alphabets wooden letter		20.00
30 lbs. Script		22.50
20 lbs. Ink		10.00
Stove and funnel		12.00
100 lbs. Flowers, etc.		3.00
600 lbs. Brevier	.30	180.00
400 " Minion	.15	60.00
150 " Nonpareil	.15	22.50
1 Press		50.00
1 Press		20.00
Trough, bank, boards, etc.		25.00
8 Sticks		3.00
Galleys		13.00
Stands		8.00
20 pr. Cases		30.00
Col. rules and head.		**15.00**

I. The Columbian Press. From *An Abridgment
of "Johnson's Typographia"* (Boston, 1828)

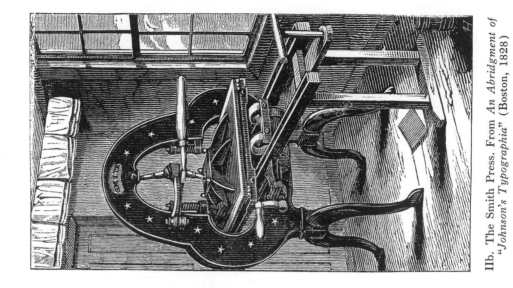

IIb. The Smith Press. From *An Abridgment of* *"Johnson's Typographia"* (Boston, 1828)

IIa. The Wells Press. From *An Abridgment of* *"Johnson's Typographia"* (Boston, 1828)

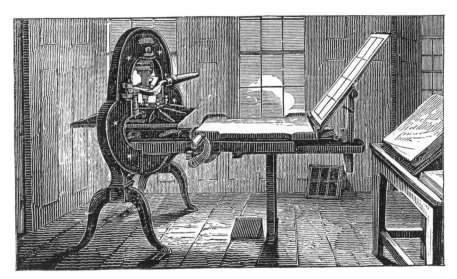

III. The Washington Press. From *An Abridgment of "Johnson's Typographia"*
(Boston, 1828)

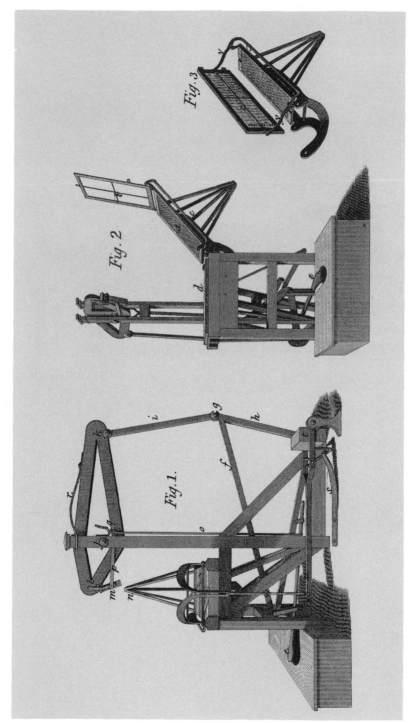

IV. Treadwell's Double-Frisket Press. From *London Journal of Arts and Sciences*, 1820

Stove and funnel   4.00
Old type in cellar   90.00[22]

These inventories convey a representative but static view of the shops without a hint that the turnover of business resulted in a natural, steady consumption of supplies and materials. In New York in 1802 two printers used a technique of ingratiation and polite self-esteem in this sanguine bid for patronage of their supply house which could have been a boon to the industry if firmly established:

Heard & Forman.—To Printers. Heard & Forman, having often heard a wish expressed, as well by City as Country Printers, that a house might be established for the accommodation of those engaged in the Art of Printing; and believing that no other than a printer is capable of judging, accurately, of the elegance and quality of Printing Materials, take the liberty of informing the whole great family of Faust, that they have now on hand, and shall continue to keep, a large and elegant assortment of Type and Printing Materials of every description.[23]

Their advertisement listed twenty-two different fonts of type and referred to other items for sale: "Two Printing Presses. Chases, Composing-Sticks, Brass-Rules, &c."[24] Perhaps because they were a little ahead of their time, they did not last for more than a few years. Until supply houses became permanent in the larger cities, maintaining a shop required the attentive energy of the boss to persuade a series of craftsmen to provide or service specialized equipment. Conscious of the ruin waiting to overtake him if orders were not filled, a printer sometimes went to immense trouble to find supplies. At times he resorted to importation with negotiations conducted by the slow mail or, infrequently, in person. As late as 1804 James Cutler of the Boston firm of Russell & Cutler "made a voyage to England at an expense of several hundred dollars, for the sole purpose of purchasing printing materials for his office."[25]

If a shop was in or near Philadelphia, a printer of 1790 could buy ink from Justus Fox, the typefounder and inkmaker of Germantown. Mathew Carey was a customer there but he also bought ink

---

[22] *Ibid.*, pp. 216–17.
[23] New York *Herald*, Aug. 25, 1802 (quoted in Rita S. Gottesman, *The Arts and Crafts in New York, 1800–1804* [New York, 1965], pp. 302–3).
[24] *Ibid.*
[25] James L. Homer, *An Address Delivered before the Massachusetts Charitable Mechanic Association* (Boston, 1836), p. 30.

from fellow printers who made it as well as from merchants who probably imported it.[26] In New York inkmakers were just as few, and printers who did not make their own used stop-gap sources. In Boston one printer described how he adapted himself to a crisis during the scarcity of ink. Writing to Isaiah Thomas in 1791, Ebenezer T. Andrews told his partner: "We imported only six kegs of Ink, and one of them I have already sold, as I did not suppose you would want above one. Will not, however, sell any more—could sell them all, as nobody has got any come but us."[27] As the number of manufacturers increased after 1800, ink became available to all but those printers whose supply lines were temporarily cut by the War of 1812. After that a printer finding himself short could easily requisition ink from a colleague. An example of this is seen in an 1816 letter from Thomas S. Shannon of Nashville, Tennessee, to William W. Worsley of Lexington, Kentucky: "There is no ink in this place except some we have made ourselves. T. G. Bradford has written to Fielding B. requesting him to send on a keg; if he has not sent it, you will confer a favor by forwarding a keg, and drawing on me for it."[28]

The designations of "summer ink" and "winter ink" used at the end of the eighteenth century seem to have been more for sales promotion than for practical advantage. In 1792 Ebenezer T. Andrews saw no difference: "I don't think there is any odds between them—imagine they only marked them differently—they are all charged alike in the Invoice."[29] Imported ink arrived from England or Germany in skins or kegs, but in this country ink was sold by the keg and priced by the pound.[30] Prices in Philadelphia varied from forty to fifty cents a pound between 1805 and 1817, with printing ink selling for less than best book ink.[31]

Since the history of papermaking in America has been detailed in other works, it may be remembered that lack of paper often vexed the printer throughout most of the period covered by this volume. Between 1750 and 1800, Dard Hunter has stated, "innumerable small paper mills were established in almost every section of the

[26] Silver, *SB*, XIX, 100.   [27] Letter of Sept. 2, 1791, in Thomas Papers.

[28] Douglas C. McMurtrie, *Early Printing in Tennessee* (Chicago, 1933), p. 39.

[29] Letter of July 1, 1792, to Isaiah Thomas, in Thomas Papers.

[30] *Am. Dict. Print.*, p. 313; letter from E. T. Andrews to Isaiah Thomas, September 2, 1791, in Thomas Papers; Silver, *SB*, XIX, 100.

[31] Silver, *SB*, XIX, 100.

eastern part of the country." Many of these, he noted, "had difficulty in surviving, because of the constant shortage of linen and cotton rags and the absence of trained workers who could produce paper suitable for writing and printing."[32] The search for rags became so exasperating that in 1810 they were imported from Europe. After the war importation of paper became so great that in 1820 the papermakers of Pennsylvania and Delaware, no longer resigned to the frustration of seeing only seventeen of their ninety-five vats in operation, sought the redress of a tariff.[33]

In the 1790's negotiations for a new press could be simplified if the printer had easy access to one of the few domestic pressmakers of the decade. The printer who preferred and could afford an English press imported it. If he could not pay for a new press, he searched for a decent second-hand one or, if he opened a business, he might buy a complete shop. Mathew Carey began business in 1784 with the contents of Robert Bell's shop and in 1792 bought another press from John Hamilton, one of the first American pressmakers, at a cost of sixty dollars.[34] Isaiah Thomas in the following year imported "a Mahogany Press Complete on the best Construction" for thirty-two pounds and "2 Common Demy Presses compleat Plated hose &c" for twenty-one pounds each from Edmund Fry & Co.[35] Thomas thought himself the victim of a long-distance swindle; a letter in reply to his accusations attempted to pacify him:

We shall be very careful in future to have the Boxes strong & well packed tho' we have very few complaints indeed—the fault is not in them or the package but in those who remove them—the difference in prices of the Presses alluded to by thee, was in consequence of the respective Charges to us from the Joiners who made them & the particular words of the Orders given them—we gave them very cautious directions respecting the Shipping them, & we are assured that they were carefully & properly packed in every respect. Thy observations on the substituting Cast Iron for the stone &c &c we shall communicate to the Joiners.[36]

Resigned to unfulfilled promises and apprehensive of costly mistakes, printers still continued to import presses. For instance, the

---

[32] *Papermaking in Pioneer America* (Philadelphia, 1952), p. 19.
[33] J. Munsell, *A Chronology of Paper and Paper-Making*, 4th ed. (Albany, 1870), pp. 58, 64.
[34] Silver, *SB*, XIX, 87–88.   [35] Bill of June 5, 1793, in Thomas Papers.
[36] Letter from Fry & Steele, January 2, 1794, in Thomas Papers.

Baltimore *Telegraphe* began in 1795 with "a new printing plant which John Hayes had lately imported from England," and in the same year a press was delivered from London to Moreau de St. Méry of Philadelphia.[37] As an example of the sale of a shop, there is the bill from John Turner to James Carey of Philadelphia, March 23, 1796, covering "a small Printing-Office, consisting of a press, minion, (Types) Long Primer, English, 2 lines Letters, flowers, chase, frame, gallies, brass rule, stone, table, furniture, &c. &c." for three hundred dollars.[38] In the cities used presses could be acquired without the high transportation costs which country printers had to pay. During the first two decades of the nineteenth century the gradual increase in the number of American pressmakers freed used presses as new ones came on the market, thus mitigating the risks of free competition for smaller firms.

As previously stated, the lack of supply houses forced printers to utilize a complexity of craftsmen to fabricate or repair equipment. At times the printer had to secure the basic material himself, as may be seen in a letter from Ebenezer T. Andrews to Isaiah Thomas, May 14, 1793: "Will, if possible, get you some mahogany for Platins."[39] Luckily, very detailed accounts of jobs and charges in the Mathew Carey Papers reveal Carey's method of equipping his shop between 1785 and 1817. Items of wood (mallets, shooting-sticks, reglet, side-sticks, etc.) were obtained from cabinetmakers. Stone-cutters provided imposing stones and press stones. A house carpenter built type cases; a turner made ballstocks. Pelts and wool for inking as well as parchment for the tympan came from a parchment-maker. Whitesmiths forged the chases. It is also of interest that Carey employed men who were seldom, if ever, mentioned as manufacturers of printing office items, namely, the inmates of the local prison. Between 1802 and 1816 the Philadelphia Prison supplied him, among other things, cases, troughs, furniture, galleys, and quoins. Additional equipment, it may be added, came to Carey from the estates of deceased printers as well as from discontinued shops.[40]

Similarly, Carey selected from a diversity of craftsmen for the frequently needed repairs. When a pressmaker was available, he

[37] Evans 28230; *Moreau de St. Méry's American Journey*, trans. and ed. Kenneth Roberts and Anna M. Roberts (Garden City, N.Y., 1947), p. 180.
[38] American Antiquarian Society, Mathew Carey Papers, VIII, 2665a.
[39] Thomas Papers.   [40] Silver, *SB*, XIX, 93–101.

could be called upon. The kind of work done is seen in a bill submitted by Adam Ramage in 1807 when Carey had a five-press shop:

1807			
March	10	To 2 pair of Points	.80
	18	To a Mallat & planner	.67
		To Work at Press	.37½
April	12	To a pair of points	.40
	14 & 16	To planing 2 plattings	.50
May	1	To 8 feet Brass rule @ 15cts	1.20
	18	To oil cup & Die steeling point of screw	1.25
June	8	To 100 quoins	.67
	16	To 6 feet Rule @ 15	.90
July	14	To a pair of ball stocks	.75
Septr.	15	To work at Timpans hooks & Eys[?] planing a platting &c	.80
		To a pair of Points	.40
October	5 & 9	To 2 pair ball stocks	1.50
	10 & 20	To planing 2 plattings cutting one at 3 times 84 yds. Reglet	5.75
Decr.	1	To planing a platting	.25
	13	To a new frisket	2.25
	18	To planing a platting	.25
		To 2 planners	.67[41]

The need for skills was relentless and endless. Every few weeks an artisan had to be pursued and cajoled to stay a press or supply a new rounce handle, or there was the platen or a new set of cramps or something else to fix. Before Ramage commenced business as a printers' joiner, repairs were done on an undefined basis, according to latent capabilities. A cabinetmaker planed the platen, stayed the press, mended the tympan. A whitesmith also mended the tympan in addition to repairing friskets. A cutler who supplied a pair of points mended the frisket, too. Even after Ramage and other pressmakers were available in Philadelphia, stonecutters attended to laying and facing press stones.[42]

Because the acquisition of type has been treated in other publications, it need not be discussed here, and it is sufficient merely to mention the tradesmen who kept the printer supplied with such quickly consumed commodities as oil for press and lamp, candles, potash for cleaning type, and flour for paste. It is apparent that with

[41] *Ibid.*, p. 89.   [42] *Ibid.*, pp. 91–93.

ingenious use of local skills all but the frontier printers could keep their shops in repair. The problems caused by a lack of strategic materials, especially paper, were much more serious.

In the first quarter of the nineteenth century, the application of new technical and scientific knowledge to the efficiency of the printing process marks the beginnings of industrialization. The wooden press became an iron press, rollers instead of balls inked the type, horse power and steam power were substituted for human energy, stereotyping became a normal procedure, lithography began to be used for illustrations. In these twenty-five years the equipment of the shop changed more than in all the past three and a half centuries put together.

It is misleading to think that shops secured new devices as soon as they appeared on the market; often many years passed before the older equipment wore out. In the meantime improvements gradually infiltrated printing shop practice and increasingly transformed tools for the craft. During this period, of course, each innovation subjected to practical use was, if found acceptable, improved in a series of progressive experiments. The printing press itself underwent severe revisions in the effort to make it a faster, less costly instrument.

Early American wooden presses may have been cumbersome, but they were long-lived; one of the first, a press built by Isaac Doolittle of New Haven in 1764, stayed in constant use for more than twenty-two years.[43] Manufacture required such competence in wood and iron that only a few men in scattered places attempted the task. By 1789, according to Wroth, presses had been built in New Haven, Philadelphia, Hartford, Charleston, South Carolina, and Fayetteville, North Carolina.[44] Many of these presses, it is interesting to note, were constructed by a partnership, one man probably a joiner, the other an ironworker. Among the first efforts to produce a better press was the "wheel press" designed by Benjamin Dearborn of Boston about 1785. The late Ralph Green stated that it "was used for a time at Newburyport, a one-pull press. The platen turned with the tympan, and the power of the lever had the additional force of a wheel and axle. Two persons worked it." Dearborn did not lose

---

[43] Letter from J. Green to Isaiah Thomas, June 10, 1786, in Thomas Papers.
[44] Lawrence C. Wroth, *The Colonial Printer* (Portland, Me., 1938), p. 84.

sight of his aim when his press failed, for twenty-five years later he tried again, also ineptly, and devised "another press on another plan with greater simplicity and more power than any then in use. It had a lever but no screw and was not patented."[45] Kainen has suggested that this press probably resembled the simple lever press patented in England by Isaac Moore and William Pine in 1771.[46] In 1786 John Goodman of Philadelphia altered the usual construction by copying an imported press. William McCulloch remembered that Goodman

while yet in the employment of his father, began to make presses. A new press, and to the Philadelphia printers, a new and simple pattern, had been imported from Scotland, and which was much admired. Young Goodman, having examined the construction, and confiding in his own talents, set about an exemplar construction. He succeeded, contrary to the anticipations of almost every one. Goodman took the pattern of the screw of this Scots press on paper; and such was his confidence in his own workmanship, that he would have engaged to have wrought a screw that would exactly fit the pattern box. In 1787 Goodman began the pressmaking business for himself, and soon obtained a sufficiency of business.[47]

Another event in the history of American pressmaking was proudly announced in 1792 when Belknap & Young of Boston told readers of the first issue of the *American Apollo* that it was printed on "the first complete Printing-Press ever made in this town—the wood-work was made by Mr. *Berry*, and the iron-work by Mr. *McClench*, it is well executed in every part, and does honor to the ingenious constructors."[48] The press delighted Ebenezer T. Andrews, who wrote to Isaiah Thomas: "Who is to make your Presses? I have seen Belknap's—it looks very well indeed—he gave 18 £ for it complete."[49] But the habit of improving the machine had taken root. On January 18, 1792, Andrews told Thomas: "I believe Presses can now be made in this town superior to the Hartford ones, and for about the same price. Belknap & Young have a very good one, and the workmen think they could now make one much better."[50] Whether or not they modified the design is not known, but in

---

[45] Information in a letter of March 19, 1947.

[46] Jacob Kainen, *George Clymer and the Columbian Press* (New York, 1950), p. 52.

[47] "William McCulloch's Additions to Thomas's History of Printing," *Proc. Am. Ant. Soc.*, n.s., XXXI (1921), 210–11.

[48] *American Apollo*, Jan. 6, 1792.

[49] Letter, Aug. 11, 1791, in Thomas Papers.   [50] Thomas Papers.

1793 Samuel McClench and Thomas Barry did advertise the manufacture of presses "on the newest, and most approved methods."[51] The same advertisement offered cases, frames, galleys, composing sticks, reglet, and furniture made by Barry. When the firm dissolved within two years, Barry continued to make presses and other equipment with a new partner, James Thompson.[52] In the New York area another pressmaker flamboyantly announced his late model to be unimpeachable:

John Hamilton, Printing & Press-Maker. Informs the printers in this and the neighboring states, that they may be supplied with presses, made on an improved plan, after the best manner, and at three weeks notice. He has made presses for most of the printers in this state, New-York, and elsewhere; and has the happiness to find that his endeavors to give satisfaction have met their approbation. His price is seventy five Dollars, which considering the manner in which he finishes his presses, he flatters himself will be considered as a moderate compensation. Elizabeth Town, N.J.[53]

While pressmakers worked on the conventional design, an American inventor, Dr. Apollos Kinsley of Hartford, tried a radical approach to efficiency. He constructed a cylinder press on which he printed apparently only one issue of a miniature newspaper, 5¾ by 4¾ inches. The only known copy of the *New Star*, February 2, 1796, now at the American Antiquarian Society, contains this notice:

This small paper is printed for the purpose of making experiments with a model of a Printing Press, on a new plan, lately invented by the Printer hereof. Though the press is by no means complicated, it puts the ink on the types, carries in the papers and prints two sheets at a time, and will deliver them well printed at the rate of more than two thousand sheets in an hour, by the labor of one person only.[54]

This press, capable of printing ten times more rapidly than the common hand press, remained experimental. "It was," said Isaiah Thomas, "a subject of much conversation among printers, but was

[51] *American Apollo*, Nov. 1, 1793.

[52] Rollo G. Silver, "The Boston Book Trade, 1790–1799," in *Essays Honoring Lawrence C. Wroth* (Portland, Me., 1951), p. 281.

[53] New York *Daily Advertiser*, June 16, 1796 (quoted in Rita S. Gottesman, *The Arts and Crafts in New York, 1777–1799* [New York, 1954], p. 272).

[54] Clarence S. Brigham, *History and Bibliography of American Newspapers, 1690–1820* (Worcester, Mass., 1947), I, 29.

never brought into use." Thomas then went on to compare it with the cylinder press previously invented by William Nicholson of London: "Nicholson placed his forms of types horizontally; Kinsley placed his perpendicularly; his method was not calculated for neat printing."[55] Kinsley's press was patented on November 16, 1796, but no precise description exists.[56] It probably looked like a Miehle Vertical with two impression cylinders arranged to print two sheets at once.[57] Perhaps if better machine tools had been available, the press would not have been a failure. It was but only one example of Dr. Kinsley's ingenuity as his other inventions included steam engines, a ship's pump, as well as machines for casting type, making pins, cutting screws, cutting tobacco, casting bullets, and currying leather.[58] In the midst of these formidable accomplishments, he kept unimpaired the hope of inventing a laborsaving press. In 1801 descriptions of three models appeared in an article about his inventions:

A Printing-Press on Three Models.—In the first of these the types are placed perpendicularly on a level stone, or plate of metal, and ink is applied to the types by means of rollers covered with soft leather, and the rollers are supplied with ink by passing under a box containing it, having a narrow aperture in the bottom. The impression is made on the paper by passing the same, with the types, under a roller covered with several folds of cloth. The whole machinery is put in motion by the turning of a crank.

In another of these presses, the plate against which the types are fixed stands perpendicularly, and has a set of types on each side. This is moved upwards and downwards between two sets of rollers, and thus prints two sheets at once.

In the third model, the types (made for the purpose) are fixed round a cylinder, and confined to it; the paper to be printed is pressed between this cylinder and a roller covered with cloth, and the ink is supplied by rollers in the same manner as before mentioned. It is calculated that by either of these modes one man and a boy will print four sheets in the same time that two men can now print one, and with more ease.

A small press on this model was made a few years since, and, on experiment, printed very well, and very expeditiously. These

[55] *The History of Printing in America*, 2nd ed. (Albany, 1874), I, 36–37.

[56] *A List of Patents Granted by the United States from April 10, 1790, to December 31, 1836* (Washington, 1872), p. 11.

[57] Ralph Green, "Early American Power Printing Presses," *SB*, IV (1951–52), 143.

[58] Newton C. Brainard, "Apollos Kinsley," *Bull. Conn. Hist. Soc.*, XXVI (1961), 20.

printing machines, and several others, have not as yet been put into operation on a larger scale, as the indisposition of the inventor for two years past has prevented him from making the necessary exertions.[59]

These projects ended with Kinsley's death in 1803. If he had lived longer, the cylinder press and the ink roller might have developed sooner.

Other pressmakers continued to improve the common press. In 1800 Henry Ouram of Philadelphia built one equipped with a screw of cleaner and more even cut, substituting screws for the cords steadying the platen, and using rollers instead of cramps for moving the carriage. When, in the next year, George Clymer, an Ouram employee, claimed the credit for these changes, he was contradicted by John S. Roebuck's statement that the improved screw had already been used at the Mint and that Ouram's partner, one Taylor, suggested the screws for the platen and the use of rollers. At least, as Kainen observes, the "priority in making the improved press must be conceded to Ouram, whether or not the ideas were originally Clymer's or Taylor's."[60] Adam Ramage also adopted the use of rollers for some of his presses; in 1803 he advertised that he "continues to make Printing-Presses, with or without rollers."[61]

Scattered and vague references to new projects indicate efforts, less successful, made by other men. In 1808 an advertisement in the Albany *Gazette* declared that A. Romeyn, who "invented a new method of locking up forms with screws," also "had a model of a printing press, on an improved plan, which he flattered himself would, if carried into effect, tend much to relieve the most laborious part of the business."[62] One year later Samuel Fairlamb of Marietta, Ohio, adopted the principle of the inclined planes which Roworth had used in England before 1800. A contemporary notice reported:

Instead of a screw he substitutes two inclined planes, moving on rollers placed in the summer, in a circle of six inches diameter. The advantage of this invention consists in avoiding the friction common to a screw, and making the pressing power much easier and more effectual. The platen is supported by two spiral springs, which supply the place of a box encircling the spindle. Some minor improve-

[59] "A Description of Various Machines and Engines Invented by Mr. Apollos Kinsley," *Am. Rev.*, I (1801), 127–28.

[60] Kainen, pp. 8, 13–14.   [61] New York *Evening Post*, March 26, 1803.

[62] Munsell, *Typ. Misc.*, p. 107.

ments are added to the above. A press of this construction can be made for about half the price of the common press.[63]

There is no evidence that Fairlamb's machine was taken seriously, but the principle of the inclined planes did not die with it. The same idea appeared in a press built by George Clymer of Philadelphia in 1811 and in a press invented by Elihu Hotchkiss of Brattleboro, Vermont, in 1817.[64] At the time that Clymer grappled with inclined planes, John P. Sawin and Thomas B. Wait of Roxbury, Massachusetts, became so intrigued with the potential of a power cylinder press that they designed and constructed one. It was patented on January 28, 1811.[65] Because all patent specifications were destroyed in the fire of 1836, a contemporary record must suffice:

The model of Mr. Wait's new invented Printing Press, is completed, and has received the approbation of all who have beheld it. The blacking of the types, and the printing, are performed by cylinders, which, with the tympan and frisket, are all operated by machinery, to which motion may be given by a horse, by steam, or by water. The same power can work several Presses. The only attention necessary is that of a lad to each Press to place and remove the sheets. The apparatus on a scale for business, is expected to be completed in a few weeks.[66]

The press which seemed practical when designed was probably found to be impractical after construction. The comprehensive interpretation of this failure is the same as for Kinsley's press: the thin machine-tool methods of the period could not produce components with the precision required for a cylinder press. Another cylinder press, patented by William Elliot of New York City on February 17, 1813, was shelved.[67] Elliot's press, according to Ralph Green, "was a hand cylinder press similar to country newspaper presses of 50 to 70 years later, with hand inking and tympans at both ends."[68] The reason that Kinsley, Sawin, Wait, and Elliot are not in the vanguard of American pressmakers may be that while their imaginations outstripped available skills, they were not practical enough to realize their predicament.

By far the best-known American pressmaker of the period was Adam Ramage, whose career has been recounted in the excellent

---

[63] *Ibid.*, p. 112.   [64] Kainen, pp. 14–15; Munsell, *Typ. Misc.*, p. 129.
[65] *List of Patents*, p. 93.   [66] New York *Gazette*, Sept. 27, 1811.
[67] *List of Patents*, p. 123.   [68] Information in a letter of July 28, 1958.

pamphlet by Hamilton.[69] Ramage began making presses in Philadelphia about 1800. Soon afterward he advertised a variety of equipment:

Adam Ramage respectfully informs his friends and the public, that he continues to make Printing-Presses, with or without rollers, Copperplate Presses; Book-binder's Presses, and Ploughs of mahogany, beach or apple-tree, on moderate terms.

A. R. has always on hand, Letter-Cases, Frames, Gallies, all sorts of Furniture, and Brass Rules of all thicknesses, and suited to any pattern at the shortest notice.

He will invariably pay the most punctual attention to orders from any part of the continent.

From the increased demand, and arangements now made, the above, particularly the Brass Rules, will be furnished considerably lower than heretofore. Riglet, of red ceder, by the 100 yards, any size under broad quotation, at 4 dollars 25 cents.[70]

Ramage gradually acquired a nationwide reputation for inexpensive, well-made presses and became "the Ford of the printing press industry in this period."[71] Because his presses were cheaper, easily repaired by carpenters or blacksmiths, and lighter in weight for transportation, Ramage survived the competition of the iron press by continuing to supply the country printers who appreciated these features. The improvements in construction attributed to him began in 1807, according to his good friend, George Bruce:

Mr. Ramage was originally a Cabinet-maker, and made the frames of his presses of Honduras mahogany, with ample substance and a good finish; so that they looked better than the foreign-made presses and were less liable to warp. Importation ceased, with an occasional exception, as early as the year 1800; for foreign presses were dearer as well as poorer than his. In 1807 he made a great improvement on the screw of the press, and the working parts connected therewith. From Moxon's time, 1683, the screw of the common book printing press was made of the diameter of 2¼ inches with a declivity of 2½ inches in a revolution. The diameter was made smaller for job presses, but the declivity was always maintained, which made the platin rise and fall ⅝th of an inch in a quarter of a revolution, a space deemed necessary for the free passage of the forme and frisket under the platin. Mr. Ramage enlarged the diameter of the screw to 3 inches, and where much power was required to 3½ inches, and at the same time reduced the declination in a revolution to two

[69] Milton W. Hamilton, *Adam Ramage and His Presses* (Portland, Me., 1942).
[70] New York *Evening Post*, March 26, 1803.
[71] Hamilton, *Ramage*, pp. 4–5.

inches, which very nearly doubles the impressing power, but made the press slower in its action. It was an improvement much wanted, and the reduction in the descent of the screw to ½ inch was met by a more careful finish of the frisket and its hinges which were made to slide very well under the platin in an opening of half an inch. The press lost in speed, but gained in power and durability.[72]

The increase in impressing power was said to have been in response to the use of hairline type made popular by Didot and Bodoni.[73] In another improvement which occurred about 1817, Ramage faced the platen with brass. A third refinement, an iron bed for a stone bed, appeared about 1820.[74] Later Ramage substituted an iron platen for a wooden one, combined the cap and head into one crossbar, and added springs to retract the platen. Always a pioneer, Ramage recognized an extension of technique in the radically different press patented in 1813 by John Ruthven of Edinburgh. It had a fixed bed with a platen that rolled on wheels to the back of the press. A toggle joint below the bed was arranged to grip the platen and force it on the tympan. The frame was wood, the other parts iron, and, to operate the press, a bar was depressed.[75] Evidently under arrangement with Ruthven, Ramage began to manufacture this press in 1818, hoping that the trade would recognize the felicity of an easily moved platen and an even pressure.[76] It was, said Adams, "much esteemed for doing fine work," but the fact that it could not be reliably converted to the use of ink rollers greatly reduced its acceptance in the following years. Until his death in 1850 Ramage continued to produce a variety of printing presses as well as standing presses and copying presses. His contribution has best been summarized by Hamilton: "His inventions were minor improvements, and generally were not revolutionary. Yet the success of his presses, and the adaptability of his designs may give him a niche equal to that of more original men."[77]

At the beginning of the nineteenth century the increased use of iron in industry and, along with it, improved machines stimulated theoretical speculations on the feasibility of a wholly iron printing press. In England, Charles, third Earl Stanhope, who expended

[72] *Ibid.*, pp. 11–13.   [73] Wroth, p. 85.   [74] Hamilton, *Ramage*, pp. 13–15.
[75] Ralph Green, *The Iron Hand Press in America* (Rowayton, Conn., 1948), p. 24.
[76] Hamilton *Ramage*, p. 25; Green, *Iron Hand Press*, p. 23.
[77] *Ramage*, pp. 26–27.

much time and money on the project, succeeded in producing such a press about 1800. Its vaunted advantage was no illusion: it was so powerful that it could print a full form with one impression as opposed to the two pulls required in wooden presses. After some modifications the Stanhope press established itself as a notable advance in the history of pressmaking. At least two were imported into the United States, one of which belonged to David and George Bruce in 1811. In that same year an article in the *Long-Island Star* implied that Francis Shield, recently arrived in New York City from London, knew how to manufacture a Stanhope press.[78] Thus did the iron printing press begin to supersede the wooden press in this country.

There is no evidence that George Clymer of Philadelphia saw a Stanhope press at that time. But even if he had seen it, it could have exerted only nominal influence on the design of his iron press. Clymer, it will be remembered, had already completed a decade of pressmaking utilizing conventional as well as experimental principles. Quite naturally his great mechanical ingenuity, depicted in the excellent monograph on Clymer by Kainen, attracted him to the superiority of iron. Clymer's iron press, the Columbian, came on the market about 1814 and is said to have been used first by William Fry.[79] Clymer's work had already aroused the curiosity of printers in remote areas. One letter, written by William W. Seaton of Gales & Seaton, Washington, D.C., to William W. Worsley, Lexington, Kentucky, on March 20, 1813, is a frank appraisal of an earlier Clymer iron press:

I do not know that I am qualified fully to offer an opinion on the Iron Press, concerning which you enquire.—There is one in our office, constantly worked on, which I have often examined, particularly since your letter was received.—Its superiority consists in its greater strength and consequent durability—the ease with which it is worked—the uniformity of its impression—and the advantage of having a *platten* large enough to cover a news[paper] form at one pull.—Ours does not possess the last mentioned advantage, but I am informed the *Aurora* is printed at *one pull.*—Your chief object, however, will not be attained in this press, as *greater expedition* is not combined in its superiority over the common presses.—Further, the cost of the one we have was $300, and its great weight would make the expence of carriage very great.—The present price may

[78] Oct. 23, 1811.   [79] Kainen, p. 18; *Am. Dict. Print.*, p. 218.

be much less, as ours was the 2d or 3d that Clymer made.—I know
not whether you will be enabled to judge of the expediency of purchasing one from what I have said—but I am as explicit as I can be.
—Mr. Gales says he would advise you against the experiment.[80]

The price, it should be noted, stayed up. Later, larger models cost
$400 to $500 at the time when Ramage's wooden presses cost about
$130.[81] Despite the expense, newspaper printers in particular appre-
ciated the large platen so much that "nearly all the newspapers in
New York," said Joel Munsell in a note about the Clymer presses,
"had adopted them."[82]

The Columbian, in the words of Kainen, bridged "the gap between the Stanhope, the first successful all-iron press, with its revolutionary compound lever actuating the ancient although improved
screw, and the Wells, Albion, Smith, and Washington presses,
which received power from the straightening of a knuckle, chill, or
toggle joint."[83] It worked by means of an iron crossbeam pivoted at
one end and pulled down at the other by a toggle mechanism. In the
middle of the beam, instead of a screw, there was a vertical member
to force the platen down. To ease the raising of the platen, a counter-
weight in the form of a cast-iron eagle rested on a bar at the top of
the press. What with the additional decoration of dragons, snakes,
and other designs on large parts of the press, there "was never a
press, before or since, which carried so much ornamentation."[84]
Elimination of the screw provided ease of pull and better impression; the iron added power and durability. Clymer's Columbian
became the best of the lever presses (Plate I).

As good as it was, Clymer could sell it to a limited number of
printers only. Compared with the Ramage, it was much more expensive, much heavier, and not as easy to repair. Country printers
balked at the price, transportation costs, and repair problems; city
printers at the price. When the American market had been satu-
rated, Clymer decided to sell his press on the other side of the
Atlantic. And so he left Thomas Barnitt in charge of domestic
manufacture, assembled some glowing commendations from American printers, and sailed for England in 1817. There he found more
customers than at home, so many that his press eventually sup-

[80] State Historical Society of Wisconsin, Draper MSS. 5CC102.
[81] Kainen, p. 20.   [82] *Typ. Misc.*, p. 126.   [83] Kainen, pp. 4–5.
[84] Green, *Iron Hand Press*, p. 2.

planted the Stanhope; on the Continent it was also popular, appearing in French and German versions.[85]

The next advance in American pressmaking was made by John I. Wells, an inkmaker of Hartford, Connecticut. While supplying printers with ink, he noticed the clumsiness of the presses and, having used a press possessing a lever and simple toggle joint in his linseed oil factory, reasoned that he could tie a printing press into the same plan.[86] Beginning in 1816, Wells spent two or three years experimenting with presses which had wooden frames strengthened with iron. Finding that the power bent the wood, he substituted iron frames.[87] His first iron press, completed early in 1819 and patented on February 8, incorporated a simple toggle joint, a very successful device:

We are pleased to state that Mr. John I. Wells, an ingenious mechanist of this city, has at length so far perfected his PATENT LEVER PRINTING PRESS, as to offer it publicly for sale. We witnessed it in operation on Thursday last, and perhaps some account of it will be acceptable to our brethren of the type.

Mr. Wells states that from the application of the power of levers end-wise, in expressing Linseed Oil, he became fully convinced that it exceeded all other mechanical powers. It is now about four years since he made his first experiment upon an old press. Since that time he has been constantly making experiments upon every part of the press which admitted of improvement, and he has succeeded in every effort. Perhaps it may be deemed high ground, after the deserved reputation which Mr. Clymer's presses have acquired;—but we are nevertheless of the opinion (and we have witnessed the operations of both for more than two years) that Mr. Well's press excels his. The construction of it is more simple and compact, and its impression is very powerful and even.

In order that a proper estimate of the power of this press may be formed, it may not be improper to subjoin a short description of it. The frame, platten, and several other parts are of cast iron; and the weight of the cast and wrought iron is about 1500 lbs. The power is obtained by two upright levers, footing in the centre of the platten; within a strong circle upon the plate. These levers are fifteen inches in length, one and three fourths of an inch square in the body, and four inches wide at the ends. They move in sockets of the semicircle of half an inch; falling back in the centre, two inches, from a perpendicular line,—this admits of the rising of the platten. They are governed in this joint, and forced neatly to a straight line, by two

[85] Kainen, pp. 21–46.
[86] Green, *Iron Hand Press*, p. 7; *Connecticut Mirror*, Aug. 2, 1819.
[87] *Connecticut Mirror*, Aug. 9, 1819.

whilſt a paſſionate man, engaged in a warm controverſy, would thunder vengeance in

French Canon

It follows of courſe, that writers of great iraſcibility ſhould be charged higher for a work of the ſame length, than meek authors; on account of the extraordinary ſpace their performances muſt neceſſarily occupy; for theſe gigantic, wrathful types, like ranters on the ſtage, muſt have ſufficient elbow-room.

For example: Suppoſe a newſpaper quarrel to happen between * M and L. M begins the attack pretty ſmartly in

Long Primer.

L replies in

Pica Roman.

M advances to

Great Primer.

L retorts in

Double Pica.

And ſo the conteſt ſwells to

Raſcal, Villain

* Leſt ſome ill-diſpoſed perſon ſhould miſapply theſe initials, I think proper to declare, that M ſignifies Merchant, and L Lawyer.

Coward,

V. Francis Hopkinson, "Plan for the Improvement of the Art of Paper War," *American Museum*, I (1787). (Reduced from 5 x 8½)

diis, alterum cum belluis commune eſt. Quo
mihi rectiùs videtur, ingenii, quàm virium
opibus gloriam quærere ; & quoniam vita
ipſa, quâ fruimur, brevis eſt, memoriam [1]no-
ſtrî quàm maxumè longam efficere. Nam
divitiarum & formæ gloria, fluxa atque fra-
gilis ; virtus clara, æternaque habetur. Sed
diu magnum inter mortali certamen fuit,
vi-ne corporis, an virtute animi, res militaris
magìs procederet. Nam & priùs, quàm [2]in-
cipias, [3]conſulto, &, ubi conſulueris, maturè
facto opus eſt. Ita utrumque per ſe indigens,
alterum alterius auxilio eget.

II. Igitur initio reges (nam in terris no-
men imperii id primum fuit) [4]diverſi, pars
ingenium, alii corpus, exercebant : etiam
tum

N O T Æ.

[1]*Noſtri.*] Notandum eſt *Salluſtium* non dicere *noſtram.* Nam *memoriam noſtram* active acciperetur, et ſenſus eſſet, quâ aliorum memores ſumus ; ſed *memoriam noſtri* paſſivè accipitur, ut ſit ſenſus, quâ alii noſtri memores ſint.

[2]*Incipias.*] Id eſt, *quilibet incipiat.* Hæ locutiones per ſecundam ſingularis numeri perſonam ſunt frequentiſſimæ & elegantiſſimæ. Iis utimur etiam cùm ad multitudinem præſentem ſermo dirigitur.

[3]*Conſulto.*] Participiorum, inquit Priſcianus, accuſativi frequentèr pro infinitis verbis ponuntur ; ut, *ſæpe celebritatem novimus te timentem,* pro *timere :* Ablativi quoque pro eorum infinitis, ut Salluſtius in Catilinario, *et priuſquam incipias,* CONSULTO, *et, ubi conſulueris, maturè* FACTO *opus eſt ;* pro *conſulere* et *facere.*

[4]*Diverſi.*] Id eſt, *diverſas vias inſiſtentes.*

VI. C. Sallustius Crispus, *Belli Catilinarii et Jugurthini historiae*
(Salem, Mass., 1805)

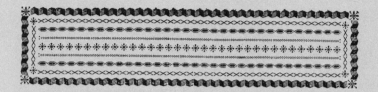

DESCRIPTION

TOPOGRAPHIQUE ET POLITIQUE

DE LA

PARTIE FRANCAISE

DE

L'ISLE SAINT-DOMINGUE.

LA Partie Française de l'île Saint-Domingue est, de toutes les possessions de la France dans le Nouveau-Monde, la plus importante par les richesses qu'elle procure à sa Métropole & par l'influence qu'elle a sur son agriculture & sur son commerce.

Sous ce rapport, la Partie Française de Saint-Domingue est digne de l'observation de tous les hommes qui se livrent à l'étude des gouvernemens, qui cherchent dans les détails des différentes parties d'un vaste état, les points capitaux qui peuvent en éclairer l'administration, & montrer les bases réelles du meilleur système de prospérité publique.

La connaissance particulière de la Partie Française de Saint-Domingue, peut encore intéresser l'homme qui, sans saisir l'ensemble dont je viens de parler, désire connaître les mœurs, le caractère, les productions, la population & le commerce d'une Colonie, que son éloignement même de la Mère-patrie,

Tome I.   A

VII. M. L. É. Moreau de Saint-Méry, *Description topographique . . . de l'Isle Saint-Domingue* (Philadelphia, 1797). (Reduced from 8 x 9⅝)

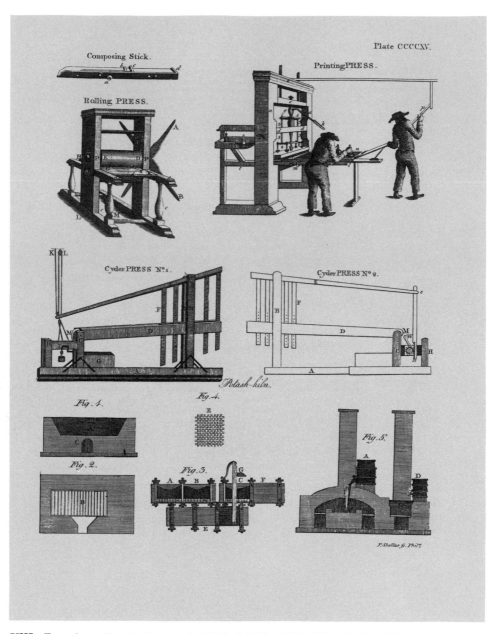

VIII. *Encyclopaedia*, 1st Amer. ed. (Philadelphia, 1790–97). (Reduced from 8¼ x 10⅝)

horizontal levers, attached in connection with the arm or bar, to the back part of the press;—which, in gaining the power are brought nearly to a straight line. The platten is raised by a spindle, suspended upon a balance lever, by a balance weight. It is governed in its movements by grooves, attached to the inner edge of the body of the Press.[88]

Until competition in New York outdistanced Wells a few years later, his press, priced at $350, apparently sold well (Plate IIa).[89]

The rival manufacturers who outsold Wells adopted his principle of the toggle joint with some upgrading of quality. They captured the market from Wells primarily through an elastic business policy and because they were located in New York rather than in Hartford. For one of them, Robert Hoe, the new press helped to build a firm which became one of the largest pressmakers in the world. Hoe, a nineteen-year-old carpenter, had emigrated from England in 1803. Two years later, he and two brothers-in-law, Matthew and Peter Smith, formed the partnership of Smith, Hoe & Co. to make wooden presses as well as other equipment including stands and cases.[90] As soon as they saw that iron presses were in use, they produced one designed by Peter Smith. This had a toggle joint similar to the Wells press, but it was enhanced by two features neglected in the archetype: springs to raise the platen and the bar on the near side.[91] With some justice, Wells bitterly felt that Smith had copied his press; he told his side of the story in a letter written in 1828:

In 1820 several of my presses were in the Bible office in N. York; and after Peter Smith had commenced the manufacture of presses, I was informed that he had examined them many times. His Patent is dated '29th Dec. 1821,' of which I have a copy. He claims that his 'improvement consists chiefly in applying the *Wedge Power*,' whereas all his power is derived from his Levers. And since then, nearly all the inventors of printing presses have adopted the principle, with some variation in the manner.[92]

The Smith press, probably with its acorn frame, appeared about 1821.[93] Heavier and stronger than the Wells, it sold well during the following years. After Peter Smith died in 1823, the press continued

---

[88] *List of Patents*, p. 203; *Connecticut Mirror*, Aug. 2, 1819.
[89] Green, *Iron Hand Press*, p. 8.   [90] *DAB*, IX, 105.
[91] Green, *Iron Hand Press*, p. 12.
[92] *An Abridgment of "Johnson's Typographia"* (Boston, 1828), pp. 302–4.
[93] Baltimore *American*, January 24, 1821; Green, *Iron Hand Press*, p. 11.

to be manufactured by the successor firm of Robert Hoe & Co. (Plate IIb).

Another New York competitor of Wells, Samuel Rust, a printer whose origins are obscure, improved the toggle joint for greater leverage. His iron press with a "figure 4" toggle joint, patented May 13, 1821, resembled the Smith press and is well known as the Washington press, so named by its inventor.[94] It was manufactured by the firm of Rust & Turney for about a dozen years (Plate III). Rust, in 1829, improved the frame by making it stronger yet lighter in weight and easy to dismantle for shipment.[95] The Hoe firm, believing the Washington press unmatched, acquired the patent about 1835 and happily manufactured it for almost a century, producing more than six thousand in that time.[96] "For simplicity and accuracy," said the *American Dictionary of Printing and Bookmaking* in 1894, "it is difficult to see how any machine can surpass it."[97] Green is explicit about its domination of American country printing:

> The name Washington, as applied to the iron press, has been in common use for over a century, but Samuel Rust has been forgotten. He invented and perfected a tool which, if its long and useful life is considered, has been of more importance and greater help to the country printer than any one item in the office.[98]

One more toggle joint press deserves mention. This was the iron press (similar to the English Medhurst) which Abraham O. Stansbury of New York City patented on April 7, 1821.[99] Although not associated with any advance in pressmaking, it belongs in an honorable category, the first of its class to be manufactured in the West. In 1822 the Cincinnati Type Foundry and Printers' Warehouse advertised Stansbury's presses made to order; in the following year it advertised cast-iron presses at two hundred and fifty dollars.[100] As early as 1822 the *Missouri Gazette* of St. Louis owned one which may have been purchased from that firm.[101] By building these

---

[94] *List of Patents*, p. 225; Green, *Iron Hand Press*, p. 16.

[95] Green, *Iron Hand Press*, pp. 16–20.

[96] *Ibid.*, p. 20; *A Short History of the Printing Press* (New York, 1902), p. 9.

[97] P. 577.   [98] *Iron Hand Press*, p. 22.

[99] *Ibid.*, p. 28; *List of Patents*, p. 225; Kainen, p. 16.

[100] Sutton, pp. 14, 17.

[101] John Clyde Oswald, *Printing in the Americas* (New York, [1937]), p. 497n.

presses, the Cincinnati foundry enabled Western printers to save the time and cost of transporting iron presses from the East.

Technological progress in the application of power soon governed further evolution of the press. Smith, Hoe & Co., in 1819, began to experiment with steampower presses, but without immediate success.[102] Two years later Daniel Treadwell of Boston designed a power press which was so profitable that by the time he relinquished it in 1829 he had earned seventy thousand dollars. Treadwell, later Rumford Professor at Harvard, had been a silversmith addicted to experimentation with machines. When he lost his silversmith business because of the War of 1812, he resorted to his hobby, inventing a screw-making machine and a nail-making machine. After a short period in which he studied medicine, he began work on an improved printing press.[103] His first press, built in 1818, was a very large, complicated machine, operated by a foot-treadle rather than a lever, with a double frisket, reversible so that half-sheets could be printed on both sides without shifting. Although, according to Green, American printers encouraged him to keep on with its manufacture, Treadwell, perhaps prompted by Clymer's foray abroad, decided instead to introduce it to the English market.[104] In London late in 1819, he had his press built by Baisler & Napier, who finished it in the late spring of 1820,[105] and obtained an English patent for it (Plate IV). English printers were careful to praise it but did not buy it. Disheartened, he returned to Boston in September, 1820.[106]

His English venture was advantageous in the long run, for he studied the new foreign steampower newspaper presses and they confirmed his ambition to design a power press of his own. Nathan Hale, the Boston newspaper publisher, fortified him with a suggestion or two, and Phineas Dow, an expert machinist who built fire engines, helped him in the construction.[107] Treadwell's power press, in all probability built by Dow and completed in 1821, used a live horse to supply the power, as steam engines were not easy to come by.[108] The press seems monstrous and an exaggeration, yet at the

---

[102] *DAB*, IX, 105.   [103] *Ibid.*, XVIII, 632.   [104] Green, *SB*, IV, 144.
[105] *Ibid.*; "Recent Patents," *London Jour. Arts and Sci.*, I (1820) 321–23.
[106] Green, *SB*, IV, 144.
[107] Edward E. Hale, *A New England Boyhood* (Boston, 1927), p. 60; Green, *SB*, IV, 146.
[108] Green, *SB*, IV, 146.

same time logically reasoned; what is more, it worked well. The spectacle is described with respectful amusement:

It was a bed and platen press of pretty large dimensions, the bed being capable of carrying a form a little larger than the ordinary hand-presses then in use. The bed was horizontal and reciprocating. The press was constructed of very large wooden timbers, about twelve inches square, and a great quantity of cast and wrought iron. Connected with its huge wooden frame was a wilderness of belts, cams, pitmen, gearings, and cranks. Its weight was enormous. A very strong rotating-reciprocating vertical iron shaft gave motion to its numerous and complicated parts. Among many devices connected with said vertical shaft, there were firmly affixed to it two very strong cams, one above the other. To each of the cams was attached one end of a very thick sole-leather belt about three inches wide. The opposite ends of these belts were secured to the bed, the office of one of them being to bring the bed to its proper place under the platen, and the other to draw it away for the delivery of the printed sheet and for the reception of a fresh one. The upper cam, with its belt, was on a plane with the top of the bed. The lower cam, with its belt, was on a plane a trifle lower than the bottom of the bed; and the lower belt, which drew the bed out from under the platen, passed over a pulley situated beyond the rear terminus of the bed's track. The cams were so contrived as to start the bed from its places of rest very gently, without producing anything like a sudden blow, and then to move it with great rapidity in or out the remaining distance of its track. Each of the belts was provided with devices for taking up any slack caused by the strain upon them. The bed rested and moved upon ways similar to those in use on hand-presses.

The press was provided with a "throw-off," to prevent an impression being made, whenever circumstances required. One end of the frisket was hinged to the front part of the bed, and one end of a reciprocating-cloth, which the inventor named a "cloth tympan," was also attached to the front of the bed. A stiff rod was fastened to each end of the "cloth tympan," which kept it stretched smooth, and free from wrinkles or folds. The impression was given by the toggle joint. The inking-rollers, for inking the type, were supported in a carriage which carried them back and forth over the type after each impression. The frisket, with a printed sheet upon it, in its movement from under the platen, ran up an inclined stationary table, or "apron," at an angle of about thirty-five degrees, while the cloth tympan, at the same time, was carried, by means of a weighted cord running over a pulley, to a perfectly vertical position,—precisely like the cloth of an ordinary copper-plate printing-press. The sheets of paper were placed on and removed from the frisket by hand. Register-points were attached to the frisket. Overlays could be secured to the cloth tympan whenever desired. When the frisket carried the sheet to be printed under the platen, the cloth tympan was carried by the same operation under the platen and over the sheet and frisket. A wooden roller about two inches in diameter, whose length was an inch or two greater than the width of the cloth tympan, was attached to the rear part of the platen, projecting a trifle beyond it; and against this roller the cloth tympan came in contact in its movements to and from its vertical and horizontal positions without chafing against the edge of the platen.

At the rear end of the press was a large, round, horizontal, inter-mittingly-rotating ink-distributing table, which made about one eighth of a revolution at each impression. The diameter of this round table was three or four inches greater than the length of the ink-distributing rollers, or the type-inking rollers, each and all of which passed over it at each impression. In the rear of the ink-distributing table was an ink-fountain, with a metal roller in it, gauged so as to give the necessary quantity of ink to the inking-rollers. The ink-distributing rollers were supported in a carriage which passed back and forth over the ink-distributing table while the type-inking rollers were passing over the form.

This press required a full horse-power to put it in operation, and the motor employed was no other than a stalwart, living horse, the horse being harnessed to some strangely contrived thills, depending from a large wooden sweep similar to those used in the old-fashioned New England cider-mills, the sweep passing over the top of the press. The circular track of the horse was about thirty feet in diameter. From some cause the inventor had failed to provide sufficient weight or momentum to the fly-wheel in order to straighten the toggle joint with ease by accumulated power; and whenever an impression was made the horse received a shock which nearly jerked him off his feet; and he soon became so familiar with these "hard spots" in his path that when he approached one of them he would often come to a dead halt, from which no amount of coaxing or scolding—nothing but whipping—would induce him to stir. Therefore it soon became necessary to employ a driver with a whip to follow him around the track. After a short time it became apparent that one horse could not endure the strain of such uninter-rupted hard labor from day to day, and especially the violent shocks caused by straightening the toggles, and a second horse was added as a relay.[109]

When the press was placed in a building, the vertical shaft could be extended through the floor to the basement, where the horse could be hitched to a horizontal lever attached to the shaft. Three people—a pressman, feeder, and driver—working at this press could print five hundred to six hundred sheets an hour, thus dou-

---

[109] *Moore's Hist. Biog. Misc. Gath.*, pp. 35–37.

bling the speed of hand presses. Green has remarked upon two interesting aspects of this invention: first, Treadwell could not adopt the impression cylinder already in use in England because of the perennial lack of adequate machine tools. The few lathes and drill presses in Boston were not yet large enough nor accurate enough, thereby obliging Treadwell to restrict himself to the scheme of the hand press; second, Treadwell's revolving disk for distributing ink to the inking rollers reappeared a quarter-century later in the job presses of George P. Gordon.[110]

To demonstrate his press to prospective customers, Treadwell set it up in Batterymarch Street, Boston, where, operated by Isaac R. Butts, it produced books for Boston publishers.[111] One such item was a New Testament printed in 1822 at "Treadwell's Power Press."[112] He then began to sell the rights to build and use the press. The rights for the Boston area were purchased by Nathan Hale and T. H. Carter, each adding four, run by horsepower, to his own plant (they jointly owned four others run by water power).[113] As the sale of his presses increased, Treadwell built two presses back-to-back so that they could be driven by a common shaft. All in all, about fifty Treadwell presses were built before 1830. Daniel Fanshaw had twenty in his New York plant, Isaac Ashmead had at least eight double machines in Philadelphia, and Baltimore and Washington printers also owned them.[114] As steampower became assured, the printers dispensed with horses. There is a touching story of one of the Harper horses which had been retired to the Harper farm only to find his empty leisure unbearable:

The first day the old horse was put out to pasture he rolled over in the grass, rushed about the meadow, and seemed to have renewed his youth. In a few days, however, the novelty wore off, and he took a long rest, spending most of his time in a shed which had been erected for him in the corner of the pasture. One morning, when Father Harper went out to the field, he heard the seven-o'clock whistle sounding, and to his surprise he saw the old horse slowly emerge from the shed and go to the center of the pasture where there was a solitary tree. Around this tree the horse traveled, round and round, as though he were turning his old-time shaft, until

[110] *SB*, IV, 145–148. [111] *Moore's Hist. Biog. Misc. Gath.*, p. 37.
[112] *The English Bible in America*, ed. Margaret T. Hills (New York, 1961), p. 71.
[113] *Moore's Hist. Biog. Misc. Gath.*, pp. 37–38.
[114] Green, *SB*, IV, 145–147.

twelve o'clock sounded, when he promptly discontinued for lunch-time and went back to his shed. At the stroke of one o'clock he returned to the tree and moved round and round again until the six-o'clock whistle blew, when he dropped work and sought the repose of his shed, where he remained for the night.[115]

After Treadwell relinquished his business, R. Hoe & Co. manufactured the Treadwell press, but less expensive and more efficient presses soon supplanted it.

In 1822 Jonas Booth, a New York printer, built the first steampower press in the United States. It was similar to Treadwell's but with a frisket frame at each end so that a sheet could be placed in one frame while another sheet received the impression from the single form.[116] By the middle of the following year Booth had printed an abridgment of Murray's English grammar for Collins & Co., which at that time was announced to be the first book printed by a steampower press in this country.[117] Booth patented the press in 1829 only to find that the competition was too strong for him to sell many presses.[118]

While Treadwell and Booth were exploiting the use of power, another hand press of an entirely new design appeared on the market. Its inventor, Daniel Neall of Bensalem, Pennsylvania, referred to it as the Vertical press when he described it to a newspaper correspondent in 1822:

I take the liberty of sending thee a sheet of paper printed on the Vertical press. Thee will perceive on examining of it, some defects, which were owing to the bed and platten being of wood, and not strong enough to resist the power applied. I made the machine in a rough manner, merely to test the principle, not with the expectation of its doing good work; and on trial it fully answers my expectation. My intention is now to make one to do its work well, the beds and platten of which will be of cast iron—the principle admits of Presses being made single or double—the single to print on one side at a time, the other to print on two at a time—the single will be for job work only—small, simple and cheap, and when not at work with, can be set aside out of the way. The large one is more complex—composed of two beds and two plattens, ranged in a line with each other, and must have two forms on at the same time, that while one form is making the first impression on a sheet, the other is finishing the one that immediately preceeded it; the person working this press

---

[115] Harper, p. 26. Reprinted by permission of Harper & Row, Inc.
[116] Green, *SB*, IV, 148.   [117] *Niles' Weekly Register*, XXIV (1823), 256.
[118] Green, *SB*, IV, 149.

puts the paper on, the press turns it, and when printed on both sides lays it snugly off. My object in planning this press has been to gain time, the operations being only to put the paper on, cause the bed and types to form a quarter of a circle, give the lever a pull, and you have a sheet printed on both sides.[119]

Three years later Neall patented the press and began to advertise it.[120] Little else is known about it other than the fact that in 1825 Kimber & Sharpless of Philadelphia had six in operation.[121]

In the use of rollers for inking the United States lagged behind England. Although Kinsley's presses, it will be remembered, were designed to have rollers covered with soft leather, the first American skin rollers were not introduced until about 1807:

In the art of printing, an important improvement invented by Mr. Hugh Maxwell, has been made and [is] in practical use in three printing offices of Philadelphia. The improvement consists of a roller used for inking the type. The advantages of which are greater regularity in the distribution of the ink, a perfect equality of colour, with a trifling attention, a considerable saving in the expense of printing, and a cleanliness, as respects picks, monks, and friars, not to be attained by the utmost care with the common balls. Another advantage which will be felt by every printer who adopts this plan, the accident of drawing letters so destructive to printing type, so injurious to part of the machinery of the press, and frequently productive of gross errours, is totally avoided.

The machine is light and pleasant work for a boy of ten or twelve years of age, and proves on actual trial a saving on each press to which it is constantly used of about six dollars per week, and the quantity of work performed on one press is more than what can be done in the usual way. One of those machines has been in constant operation for seven months, and during that period has not required one hour's attention. There is no preparation necessary, but cleaning, which is performed in a few minutes. The trouble of preparing new balls, and knocking up balls, which on the old plan consumes so much time is in this machine totally saved. It is computed, that in saving of time one fifth more can be done per day than on the old plan, with all the superiorities enumerated.

Two of those machines are now in constant use in the printing office of Smith and Maxwell, one in the office of Benjamin Johnson, and one in the office of Thomas S. Manning, where they may be seen at work.

The machine is furnished complete for one hundred dollars.[122]

[119] Baltimore *Federal Gazette*, May 11, 1822.

[120] *List of Patents*, p. 298; Baltimore *American*, Nov. 18, 1825.

[121] Baltimore *American*, Nov. 18, 1825.

[122] Thomas G. Fessenden, *The Register of Arts* (Philadelphia, 1808), pp. 363–64.

They were said to have been abandoned because they were awkward to manipulate. About 1815 Daniel Fanshaw of New York reintroduced them, and again their reputation discouraged many printers. An account written thirteen years later supplies one reason: "They have never been considered so good as balls: being too heavy for the hand."[123] Another reason may have been the problem of the seam, which could easily make an ugly blotch. Other than the patent obtained by Hugh Maxwell in 1817, a mere formality, the idea of the roller was buried until news of the composition roller arrived from England.[124]

At least four different printers have been credited with introducing composition rollers. One source declares that William Brown of Philadelphia first tried them; another that Isaac Ashmead of Philadelphia was the first to use them. The notes of Ralph Green, now at the College of William and Mary, say that Thomas Palmer introduced them in Philadelphia in 1823–24 after his return from England.[125] A fourth source states that in 1826 or 1827 Jonas Booth of New York "began using composition rollers, casting them himself. They had previously been unknown on this side of the water."[126] This ambiguity may eventually be clarified. In the meantime it may be proved that composition rollers were introduced about 1825 because Van Winkle described both skin and composition rollers in his 1827 edition of *The Printers' Guide* and because *An Abridgment of "Johnson's Typographia"* (1828) discussed composition rollers "with the observations resulting from a practice of nearly three years."[127]

In addition to printing from type, American printers began to utilize stereotyping and lithography. Their knowledge of stereotyping technique, as of composition rollers, came from England. In 1811 the *Long-Island Star* noted that Francis Shield of London, who had just established himself as a press manufacturer in New York, "is also in possession of the art of taking *Stereotype plates*, and has specimens in his possession."[128] During the following year at

---

[123] *An Abridgment*, p. 309.   [124] *List of Patents*, p. 184.
[125] *Am. Dict. Print.*, p. 434; *Typographic Advertiser*, XV (1870), 436.
[126] *Am. Dict. Print.*, p. 63.
[127] Cornelius S. Van Winkle, *The Printer's Guide*, 2nd ed. (New York, 1827), p. xxi; *An Abridgment*, p. 310.
[128] Oct. 23, 1811.

least three others were working on the process: David Bruce sailed for England to learn about it; John Watts, an Englishman who had worked with Andrew Wilson in London and whose brother was one of Earl Stanhope's first pupils, experimented with stereotyping in New York; at Baltimore S. W. Johnson offered lessons in stereotype founding.[129] In December, Whiting & Watson of New York announced a forthcoming Hebrew Bible for which stereotype plates would be cast by John Watts.[130] Only the first few parts of the Bible, stereotyped by D. & G. Bruce in 1815, were printed, but *The Larger Catechism*, stereotyped and printed by J. Watts & Co. and published in June, 1813, bears a statement on the title page: "The first book ever stereotyped in America."[131] This, though, is not the first book printed from stereotype plates in America; in 1812 the Philadelphia Bible Society had printed a Bible from plates imported from London.[132] Watts continued stereotype founding for a few years, turning out an edition of Murray's English grammar in 1814.[133] When the competition of the Bruces in 1816 became alarming, he disposed of his foundry to B. & J. Collins.[134]

A touch of speculative fever accompanied the introduction of stereotyping in America. In Connecticut a group which included Hudson & Goodwin, publishers, Eli Whitney, and Benjamin Silliman was incorporated in 1813 as The Stereotype Company for "the purpose of manufacturing stereotype plates and other plates and types, and of printing and vending literary works maps and charts." The capital could not exceed $500,000 and operation could not begin until $100,000 was subscribed.[135] A similar company was incorporated in the same state two years later with a capital of $150,000.[136] Neither apparently achieved success.

[129] Rollo G. Silver, *Typefounding in America, 1787–1825* (Charlottesville, Va., [1965]), p. 76; E. B. O'Callaghan, *A List of Editions of the Holy Scriptures* (Albany, 1861), pp. 128–30; *Catalogue of the Books in the Library of the Typothetae of the City of New York* (New York, 1896), p. 28; *Am. Dict. Print.*, p. 578; Silver, *Balt. Book Trade*, p. 36.

[130] New York *Commercial Advertiser*, Dec. 26, 1812.

[131] M. Vaxer, "The First Hebrew Bible Printed in America," *Jour. Jewish Bib.*, II (1940), 25–26.

[132] *Eng. Bible in Am.*, p. 37.

[133] *American Bibliography . . . for 1814*, comp. Ralph R. Shaw and Richard H. Shoemaker (New York, 1963), p. 189.

[134] *Cat. Books Typothetae*, p. 28.

[135] Connecticut State Library, Connecticut Archives, Industry, 1747–1820, 2nd ser., Vol. II, Docs. 145–46.

[136] William Charvat, *Literary Publishing in America, 1790–1850* (Philadelphia, [1959]), p. 19.

Despite the fact that Earl Stanhope courteously refused to tell David Bruce much about the process of stereotyping, Bruce returned from England with some knowledge of the technique. After a period of experimentation Bruce mastered the process and, in doing so, improved it at three stages: he invented a planing machine, he used mahogany shifting blocks, and he devised a method of packing plates in boxes. Finding it necessary to obtain type with the square shoulders required for stereotyping, the firm of David and George Bruce, the largest printing office in New York, purchased a foundry. At the beginning they did not intend to make a general business of stereotyping, but success soon changed their minds. In 1816 they relinquished the printing business so that George Bruce could devote his attention to typefounding and David to stereotyping.[137] With the invention of the planing machine "stereotyping became an art useful everywhere."[138]

Aggressive printers quickly adopted it for large editions, such as Bibles and textbooks, which had a large national market. As early as 1814 Mathew Carey purchased the plates of a New Testament from the Bruces for $756.00 and the plates of a grammar (probably the Watts plates of Murray) from Collins of New York for $802.50.[139] Within ten years classical texts, previously imported, were also stereotyped; in 1823 the Carey firm wrote: "We have stereotyped Virgil Delphini & Horace Delphini at an expense of nearly $6000. Mr. Warner of this place had Ainsworth's Lat. Dict. stereotyped for which he paid $4500. Ovid & Caesar Delphini have been stereotyped in New York. Graeca Minora is now stereotyping there for a house in Boston."[140] By 1825 the stereotypers of New York, Philadelphia, and Boston were supplying printers with popular texts which could be published in each city simultaneously without the labor of composition or the expense of standing type.

It was in this period, too, that lithography was introduced into the United States. Using a stone from Munich which had been presented to the American Philosophical Society by Thomas Dobson, Bass Otis drew a lithograph in Philadelphia for the July, 1819, issue of the *Analectic Magazine*. It appeared with this note:

---

[137] Silver, *Typefounding*, pp. 69–70, 76, 82.   [138] *Am. Dict. Print.*, p. 527.
[139] Silver, *Typefounding*, pp. 77–78; American Antiquarian Society, Mathew Carey Papers, XXVIII, 4149.
[140] Earl L. Bradsher, *Mathew Carey* (New York, 1912), p. 36.

In this number, we present our readers with a specimen of *American Lithography:* the design and the execution from beginning to end—from the drawing to the impression inclusive—is by Mr. B. Otis; who, following the suggestions of judge Cooper, and Dr. Brown, of Alabama, has by means of their hints, and his own more successful improvements, produced the specimen now submitted.[141]

The note went on to describe other experiments:

But the art has been successfully tried on specimens of stone from Frankfort, in Kentucky, procured by judge Cooper, Dr. Brown, and Mr. Clifford—from Doe run in Kentucky, furnished by Dr. Blight —from a quarry about two miles from Maytown, Lancaster county —and also on some pieces of white marble from White Marsh, commonly found at the stone-cutters in this city. Dr. Brown in particular has felt great interest in the progress of this trial, and has written to various places in the western country for pieces of stone as similar as may be, to the stone of Munich; which are now on the road: so that the next print will probably be from a limestone of our own country.[142]

As will be seen later, lithographs thereafter appeared as book illustrations.

Thus, as the first quarter of the nineteenth century ended, the American printer was becoming familiar with iron presses, stereotyping, lithography, and the use of power. These were ingredients of the industrial revolution in printing.

[141] "Lithography," *Analectic Mag.*, XIV (1819), 67.   [142] *Ibid.*, p. 68.

CHAPTER 3

THE PRACTICE OF PRINTING

THE Revolution compelled a good many printers to face a recurring ethical problem, whether to print views contrary to their beliefs if ordered by their patrons or to refuse, and risk political and economic misfortune by printing only the opinions which they supported. Some printers, among them Hugh Gaine, made the best of both worlds by remaining Tory partisans during the Revolution and sliding into a new alliance as the new republic began. This ability to keep on good terms at both periods with both parties enabled some former Tories to prosper, whereas Benjamin Edes, who printed much revolutionary propaganda for a cause which must have seemed at times hopeless, died a poor man. His final editorial, written when his Boston *Gazette* ceased publication in 1798, concludes with these paragraphs, which do him honor:

But, alas! the cause of Liberty is not always the channel of preferment or pecuniary reward. The little property which he acquired has long since fell a sacrifice;—the *paper-evidences* of his services were soon consumed by their rapid depreciation, and the cares of a numerous family were too powerful to be resisted, though he fed them with property at *four shillings and sixpence in the pound*, which he faithfully and industriously earned at *twenty shillings*.

However, it is beneath a patriot to mourn his own misfortunes. The Independence of America being obtained, he enjoys the pleasing contemplation, that the *same virtuous sentiments* which led to the *acquisition* will not cease to operate for its *continuance*—That his fellow-citizens will ever revere the First Principles of the Revolution; and it is his earnest prayer to Heaven, that the Rising Generation will remember the exertions of Their Fathers, in opposing the lawless attempts of Britain for their subjugation.

Let the citizens of America Reverence Themselves. Let them strive to maintain the Republican Principles of their own Constitution; and while practising these duties, we may trust to the Guardian Angel, which has conducted us through dangers, the most alarming and distressing.

And now, my Fellow-Citizens, I bid you FAREWELL! Maintain your Virtue—Cherish your Liberties—and may The Almighty protect and defend you.[1]

Similar personal courage is seen in those printers who left the easier life of cities and towns after the Revolution to establish presses in the remote new settlements. Often without funds and dependent on the good will of strangers, they managed to gather up enough equipment to print the newspaper and other items needed in a community which frequently could not afford their product. Hamilton has said that there were three possible methods by which a printer might secure financial aid: he might appeal to the village inhabitants, he might appeal to a single patron, or he might be sought out by a group of public-spirited persons who felt that a newspaper was needed in the area. However financed, return on investment was not assured. Sometimes the sponsors mortgaged the equipment. When a group of inhabitants realized the necessity of a printer and combined to obtain one, they sometimes did this without thought of realizing a substantial profit; they primarily wanted to improve their own community. Therefore they later withdrew from ownership. One example, cited by Hamilton, is that of a newspaper declaring it "was originally purchased and set in operation by a company of gentlemen, without distinction of party; and who had in view, probably, the benefits resulting to the country from a Press located in this village."[2] If a single patron supplied funds, he may have been the leading citizen or a worldly man with political ambitions or financial power.

Hamilton believed that it must have taken at least several hundred dollars to set up a small office in New York state about 1805. After that, in some instances, additional subsidies would be required to continue operation. The printer beginning in debt had to earn

---

[1] Rollo G. Silver, "Benjamin Edes, Trumpeter of Sedition," *PBSA*, XLVII (1953), 266.

[2] *Country Printer*, pp. 51–54.

enough to support himself and his family while paying off his loan. Usually he had to contend with a too-small subscription list, rival publications, a scarcity of money, and people who did not pay the bills he sent out. His income from advertising and subscriptions could be supplemented by job printing, which, Hamilton found, "sometimes represented the difference between success and failure." In small offices where the press was needed only a few days every week for the newspaper, jobs could be turned out in the remaining time with an obvious reduction of overhead costs. Added to the usual mercantile jobs, political literature, if the printer gained the favor of a solvent party, might be particularly profitable. But although these country printers willingly accepted commodities instead of cash, their numerous appeals for payment testify to their forever precarious financial condition. Cognizant of this, papermakers required cash. This in itself was burdensome; in 1813 a Poughkeepsie, New York, newspaper used weekly "nearly two reams, at *four dollars and fifty cents* a ream."[3] The inkmaker, post rider, and landlord also had to be paid; repairs and new equipment constituted additional expenses. Consequently, little money was usually left for the printer. In 1825, when Thurlow Weed, a printer in Manlius, New York, was elected to the Assembly, the rising politician "had to borrow clothes to give him an appearance befitting his talents."[4] In the constant struggle to make a living the printer's wife worked in the shop as well as the house. If there were apprentices, she became their foster mother. Sometimes she set type or folded sheets or stitched them. And since many newspaper offices sold theatre and lottery tickets along with household goods, she guarded the cashbox at the sales desk. In his study of New York country printers Hamilton arrives at the conclusion that a wife was a necessity if the printer wanted to succeed in business.[5]

The comparatively few country printers who achieved prosperity were, according to Hamilton, entrepreneurs rather than craftsmen.[6] By expanding to newer markets they managed to take advantage of the growth of their regions. Some became wholesalers of books and printing supplies; others published religious periodicals; others became book publishers or established additional printing offices in

[3] *Ibid.*, pp. 57, 64, 68.   [4] Henry B. Stanton, quoted, *ibid.*, p. 70.
[5] *Country Printer*, p. 71.   [6] *Ibid.*, p. 72.

nearby localities. The imaginative and aggressive entrepreneur chose the most responsible of his former apprentices as managers of the branches of his organization.

In the cities and larger towns the printer's economic situation was less precarious. If his own business kept him poor, he could usually find employment in a nearby shop without the expense of moving family and possessions. Furthermore, he had a refreshing change of role: "a journeyman one month was an employer the next, and frequently two or three journeymen would pool their cash and publish a book, divide the profits on its publication, and then dissolve partnership."[7] Despite these advantages, the craft of printing offered little chance of getting rich.

Printing for political parties afforded extra income if the party was solvent; but in any community, small or large, if the printer received work from the government, he was safe in a customer whose jobs came regularly and whose credit was good though sometimes slow. In addition to public notices in newspapers, local authorities needed such jobs as tax bills, bylaws, ordinances, and financial statements. Obviously the printer who published a newspaper could negotiate from advantage for this lucrative official patronage. As competition increased, bidding for orders from politicians intensified and eventually there were occasional lively scandals. In 1829, for example, Isaac Bunce of Salina, New York, was found to be charging twice as much as another printer for the same work.[8] But who pocketed the difference? Examination of printing bills still extant in local, state, and federal archives will increase our knowledge of government printing as well as add to the comprehension of our social and economic past.

In the East where printing was a respectable institution and the people were becoming sophisticated and cooperative, a few states tried various experiments to combat the political deals being made for printing contracts. Delaware sometimes divided contracts among the leading printers, but at other times only one printer was selected.[9] For an interval the Massachusetts legislature ordered its secretary and clerks to designate a printer, but then finding that solution just as disagreeable, returned to having its membership

[7] R. H. Cressingham, quoted in Stevens, p. 39.
[8] Hamilton, *Country Printer*, p. 64.   [9] Hawkins, pp. 49–50.

select one.[10] New York, between 1805 and 1809, spread the business by having the laws printed in the newspaper of the state printer and in newspapers in four districts. But in 1820 political morality in that state fell so far that two politicians who were not printers secured the printing contract after buying a newspaper and submitting a bid—which was not even the lowest. New York sheriffs played favorites in dispensing printing jobs to such an extent, Hamilton found, that loss of a sheriff's patronage might stop publication of a newspaper.[11] In North Carolina, although some official printing was occasionally farmed out, the state printer was elected by both houses. His contract in 1785 specified the number of copies to be printed for each major document and his salary was set at five hundred pounds a year, exclusive of the cost of paper. During the next fourteen years his salary ranged from five hundred to six hundred pounds a year, with extra appropriations for printing documents not specified in the law. In 1787 these included 150 copies of Baron Steuben's *Military Instructions* and 1,500 copies of the Federal Constitution. By the turn of the century the Federalists and Republicans publicly and privately were fighting, to a degree unthinkable earlier, for state printing for their own members.[12] And in Alabama in the 1820's the position of state printer "became the principal plum for which the newspaper presses of the state contended."[13] In one instance, rare if not unique, a state legislature rewarded a printer for exceptionally good work. This occurred in 1825 when the Vermont legislature examined copies of the *Compiled Statutes* printed by Simeon Ide and "voluntarily, and almost unanimously, passed a resolution awarding him $500 more than the contract price."[14]

The frontier territories had neither the volume of work nor enough printers to solicit official printing. As will be seen later, when a territory was organized it was sometimes necessary to search for a printer and induce him to come. Thus Lexington provided John Bradford with land for his shop when he began to print for the

[10] Rollo G. Silver, "Government Printing in Massachusetts, 1751–1801," *SB*, XVI (1963), 170–72.

[11] *Country Printer*, pp. 128, 133.

[12] Mary L. Thornton, "Public Printing in North Carolina, 1749–1815," *N. Car. Hist. Rev.*, XXI (1944), 193–97.

[13] Rhoda C. Ellison, *Early Alabama Publications* (University, Ala., 1947), p. 9.

[14] Flanders, p. 51.

District of Kentucky.[15] As soon as a second printer arrived in a territory, competition automatically started, as it did in Missouri, where Joseph Charless was comfortably ensconced as territorial printer until Joshua Norvell's arrival in 1815 prompted the legislature to solicit bids.[16] As more printers entered the territories, the battles for patronage resembled those in the East.

At the beginning, national government documents, with few exceptions, were printed and paid for only on order of Congress. What with the Old Congress moving from city to city, changing Presidents, and frequently finding itself short of money, Powell has concluded that "in the years after peace no printer could hope to make a profit by contracting with the Confederation Congress." But the mark of status in being an official printer apparently sufficed to compensate him so that he worked for nothing in order to feel superior to his fellow citizens of the revolutionary state. John Dunlap and David C. Claypoole were the principal printers to the Old Congress, occasionally subcontracting a job or acting as collection agent for work done by another printer. It is amusing that although these were the official publications of the Confederation, the printer called himself "Printer to the Honourable the Congress of the United States," an appellation which survived after the Constitution was adopted.[17]

Very soon after the First Congress assembled in 1789, it passed a Joint Resolution giving the secretary of the Senate and the clerk of the House the responsibility for obtaining printing "on the most reasonable terms, the paper being furnished by the said Secretary and Clerk . . . at the public expense."[18] The custom of having the government furnish the paper continued "for a long time." New York printers who owned newspapers were particularly anxious to secure these contracts because they placed in their hands much source material for their columns and put them in line for more government business. Within a short time more than one printing firm produced government documents—acts, journals, individual laws, and newspaper publication of the laws. The constant increase

[15] William H. Perrin, *The Pioneer Press of Kentucky* (n.p., 1888), p. 9.
[16] David Kaser, *Joseph Charless* (Philadelphia, [1963]), p. 123.
[17] Powell, pp. 71, 74, 83.
[18] James B. Childs, "Disappeared in the Wings of Oblivion," *PBSA*, LVIII (1964), 94.

in documents which required more printers and, in turn, gave rise to problems (demands for overnight production, slow payment, poor help) is described by Powell. It should be realized that official printers were not the only printers of government documents. Popular governmental publications such as import rate and drawback schedules were frequently reissued by other printers. Even some official government documents came from printing shops which did not regularly do government work.[19]

As long as Congress remained in Philadelphia, demand and supply of labor were adjusted to satisfy the increasing printing requirements of the government. Then, when the government went to Washington, printers followed. Eight or nine men soon set up shops in the village designated as the national capital. Where there had been two newspapers, there were, within six weeks, four dailies, two triweeklies, and one magazine—established in Washington, Georgetown, and Alexandria. Some printers, especially the friends of the powerful, succeeded in getting government work; others eventually failed. Printing in Washington, at best, hardly returned the outlay involved, as it flourished in the periods of Congressional sessions and slackened in the recesses. Journeymen thrown out of work between sessions had to find jobs in other places. Between 1804 and 1819 the printing contracts, by order of Congress, were given to the lowest bidder. This policy, although economical, became an annoyance to Congress, for it resulted in shoddy work and inaccurate texts, often delayed. When, in 1818, a committee was appointed to "consider and report whether any further provisions of law are necessary to insure dispatch, accuracy, and neatness in the printing," the report recommended the creation of a national printing office. Congress took no action, but in the following year a Congressional resolution admitted the inadequacies of the printing supplied by specifying type sizes, page sizes, and prices for various kinds of work. The resolution also stated that the House and Senate should each elect its printer by ballot.[20] Not until 1860 did Congress create a government printing office.

Printers in the several states cut into a share of government

[19] Pp. 85–86, 94–96, 101.
[20] U.S. Government Printing Office, *100 GPO Years* (Washington, D.C., n.d.), pp. 9–10, 14–16.

patronage by obtaining appointments to print the laws of the United States in their newspapers. These annual appointments, ranging from one to three in each state, were made by the Secretary of State and yielded about one hundred dollars a year.[21] Again the glamour of the legend "Printer of the Laws of the United States" on the masthead added to the attractiveness of the position. On the frontier "District Printers" also obtained this patronage. A typical letter of renewal is:

Department of State,
Dec. 20th, 1803

To the several District Printers.
Sir.

Being desirous of continuing your Gazette as a medium of promulgating the laws of the present Congress within the State of——. You will find enclosed copies of the first laws passed by them. The compensation like that of the last will be at the rate of 50 Cents p. page of the octavo edition of the laws printed at the seat of Government a specimen of which was sent you in my last. You will be pleased to inform me without delay of your determination to accept or decline the reappointment. If you accept you will commence the printing as soon as possible and during its continuance, as heretofore, forward your paper to this office free of expense as part of the contract.

I am Etc
James Madison[22]

Printers lobbied heavily for this privilege; as Lucke has shown, the State Department leaned on the endorsements of Congressmen.[23] The limited number of appointments permitted assures that this was no attempt to control the press. Government printing at this time was merely an early communications network.

Once a successful shop was in operation, with or without the aid of official work, the printer could direct his profits toward bookselling, publishing, or branch printing offices. He could quickly set up a bookstore by printing some books and exchanging them with other booksellers. When his wholesale interests expanded so that he could no longer manage the printing shop himself, he hired a manager

---

[21] Hamilton, *Country Printer*, p. 134; Jessie R. Lucke, "Letters from John Quincy Adams and Others," *Va. Mag. Hist. Biog.*, LIX (1951), 34–35.

[22] Douglas C. McMurtrie, *The Need of a Printer in Indiana Territory* (Bloomington, Ind., 1936), p. 35.

[23] *Va. Mag. Hist. Biog.*, LIX, 34–35.

who assumed complete control of it. With these new expansionist factors developing, printers wisely insisted on formal contracts such as the following:

Articles of Agreement mutually entered into this fifteenth day of May, in the year, one Thousand seven hundred and ninety five, by and between Isaiah Thomas and Ebenr. T. Andrews of Boston, Printers & Copartners, on the one part; and Wm. Manning of said Boston, Printer, on the other part, namely,—

First. The said Isaiah Thomas and Ebenr. T. Andrews covenant and agree with the said Wm. Manning, that they will, on the eighth day of June next, deliver up to him the rooms now occupied by them as a Printing Office, with all the Printing Apparatus, therein contained, agreeably to the Schedule hereunto annexed, in complete order and repair, and also that they will furnish him with constant work in said Office, for himself and eight apprentices or a number of Journeymen equal to eight apprentices, that is to say, to the amount of seven hundred and fifty pounds per annum, on the terms and conditions herein specified.

Secondly. They engage that the said Manning and his eight apprentices or a number of Journeymen equal thereto, or any of them, shall never be idle for want of work or paper, for a longer term than two or three days, at any one time; but if it should so happen, that they or any of them should be out of employ, for more than two or three days at any one time, either for want of work or paper, the said Thomas & Andrews engage to pay said Manning one half as much for the time, he and his hands, or any of them, may be so out of employ, as they would have earned, had they been employed; the amount of such allowance to be ascertained by the amount of the work usually done, by said number of hands, so unemployed, in the same term of time—Provided, however, that this allowance of half pay for the time said Manning and his hands, or any of them may be so unemployed, shall not extend to any instance where said Manning, by unusual exertion, without the particular request of said Thomas & Andrews, shall have done more work than the ratio of sixty two pounds per month from the time of their last settlements—

The said Wm. Manning, on his part, covenants and agrees, that he will after said eighth day of June next, receive the care & charge of said printing Office, and provide himself with sufficient help to carry it on as before mentioned, and that he will conduct it for said Isaiah Thomas & Ebenezer T. Andrews, to the best of his knowledge and ability, with care and fidelity, on the following terms & conditions, viz.

First. He will execute all common work, as it usually occurs in the course of business, at the rate of two shillings for every thousand m's, including composing, correcting, distributing &c. & four shillings for every token, or every two hundred & fifty sheets of white paper, worked at press, on both sides; and he will execute all unusual and extraordinary work, such as Latin books, French books, works wholly composed of figures &c &c— at proportionable prices.

Secondly. He will furnish every consumable & wastable article required in the Office, such as wood, Candles, Ink, balls, Oil, Rules, Furniture, Tympans, blankets, Soap, and other articles of a similar nature at his own expense—He will also repair all damages done to the presses, windows in the building &c &c, so that every thing in the Office may always remain in as good repair and order as he receives them common wear excepted—

Thirdly. He will keep a regular account of all paper delivered to him from time to time, and account for the same, reasonable allowance to be made for what is necessarily consumed for proof sheets &c &c—

Fourthly. Whenever the number of copies shall fall short more than twelve of the number which the paper used, would complete, then said Manning is to reprint such sheet or sheets as may be deficient without making any charge thereof, or otherwise to pay for such deficient copies more than twelve, at the price such books may sell for in sheets—

Fifthly. Said Manning is to cause all the books as fast as they are printed and dried to be accurately counted out into quires of twenty five sheets each, and delivered at the bookstore of said Thomas & Andrews—

Sixthly. Any material injury that may accrue to the printing Materials, paper, or books, when printed, before they are delivered as in the last article mentioned, by the neglect or inattention of said Manning, or any person in his employ, shall be made good by said Manning, and any articles lost or broken, by careless or improper usage, shall be paid for by him or replaced—fire & unavoidable accidents, only, excepted—

Seventhly.   No work to be done in the said Office, except for the said Thomas & Andrews, and the imprint of all books &c to be in their name, as printed by them as usual—

Eighthly.   The said Manning to keep a particular account of all work done, and to allow said Thomas & Andrews, one third part of the amount thereof for the use of said Office & materials—

Ninthly.   No more copies of any work to be printed by said Manning than are delivered to said Thomas & Andrews—

Tenthly.   All work that shall be badly executed, or done in an unworkman like manner, shall be paid for by said Manning at twenty five perCent advance upon paper & print, and destroyed and not suffered to be sold by either party—to determine when work is badly executed, each party agree to submit to the decision of three disinterested, judicious printers, provided they cannot agree between themselves—

Eleventhly.   Said Manning engages that he will be particularly careful in guarding against fire, and that when Candles or fire have been used in the Office, he will himself, after work is over, see that they are properly taken Care of—and in case of his not being able to attend to it himself, that he will have it done by some suitable, confidential person—

The said Thomas & Andrews agree that they will pay said Manning, for all work he may do at the rate before mentioned after deducting one third of the amount for the use of the printing materials, and farther that they will pay him the said Manning one third of the amount of all consumable articles as before expressed, including repair, &c—

They will also furnish the said Manning with money from week to week to the amount of one half or two thirds of the work done in each week, and make settlements quarterly, or otherwise, as shall be most convenient to said Manning—

They will furnish said Manning with a copy of each different work he may print for them bound decently, free of expense,—No copies to be allowed to be saved by boys or Journeymen—

It is mutually agreed between the parties, that this agreement shall continue and abide in force for the term of eight years from the date hereof, unless they should mutually agree sooner to part

—And in Case either party contrary to the wishes and interest of the other should insist upon a dissolution of the contract before the expiration of eight years, the party so insisting thereon, shall pay to the other the sum of three hundred pounds, unless the aggrieved party shall consent to receive a less sum as a compensation—

In witness of all which the parties have hereunto affixed their hands & seals this fifteenth day of May, in the year, one thousand seven hundred & ninety five—

Willm. Manning
Isaiah Thomas
Ebenr. T. Andrews[24]

This contract shows the proprietor's concern over wastage of paper, theft by employees of works printed, the wayward damaging of stock, and the threat of destruction by fire—any one of which could upset the precarious balance at which he struck for his livelihood. (Many printers were not as fortunate as Anthony Haswell, who secured permission from the General Assembly of Vermont to run a public lottery in order to recover his loss when fire destroyed his Rutland shop in 1792.[25]) Another clause stipulates the deduction of one-third of the price for the use of the shop, evidently the evaluation of the overhead. The definition in the contract of the token as 250 sheets printed on both sides conformed to common but not invariable New England usage; in other sections the token was considered to be 250 sheets printed on one side.[26] After the expiration of the contract Manning continued to manage the shop of Thomas & Andrews for about a year. In February, 1804, Andrews discussed the arrangement in a letter to Thomas:

We now give Mr Manning 25 Cts. per 1000 and 50 Cts, per token—find office, ink, wood, candles and every material—run all risks, lose the interest of the amount of the office which is between 4000 and 5000 Dolls (besides the Bible) and sustain the wear and tare. From this data you can determine the difference between what we give now and what we should pay if we had no office, admitting that we paid the present price of 2/6 thousand and 5/ token, which is what we should probably have to do.[27]

[24] Thomas Papers.

[25] John Spargo, "Early Vermont Printers and Printing," in *A New England Keepsake* (n.p., 1938), p. 11.

[26] *The Cost Books of Ticknor and Fields*, ed. Warren S. Tryon and William Charvat (New York, 1949), p. 1; *Am. Dict. Print.*, p. 545.

[27] Letter, Feb. 8, 1804, in Thomas Papers.

One week later Andrews told Thomas of his decision: "I find that on an average we save about 1000 D per ann. besides paying rent, wear and interest of materials, which added to the convenience, makes it an object worth retaining."[28] Manning left Thomas & Andrews soon after to take an active interest in his firm of Manning & Loring. Thomas & Andrews replaced him with Joseph T. Buckingham who, in his memoirs, continues the story:

In the spring of 1804, I contracted with Thomas & Andrews to carry on their printing business for a term of five years, at certain fixed prices. The prices allowed me but a small profit above the rate of journeymen's wages; but that small profit, added to the earnings of my labor at *the case*, enabled me at first to gain a decent livelihood. Before the term expired I married and became a housekeeper. The additional expense thus created, induced me to take advantage of a condition in the contract, by which I was permitted the use of the types and presses to execute printing on my own account. Beside, though I had ample employment as a printer, in superintending the largest printing concern in Boston, I found it difficult to repress my aspirations to display my intellectual as well as my industrial and mechanical abilities . . . .

The contract with Thomas & Andrews expired at the end of five years, and was renewed on rather more favorable conditions for another term of the same length; but before it terminated, the whole printing apparatus was offered to me on conditions which seemed to promise better fortune. The price was set at $4500. I was to be furnished with printing to the amount of $9000, one half of which was to be paid for in cash,—the other half to balance the price of the printing materials. But this, like former projects, ended in trouble. The amount of work contracted for was not sufficient to employ so large an office, and work was undertaken which proved unprofitable, and severe losses were sustained by publishing, on my own risk, works, which, though valuable in themselves, did not meet with a ready sale,—unless it were to booksellers, at a ruinous discount. Before all the notes given for the printing apparatus were due, debts had been contracted for paper and labor, and attachments were laid upon the whole stock, and a part of it was sold at auction.[29]

In fairness to Buckingham it must be remembered that he purchased the shop when the War of 1812 was approaching and when Thomas & Andrews were shrewd enough to dispose of it.

Manning's carefully drawn and precise contract for managing a very large office may be compared with a simpler contract for man-

[28] Letter, Feb. 15, 1804, in Thomas Papers.
[29] *Pers. Mem.*, I, 52–53, 62–63.

aging the small shop of a country firm such as that of Thomas &
Thomas in Walpole, New Hampshire:

The said Cheever Felch hereby convenants and engages that he
will execute in a correct and workmanlike manner, for the said
Thomas & Thomas, in said Walpole, such work in the printing business as may be furnished by the said Thomas & Thomas, equal
to what himself and another hand can perform, reckoning said
work at 25 cents per 1000 ms, and the same sum per token, and
that he will hang up and take down the sheets and deliver them at
the bookstore; that he will use with care and prudence all such
materials as are used in the office; that he will do no work in said
office, except such as may be furnished from time to time by the
said Thomas & Thomas, and that he will keep the press in good
working repair & in general see that balls and ball stocks &c are
prepared, as are necessary for said office, and that he will take good
care of the fire & close the office as early as nine oClock each
evening.
And the said Thomas & Thomas, on their part promise and engage to furnish a suitable office room for carrying on said printing
business, and also types, press and other necessary materials such
as ink, paper &c. that they will be at the expense of balls, ballstocks,
firewood, candles &c, and all articles that are used and necessary
for said office, and that they will furnish work, sufficient for himself
the said Felch and one other hand; and that they will allow him the
sum of twenty five cents per 1000 ms, & the same sum per token for
such work as they may confide to his care.
And it is mutually agreed that this copartnership shall continue till
one of the parties gives the other three months previous notice of his
inclination to dissolve this agreement at which time the said Felch
agrees to relinquish the office in good order, and the matter all distributed—
In testimony of all which the parties have hereunto set their
names interchangeably, and affixed their seals this thirtieth day of
March, A. D. one thousand, eight hundred and eight—

Cheever Felch
Thomas & Thomas[30]

The price a printer charged customers for his work rose or fell in
response to his costs, the amount of work on hand, the growth rate
of the local economy, and his own competitive instinct. If no work
was on hand, an ambitious printer would find some work to do:

In 1810, a copy of the "Elements of Elocution," by John Walker,
attracted my notice in the bookstore of Mr. William Wells I
purchased the Elements of Elocution, and immediately put it to

[30] Thomas Papers.

press, without making a single effort to dispose of the edition when it should be completed. Before the printing was finished, however, the entire edition was sold to a bookseller, at a small advance on the cost. Encouraged by this success, I undertook to publish Locke's "Essay on the Human Understanding," in two volumes octavo. All the American editions of this work, then in the market, were in duodecimo, on cheap paper, and clumsy typography. When my edition was about half printed, some of the sheets were seen by Messrs. Cummings & Hilliard, who immediately made a bargain for the work. It was completed in about sixty days from the commencement, and delivered to them at a small advance on the cost. . . .

No great profit was made by publishing either of the works above-mentioned; but there was no loss, and the printing furnished employment for several apprentices, and for types and presses, that had cost something like eight thousand dollars. I did not like that so much capital or so many good apprentices should be idle; and as booksellers gave me no employment, the publishing of other works was prosecuted.[31]

In determining their charges, some printers calculated their expense, considered the bargaining power behind their proposition, and then added as much profit as the traffic would bear. E. T. Andrews, in 1791, gave his partner the reasons for establishing a price:

Would you consent to do Morse's Geography under £6 per sheet? it is only one price and a half—that is, the expense of a sheet is £2.. 8..0.... I do not think it will be worth while to offer less, as we shall have other work enough, and I doubt whether any body here would undertake so large a work—besides, I offered to take one third of the payment in the books when done.—Mr. Hall says he cannot think of undertaking so large a work and Belknap and Young I think cannot afford to take one third in books, nor to wait so long for pay as we can.[32]

In this instance, Andrews wanted "one price and a half." Two weeks before he had written to Thomas about hoisting a price for another work:

Morse, and Kellogg print Hemmenway's work—believe they have, or are like to have, a considerable number of subscribers. I don't know how I came to make so good a bargain with Morse—upon calculation find we have above 4 *prices* for it—that is, 4 times the expense.[33]

[31] [Joseph T. Buckingham], "Croaker—No. XLVIII," Boston *Courier*, March 23, 1850.
[32] Letter to Isaiah Thomas, Sept. 2, 1791, in Thomas Papers.
[33] Letter, Aug. 21, 1791, in Thomas Papers.

With such rule of thumb cost accounting, the relationship between wages and prices went askew. Indeed, to analyze printer's invoices between 1787 and 1825 at various times in different places would require a volume in itself. Quantities, too, varied according to demand and circumstance. To provide approximations of the sizes of editions in a major city, some examples are listed in the Appendix.

A wise purchaser of printing shopped around before he bought, as Ezra Stiles did in 1794: "Delivered 60 pages MS. Copy of my Hist' to Cap' Throop to be sent off to Hartfd to be printed, as the Work could be done there cheaper than at N Haven, £3 per sheet & 15/ per thousd for as many Copies as they please."[34] Some patrons, of course, did not wish to subject themselves to the delay of sending work out of town. Those in large cities examined prices most critically, with the result that in New York, Boston, and Philadelphia competition became so keen that the master printers, already confronted by demands of journeymen, decided on a collective price reform. Eleven of the major New York printing firms, in 1795, announced the establishment of a list of prices which included:

	L.	s.	d
For Every sheet of common-work, on demi paper, printed on brevier, of which 1000 copies are printed,	6	10	0
For every sheet of ditto, on burgeois, of which 1000 copies are printed,	6	0	0
For every sheet of long primer, or small pica, on demi paper, of which 1000 copies are printed,	5	0	0
For every sheet of pica or english, of which 1000 copies are printed,	4	10	0
For every additional thousand,	1	10	0

If the work should be French, Latin, Rules, Figures, &c. an advanced price to be paid. (of one fifth at least.)

N. B. In the above cases, the person employing the printer to furnish paper.[35]

Additional prices were given for cards, handbills, and blanks. The announcement concluded with the statement: "We do further agree, That if either of us shall do work at a less rate than is here es-

[34] *The Literary Diary of Ezra Stiles, D.D., LL.D.*, ed. Franklin B. Dexter (New York, 1901), III, 529.

[35] Charlotte E. Morgan, *The Origin and History of the New York Employing Printers' Association* (New York, 1930), p. 29.

tablished, we will forfeit the sum of twenty pounds, to be appropriated as a majority of us shall think proper."[36] One wonders whether this price-fixing strait jacket was completely workable. Most likely it was not. A Boston scale of 1805 was, according to Buckingham, "faithfully adhered to," for a few years at least, but a Philadelphia scale, McCulloch recalled in a letter of 1814, was immediately violated:

Some ten or fifteen years ago, the printers of this city convened for the purpose of fixing on a regular undeviating rate of prices. The resolutions were unanimously adopted, and it was anticipated that there would be a new era of printing. But one of the pledged members, on his return from the meeting, called on Robert Campbell, then a principal bookseller in the City, and told him that the printers had entered into an obligation to each other, to print at such and such prices only: "but," continued this disinterested man, "if you will give *me* your work, I will do it for such and such a price."[37]

The New York scale may not have been annulled as quickly, but it is most probable that some printer, under strain of competition, soon offered a lower price. Pricecutting sometimes cloaked itself in the guise of benevolence, for undoubtedly other printers as well as Samuel Armstrong advertised "An allowance made on Printing to those who publish Religious Tracts for Charitable Distribution."[38] Deterioration of prices apparently became a trend in small towns, too, as Anson Whipple, a Walpole, New Hampshire, bookseller remarked in 1816: "The common price of printing is 100 Cents for the *white token* of 10½ qrs worked on both sides, and 50 Cents per 1000 m.—perhaps he would do it cheaper, as printers frequently do work under the nominal price—."[39]

Meanwhile the New York printers attempted a new solution to pricecutting. A list, "agreed upon by the Master Printers of the City of New-York, at a meeting held the 18th of September, 1815," covered book and job work in detail. The section on book work specified these prices:

[36] *Ibid.*

[37] [Joseph T. Buckingham], "Croaker, No. XXXIX," Boston *Courier*, Jan. 12, 1850; "William McCulloch's Additions," pp. 136–37.

[38] *The School of Good Manners* (Charlestown, 1809), a broadside in the American Antiquarian Society.

[39] Letter to Isaiah Thomas, Jan. 29, 1816, in Thomas Papers.

Composition.

Brevier, or larger type, common matter, from printed
    copy, per 1000 ems, $0   56¼

Minion,   62½

Nonpareil,   75

Pearl and Diamond,   1   00

Works from manuscript copy, or printed copy containing alterations, interlineations, and erasures, an addition of 6¼ cents per 1000 ems.

Rule and figure work must be charged two prices.

Work part in figures and part plain matter, such as common arithmetics, one price and a half.

Rule work, with columns blank, one price and a half.

Greek and Hebrew, without points, one price and a half—with points, two prices; the asper not to be considered a point.

French, Latin, or any other foreign language, in common type, 18¾ cents more per 1000 ems than the prices for the English language.

*Press Work.**

Medium paper, or less size, on Brevier or larger type,
    per token, $0   56¼
        On Minion,   0   62½
        On Nonpareil, and all less,   0   75

Royal paper, on Brevier or larger type,   0   68¾
        On Minion,   0   75
        On Nonpareil, and all less,   0   87½

When a form contains one or more wood engravings, an addition of 6¼ cents per token to be charged.

Rule work must be charged one price and a half.

Pressing sheets, single, one dollar per 1000; double, 75 cents.

The credit on Book Work shall not exceed four months, nor shall more than seven per cent. be deducted from the face of the bill for cash.

* These prices are calculated for an edition not exceeding two thousand copies, or eight tokens on a form. For each token exceeding eight on a form, on type larger than Minion, 6¼ cents advance; if on Minion, 12½ cents; on Nonpareil, 18¾ cents; if on type less than Nonpareil, 25 cents.

The "General Remarks" at the end included:

Fitting up furniture for an octavo pamphlet or book not exceeding five sheets, to be charged one dollar; all other impositions 25 cents extra, progressively, in proportion to the size. For all works exceeding five sheets, no charge to be made.

Title pages, or Proposals, to be charged at the rate of 1 dollar and 50 cents per 1000 ems, and 75 cents per token.

Alterations from copy, made by authors or publishers, to be charged for at the rate of 40 cents per hour.

All type larger than English to be calculated as English.[40]

Until evidence proves otherwise, these prices can be considered good approximations of what the New York printers received rather than the rates charged every customer. It would be difficult to believe that these individualistic shop owners worked in concert to maintain trade agreements to the letter. Another price list, in or before 1825, is implied in an announcement of a meeting of the Boston Master Printers Association:

Boston, May 25, 1826.

The Committee to whom was recommitted the 12th article of the Constitution for revision, have made such alterations as they deemed necessary, and submit the following for your consideration.

Composition.

Plain Book Printing, printed copy, per 1000 ms	50 cts.
" " " MS. " "	56 1–4
Common Arithmetic, printed copy, per 1000 ms	70
" " MS. " "	87 1–2
Works in Foreign Languages, (Roman Type) per 1000 ms	67
Greek and Hebrew, per 1000 ms	1 00
Almanacks, per page	1 50
Rule and Figure work, per 1000 ms	1 00

All marginal notes at the sides of pages, to be charged in the letter in which set, the whole margin to the cast.

Press Work.

Medium paper, or less size, per token,	1 25
Royal per token,	1 37 1–2
School Books or Almanacks, medium or less	1 10
Royal	1 15
Pressing in single sheets, per token	25

Then follows a detailed list for job work, concluding with:

Title Pages, Proposals and other displayed work, $1 per 1000 ms and $1 50 per token.

Alterations from copy, made by authors or publishers, to be charged at the rate of 33 cts. per hour.

All type larger than English to be counted as English.[41]

[40] Cornelius S. Van Winkle, *The Printers' Guide* (New York, 1818), pp. 212–19.

[41] Broadside in the Boston Public Library.

These three sentences bear a clear resemblance to the New York scale of 1815, suggesting that this model was carried on with revisions during the decade. The existence of intervening scales is quite possible because a master printer as a good businessman would prefer less price competition and would, therefore, substantially cooperate in the preparation of price lists. Ideally, they would assure good profits; practically, they supplied guidelines and were the logical reactions to the rising wage scales of the journeymen.

The majority of master printers, at times embroiled in feuds with those who did not maintain agreements, had an emotional commitment to their craft which was rekindled in times of emergency. When Thomas & Andrews needed a great many mathematical characters for a textbook they published in 1801, they borrowed from almost every shop in Boston, Worcester, Charlestown, and Cambridge.[42] After fire damaged the office of the Raleigh, North Carolina, *Register* in 1804, the newspaper was printed in the office of its rival, the rancor between owners notwithstanding.[43] To cite one more example, the firm of George Dobbin & Murphy publicly acknowledged the "generous and friendly offers of our brother printers in Baltimore" when fire destroyed their printing office in 1809.[44] At other times the printers stood in practical alignment to help the poverty endemic in the profession. This first occurred in Philadelphia on March 8, 1788, at the suggestion of the most famous American master printer. It was a benevolent society whose constitution declared that "this Society be entitled the Franklin Society; the propriety of such an institution in this city having been first suggested by the late Dr. *Benjamin Franklin*—that patriot, philosopher, and friend to the arts, particularly the typographical." The objectives were "to provide, in the time of health and strength, against the infirmities of old age, distress and want, among their own members,—to support their widows, and educate their orphan children." To become a member, one had to be "a printer, of a good character, and who has served an apprenticeship to the printing business—free from any bodily infirmity at the time of entrance, and not above forty-five years of age."[45] While he lived, Franklin

---

[42] Buckingham, *Pers. Mem.*, I, 51.

[43] Robert N. Elliott, Jr., *The Raleigh Register, 1799–1863* (Chapel Hill, N.C., 1955), p. 27.

[44] Silver, *Balt. Book Trade*, p. 25.

[45] *Constitution of the Franklin Society* ([Philadelphia], 1792), pp. 3–4, 11.

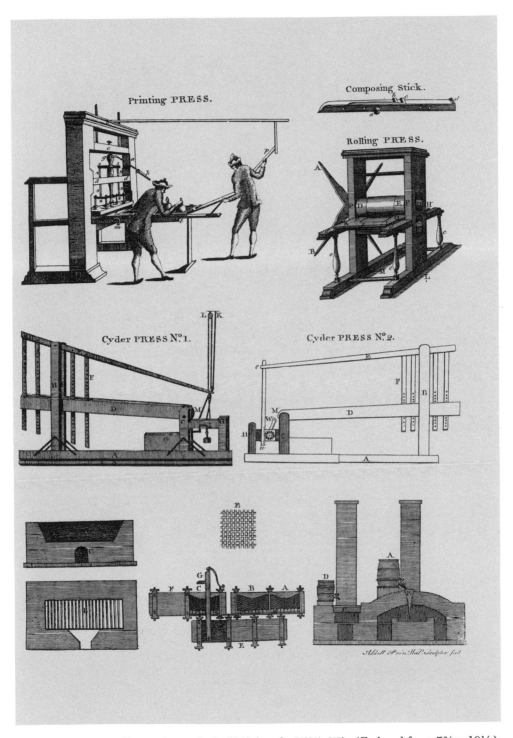

IX. *Encyclopaedia Britannica*, 3rd ed. (Edinburgh, 1787–97). (Reduced from 7⅜ x 10½)

THE

Holy Bible,

CONTAINING THE

OLD AND NEW

TESTAMENTS:

WITH THE

A P O C R Y P H A.

TRANSLATED

Out of the Original Tongues,

AND

With the FORMER TRANSLATIONS diligently COMPARED and REVISED,

By the special Command of King JAMES I, of *England.*

WITH AN

I N D E X.

Appointed to be read in Churches.

VOL. I.

United States of America.

PRINTED AT THE PRESS IN *WORCESTER*, MASSACHUSETTS,
BY ISAIAH THOMAS.

Sold by him in **Worcester**; and by him and Company, at FAUST'S STATUE, No. 45, NEWBURY STREET, **Boston.**

MDCCXCI.

X. The Isaiah Thomas Edition of *The Holy Bible* (Worcester, Mass., 1791). (Reduced
from 9⅜ x 15¼)

OF

COMMERCE

AND

LUXURY.

Quid leges fine moribus
Vanæ proficiunt ? fi neque fervidis
Pars inclufa caloribus
Mundi, nec Boreæ finitimum latus
Duratæque folo nives
Mercatorem abigunt ?

HORAT. L. III. Od. XXIV.

Printed, FROM THE LONDON EDITION,
BY T. LANG, No. 21, CHURCH-ALLEY,
PHILADELPHIA.
M,DCC,XCI.

XI. *Of Commerce and Luxury* (Philadelphia, 1791)

Christliche
Betrachtungen
über die
Evangelischen Texte,

so man pfleget zu lesen

an denen

Sontagen und hohen Festen,

Christlich und aufrichtig gepredigt und beschrieben

durch

Erasmum Weichenhan,

Pfarrer zu Langen=Bielau.

Germantaun: Gedruckt bey Michael Billmeyer, 1791.

Auf Kosten vereinigter Freunde.

XII. Erasmus Weichenhan, *Christliche Betrachtungen über die Evangelischen Texte* (Germantown, Pa., 1791). (Reduced from 6⅜ x 8⅛)

made sure that members came to meetings by simply holding them at his home. After his death the society, missing Franklin's infusion of vitality, lost its motivation and was dissolved in 1795.[46]

The Franklin Society, created for mutual benefit and offering aid to journeyman and master alike, tended to be more comforting to the journeyman because his misfortunes were immediate and easier of solution. The masters, finding themselves crippled by unstable prices, pressed for trade regulation as the utmost necessity, and to that end they combined with the booksellers in organizing the Philadelphia Company of Printers and Booksellers. The constitution, recently discussed by Edwin Wolf, 2nd, boldly detailed the objectives of the members.[47] Under a date of questionable appropriateness, July 4, 1791, it provided for membership, dues, officers, and an "acting committee." Then followed five clauses specifying the regulations:

IX.

The acting committee shall meet on the *second Monday* in every month, or oftener if necessary, and determine what books it may be advisable for the company to print. Notice of such their determinations, shall be sent to the respective members of the company, who shall have the option to subscribe for as many copies of each as they shall see fit; which subscriptions shall be lodged with the secretary, before the next monthly meeting. The members who subscribe for each work, shall decide, by vote, who shall print it, and in what manner; the votes to be taken in proportion to the numbers respectively subscribed for.

X.

The copy-rights of any books which have been printed by any of the members of this company, before the adoption of this constitution, shall be vested in the printers of them, their heirs, or assigns, respectively.

XI.

The earliest claimant of any book, not already printed by the company, nor by any member thereof, shall be invested with the copy-right, which right shall descend to the heirs, or assigns, of the holder. The claim shall be made by entering the title thereof in the secretary's book, and the claimant shall immediately send notice to the different members of the company.

[46] James Mease, *The Picture of Philadelphia* (Philadelphia, 1811), p. 272.
[47] *The Annual Report of the Library Company of Philadelphia for the Year 1965* (Philadelphia, 1966), pp. 40–41.

XII.

Any member of this company shall be entitled to subscribe for any work, which any other member is about to print; the number of copies, and the terms of subscription, shall be regulated hereafter, by the bye-laws of the company.

XIII.

Each member of this company shall fix the prices to the trade, to shopkeepers, and to the public at large, of every book, of which he is invested with the copy-right. A list of these prices shall be given in to the secretary of the company, who shall have a like list of all the prices of the company's books. Any member who sells books below these prices, shall be expelled the company, and forfeit all its privileges; and what copy-rights he may have been possessed of, shall belong to the company.[48]

The minutes appended to the constitution recorded the activities of the company. After recruiting more members under threat of noncooperation, it planned for joint publication:

Resolved, That in the inprint arrangement of names, those printers who subscribe for the greatest number, shall have precedence—and in case of equality of subscription, the oldest standing shall give precedence.

Nevertheless, the names of the present members of this company, shall always take the lead of those members, who may be hereafter chosen.

It arranged to have the book trade petition Congress to take off the duty on paper, later noting that "the prayer of their petition was not granted." It discussed a cartel so that sales and exchanges remained within the membership as much as possible; in 1794 it approved an increase in book prices because of "the great advance on the prices of almost every article of consumption in this city;" it established a procedure for keeping a title in print after the death of the printer.[49] There are also references to two books printed under the auspices of the company: Cicero's *De Officiis* and Johann Zimmermann's *Solitude Considered*. In 1794 the company printed a catalogue of the books published by its members.[50]

[48] *The Constitution, Proceedings, &c. of the Philadelphia Company of Printers & Booksellers* ([Philadelphia], 1793), pp. 4–5.

[49] *Ibid.*, pp. 8, 10–17.

[50] *A Catalogue of Books, Published by the Different Members of the Philadelphia Company of Printers and Booksellers* (Philadelphia, 1794).

The date of dissolution is not known, but two bits of evidence show that the company continued for at least five years. One is a bill to Mathew Carey for the admission fee (7/6), the annual dues for four years (1/10/–), and three fines for nonattendance (1/10½ each) covering the period between July 4, 1791, and July 4, 1795.[51] The other is a printed broadside letter, dated July 4, 1796, in which Mathew Carey stated his reasons for withdrawing from the company. It had failed, he said, to attain its two objectives. The first objective, "to produce an union in the expense and risk of publishing Books that might be beyond individual exertion," was not achieved: "The Company have printed but one valuable Book—and the small number of the edition reduced the profits to a very low scale." As for the second objective, "to secure the copy-rights of the members against invasion by printers at a distance, or by the associators individually," Carey felt that "its operation has been pernicious to me."[52] Because of the rules of the company, he could not obtain out-of-city reprints of Philadelphia books in exchange when Philadelphia editions were not obtainable.

The Philadelphia Company of Printers and Booksellers provided defensive arrangements for the book trade but did not follow through enough to satisfy the master printers who wanted more strict regulation of the printing trade. So to advance their own policies these men organized their own employers' association under the name of the Company of Philadelphia Printers. This was one of those "companies" which, as Stewart wrote, "formed a link between the merchant guilds of the late Middle Ages and the employers' associations of to-day."[53] Its purpose candidly appeared in the constitution, adopted on September 11, 1794:

When the Company are organized, they shall have power to regulate the prices at which its members shall execute printing work; to determine the terms of employing journeymen; to fix penalties for the violation of their regulations; and, in general to adopt such rules as may be considered conducive to the prosperity of the printing business.[54]

[51] Silver, *SB*, XIX, 101–2.
[52] *Sir, Having, on mature deliberation . . .* (Philadelphia, 1796).
[53] Stewart, p. 861n.
[54] *The Constitution of the Company of Printers, of Philadelphia* (Philadelphia, 1794), p. 6.

Apparently pricecutting had become excessive, and perhaps they were wary of the journeymen who, having created a strike-benefit fund in 1786, were about to make tougher demands. Neither the precise circumstances of the establishment of the company, nor the nature of the company's transactions, nor the date of dissolution have been ascertained.

A better-documented and more fascinating organization of employers later appeared in Boston:

In the summer of 1805, there was an informal and rather accidental meeting of three or four printers at the office of Munroe & Francis. Certain evils to which they and the members of the profession generally were exposed, became the subject of a conversation, which resulted in a request to Mr. Francis that he would call a meeting of the printers, to consider the expediency of forming themselves into a society for purposes of mutual protection and advantage. He complied with the request, and on the 16th of July a meeting was accordingly held [at] Vila's Hotel. Not more than ten or twelve persons were present. David Carlisle was the Chairman, and David Francis the Secretary of the meeting. After mutual expression of opinions, it was agreed to form an association, to establish uniform prices of printing and some general rules in respect to apprentices and journeymen, and a committee, . . . was "appointed to draw up articles for the regulation of the profession." This committee, on the 2d of August, reported a constitution for "the Society of Printers of Boston and its Vicinity," which was accepted and signed by all the persons present. The constitution provided that there should be a President, Secretary, and a Standing Committee of five members.[55]

. . . . .

The constitution of the association was very brief, and its provisions were not very stringent. If I remember rightly, a scale of prices for printing was adopted, by which all agreed to be governed, and which was faithfully adhered to. But these prices had reference only to work done for booksellers and authors—at least, they had nothing to do with the compensation made to journeymen or apprentices. In that respect, every one was left at liberty to make his own arrangements. But they had one rule, which all were pledged to observe, namely, no member should take an apprentice from another, or receive an apprentice into his employ from another member, without the consent or approbation of said apprentice's employer. And this, I think, was the first motive, that brought the association into existence.[56]

[55] J[oseph] T. B[uckingham], "The Faustus Association," Boston *Evening Transcript*, Sept. 7, 1859.
[56] Buckingham, "Croaker, No. XXXIX."

Buckingham recorded that the standing committee initiated the establishment of dues and a library—"the members being expected to give a copy of each of the books, pamphlets, and newspapers that they printed."[57] The standing committee also plumped for quality control:

> The association, through the agency of its Standing Committee, made great exertions to secure improvements in the manufacture of paper,—recommending the exposure of all instances of fraud in counting, the interpolation of imperfect sheets, and broken quires. The qualities and composition of ink were also a subject of investigation; and that manufactured by J. M. Dunham at Cambridgeport was recommended, both for book and newspaper printers, as superior to all other specimens then in the market. Some of the types from the foundry of Binney & Ronaldson, of Philadelphia, had been complained of by one of the members, as of *bad quality*, and a chemist was employed by the committee to analyze the metal and determine whether it was inferior to that used in other foundries. The chemist reported that the specimens of Scotch type were by far the most durable, that the English was less so by 15 or 20 per cent., and that the American had an alloy surprisingly great. Whether the result of this investigation was transmitted to the Philadelphia founders or not, I do not recollect; but I find the record states that the difficulty in which it originated had been adjusted.[58]

In April, 1808, the standing committee reported on dressed leather balls:

> Your committee have examined the use of what are called patent or dressed leather balls. They find them to be a valuable substitute for pelt balls, particularly in cases where new letter is used; that they are attended with little trouble in keeping soft, requiring nothing more than to have the ink taken off with pearl-ash lie, and to be covered with a woollen capper wet with clean water, when out of use; that they require knocking up but seldom, say fortnightly: that a skin will last from one to two months; and during that time will need but about one new supply of wool. Though made of dressed leather instead of pelts, they are not, in the first cost, more than fifty per cent. higher.[59]

For the annual banquets of the society which began in 1807, it was hoped to have an orator who would "exhibit the result of ingenious researches in the ample history of our profession." Only one speech was written, and that by John Russell, who had suggested the annual oration, but the banquets continued. Leading booksellers were

[57] Buckingham, "Faustus Association."   [58] *Ibid.*   [59] *Ibid.*

among the guests, helping to enjoy the food, drink, and entertainment. Luckily, three members were "capital vocalists."[60]

As they launched into activities broader than trade regulation, some members felt that the name of the society was "too narrow and confined to embrace the higher branches of our profession, which are not *mechanical*, nor bounded by rules, but which soar to improvements as valuable to science and humanity, as those which have immortalized the discovery of Faustus, whose name we propose to bear."[61] The other members concurred; in 1808 the name was changed to the Faustus Association.[62] The standing committee tackled the job of helping printers to save their shops from fire: in 1811 it organized the Conservative Fire Society, comprising printers, bookbinders, and booksellers, "for their mutual assistance and benefit, when endangered by Fire." When called out, the members would rush to the fire with their buckets, bags, and bedkeys (an iron tool for screwing and unscrewing the nuts and bolts of a bedstead—*O.E.D.*) and proceed to use their "best endeavours to preserve the building, and to remove and secure the goods and effects."[63] It disappeared after the creation of the Boston Fire Department in the 1830's reduced the need for fire societies.

At the end of seven years a mutiny among the newer members, who deprecated the social and commercial rules of the Faustus Association, brought about its decline:

The meetings had been harmonious, and the provisions of the Constitution and the principles of the compact observed and practised, at least so far as the original members were concerned. Some, of more recent standing, were less scrupulous in acting up to their social obligations. Some of the rules in respect to prices of work were treated with indifference, and in one or two instances, boastingly violated,—in consequence of which two members took up their connections with the society. In 1812, the cry of *Hard Times!* and the approach of the war, led some to complain of the unnecessary expenses of the association, although *all* the assessments amounted to no more than *four* dollars a year.[64]

---

[60] J[oseph] T. B[uckingham], "The Faustus Association," Boston *Evening Transcript*, September 12, 1859.

[61] *Ibid.*

[62] C. L. Nichols, quoted in Clarence S. Brigham, "Report of the Librarian," *Proc. Am. Ant. Soc.*, n.s., XXIV (1914), 251.

[63] Rollo G. Silver, "Buckets, Bags, and Bed Key," *Am. N. & Q.*, VIII (1948), 5.

[64] J[oseph] T. B[uckingham], "The Faustus Association," Boston *Evening Transcript*, Sept. 16, 1859.

The breach was never healed, and as it was as fundamental as the calamity of war, the association dissolved. The last meeting noted in the record was held on October 3, 1815.[65]

In all of the larger cities printers were closely involved in literary fairs and in facilitating the interchange of publications; printers formed combinations to petition Congress on proposed tariffs and they supported the apprentices' libraries so popular at that time.[66] Rather consistently the master printers as individuals or in groups conducted themselves with scrupulous nicety and a dignified courage, sometimes contributing to the support of a dying journeyman, sometimes contributing to the national effort as did William Pechin when he closed his office to take the entire staff to help in the Battle of North Point.[67]

As domestic manufactures increased and lines of supply improved, city printers, no longer confronted with a shortage of materials, could manage their business with reasonable efficiency, free at last of breakdowns in their primitive assembly lines. In 1791, for example, E. T. Andrews of Boston had feared that a shortage of paper would oblige him to print an edition of only ten thousand copies of a spelling book instead of the twenty thousand he had planned.[68] In the following year he needed enough type for a reader so that he could set up two half-sheets, in order that one might always be "at press."[69] A half-sheet sometimes enabled a printer to maintain production: Andrews observed that in Hugh Gaine's prayer book "every other one is a half sheet, so that I suppose he keeps a press going all the time."[70] These printers were indeed adaptable men: John C. Clark, who composed the text of Alexander Wilson's *American Ornithology* (1808–14), is said to have lacked a sufficient number of accents, so he used a penknife to improvise them from hair spaces.[71]

As master printers took for granted normal supply lines, they began to resist poor quality in materials and workmanship. Samuel

---

[65] *Ibid.*

[66] Charles L. Nichols, "The Literary Fair in the United States," in *Bibliographical Essays: A Tribute to Wilberforce Eames* (n.p., 1924), pp. 85–90; Silver, *SB*, III, 208–28; Silver, *PBSA*, XLVI, 33–44; Rollo G. Silver, "The Boston Lads Were Undaunted," *Lib. Jour.*, LXXIV (1949), 995–97.

[67] Buckingham, *Pers. Mem.*, I, 36; Minick, pp. 63–64.

[68] Letter to Isaiah Thomas, Sept. 22, 1791, in Thomas Papers.

[69] Letter to Isaiah Thomas, Jan. 8[?], 1792, in Thomas Papers.

[70] Letter to Isaiah Thomas, April 21, 1793, in Thomas Papers.

[71] *Am. Dict. Print.*, p. 99.

Etheridge of Charlestown, Massachusetts, complained to William
Bentley in 1807 of "the great difficulty of getting good printing
paper & ink & the disadvantages to the Am. printing from having
the same hands at all branches of the business."[72] Supervision of
quality of materials, it will be remembered, was also recommended
by the Society of Printers.

The frontier and many small towns naturally endured shortages
of paper and type for a longer period. In 1800 John Scull of Pittsburgh borrowed cartridge paper from the commandant of Fort Fayette, and in 1809 Joseph Charless in St. Louis used writing paper.[73]
Printers engulfed by emergency reduced the size of the sheet or, as
the Wheeling *Repository* did in 1807, suspended publication until
paper arrived.[74] Type was so limited in places that at the beginning
of the nineteenth century Alden Spooner of Sag Harbor, New York,
printed sermons at night so that the same type could be used in his
newspaper.[75] As late as 1819 the Rochester, New York, *Gazette*
worked off one side, distributed the type, and then used it for the
inner form.[76]

In marked contrast, the wealthier firms could afford to keep type
standing for religious or educational texts in answer to progressively
increasing demand. Beginning in 1789, Thomas & Andrews probably printed Noah Webster's *American Spelling Book* from standing
type, a very practical method to keep pace with the accelerating
sales of the schoolbooks of Webster and Caleb Bingham.[77] When
Joseph Charless of Lexington, Kentucky, purchased the "western
rights" of the speller in 1806, he had the forms of standing type
shipped to him from Philadelphia.[78] A much larger investment was
required for standing Bibles, some of which were composed abroad
and imported in forms. Hugh Gaine's Bible of 1792, according to
Evans, was "said to have been set up in Scotland, and imported, in
page-form, ready for printing."[79] Five years later Isaiah Thomas

[72] *Diary of William Bentley, D.D.* (Salem, Mass., 1911), III, 325.
[73] Reuben G. Thwaites, "The Ohio Valley Press before the War of 1812–15,"
Proc. Am. Ant. Soc., n.s., XIX (1909), 312; Kaser, p. 83.
[74] Kaser, p. 85; Hamilton, *Country Printer*, p. 16; Otis K. Rice, "West Virginia
Printers and Their Work, 1790–1830," *W. Va. Hist.*, XIV (1953), 337.
[75] Hamilton, *Country Printer*, p. 79.
[76] Edwin Scrantom, quoted, *ibid.*, p. 33.
[77] *A Bibliography of the Writings of Noah Webster*, comp. Emily E. F. Skeel
and ed. Edwin H. Carpenter, Jr. (New York, 1958), p. 15.
[78] Kaser, pp. 51–52.   [79] Evans 24098.

advertised that he had four Bibles (folio, royal quarto, large demy octavo, demi-duodecimo) "now all standing, and are to be kept ready at all times for the press, in the same manner as they are at the Royal Printing Offices in London and Edinburgh, and the University Printing Houses of Oxford and Cambridge."[80] The demi-duodecimo or "Common School Bible" appeared in 1797, seven years after Thomas ordered it from the Fry foundry on receiving their quotation of £1,444 for the type, composition, reading, and correction.[81] Another school Bible, issued by Hudson & Goodwin in 1809 and also imported in corrected pages, came from the Wilson foundry at a reputed cost of six thousand crowns.[82] Mathew Carey, too, kept his Bibles in standing type, and by the beginning of the nineteenth century Thomas & Andrews had enlarged their stock of standing type for educational books:

Of several books, used in schools, the forms were kept standing. Webster's Spelling-Book kept one press constantly employed, and often two or three. Of the duodecimo Bible, two or three large editions were published every year. Webster's "Third Part," commonly so called, (a reading book once popular, and in many parts of the country almost the only book used in the higher classes of the common schools) was also one of the books, the types for which were kept standing.[83]

When the need for standing type disappeared with the introduction of stereotyping, money tied up began to be released for other investment.

Conservatives in the trade shied away from the new technique until their more hardheaded colleagues demonstrated that it was no longer experimental, but practical to use. Uriel Crocker told of the miscalculation of leading Boston firms who refused to join him when, about 1820, he suggested stereotyping a Family Bible in six volumes. Two editions of this large work printed from type had lost money, and Crocker reasoned that if plates were used a radical saving could be made in paper because only five hundred copies need be printed at one time instead of three thousand. Cummings & Hilliard, Manning & Loring, Lincoln & Edmands all declined to join, but Crocker's firm made a crucial decision to publish it against

---

[80] Evans 31806.   [81] Silver, *Typefounding*, p. 112.
[82] O'Callaghan, p. 96.
[83] Silver, *SB*, XIX, 103–22; Buckingham, "Croaker, No. XXVI."

their advice. For an investment of twenty thousand dollars, their confidence was well rewarded: "Probably we printed and sold in all twenty or thirty thousand copies of the work. It cost us about six dollars a copy to manufacture them, and the retail price at which they were sold was twenty-four dollars a copy. We got about twelve dollars for those we sold to the trade."[84]

The use of press figures is now being investigated by Professor G. Thomas Tanselle. After examining more than a thousand books printed in America between 1775 and 1825, he summarized his findings in his first report:

> On the basis of these examples of American books with press figures, drawn from the twenty-five year period between 1790 and 1814, a few observations may be made: (1) press figures do not occur in American books of this time with great frequency, but they appear regularly in the work of certain printers; (2) the two most extensive examples thus far discovered are volumes printed in Philadelphia by several printers (especially Thomas Dobson) in the 1790's and books printed in New York by Isaac Riley and Charles Wiley in the 1810's; (3) Dobson, using four figures, figured about 66% of the quarto formes he printed for his *Encyclopaedia*, figured 36% of the sheets in both formes, and figured 85% of the outer formes; (4) Riley, using six figures, figured 73% of the formes in his legal octavos in half-sheet, Wiley 93%; (5) Dobson generally figured inner formes on 4^r and outer on 4^v, while Riley and Wiley placed their figures on 3^v of the half-sheet gathering; (6) evidence exists, in the press figures, for possible detailed reconstruction of the printing history of several large projects, such as the Dobson *Encyclopaedia*, the Riley legal reports, and the Mathew Carey Bibles, as well as many smaller works turned out by these printers during the same years. Furthermore, the data lean slightly toward the conclusion that press figures stand for men and that unfigured formes are the work of at least one additional press crew, working without a number. Press figures have not yet been located in American books before 1790, but further search is obviously called for.[85]

The mechanics of reprinting books could be facilitated by issuing a page-for-page edition. Using the printed text rather than a manuscript, printers easily calculated the amount of paper and scheduled work to be needed, thus cutting capital costs at the source. Composition from print was more efficient and cheaper, imposition more

[84] *Mem. U. Crocker*, pp. 38–40.
[85] "Press Figures in America: Some Preliminary Observations," *SB*, XIX (1966), 157.

rapid. For examples, William Hayley's *The Triumphs of Temper* (Newburyport, 1794) and Samuel Rogers' *The Pleasures of Memory* (Boston, 1795) were page-for-page reprints of London editions.[86] Domestic books also appeared in page-for-page editions. In consultation over one such book Alexander Thomas suggested a change in size to Isaiah Thomas: "Shall issue proposals of printing Espinasses Reports 3 vol. R. 8vo.—We can do it, I think in Royal 12mo. p. for p. with Byrne's edition. His sells at 3 dol. per vol. We can afford them at 1.50 very well."[87] On the other hand, under certain circumstances printers saw disadvantages which overrode the convenience of page-for-page editions. E. T. Andrews pointed this out to Isaiah Thomas:

I do not think it best to print Zoonomia [by Erasmus Darwin] page for page with the English Edition. I have been thinking to get it into two good sized 8vo. Vols. to sell at about 6 Dolls.—As it is a professional book, and physicians, in the country especially, are not full of Cash, I think it would answer much better in two Vols. than four, and they can be made more profitable, in proportion to the cost of them.[88]

The baffling experience of setting bad manuscripts, already mentioned in the first chapter, sent compositors into spasms of confusion and irritation. Uriel Crocker, horrified at the illegibility of the manuscripts of several ministers, remembered that "hours were spent by us in deciphering their words. Frequently, if we could not succeed in making out the words, we would put in words of about the same length that made nonsense, or would leave a vacant space or turn the type upside down."[89] More liberties were taken with John Neal's outrageous manuscript of *Logan* by printers who, Carey & Lea told the author, "pronounce your manuscript the worst they ever had & it is shoved out of the way at every opportunity."[90] With the rate of pay based on a thousand ems, compositors could not afford to spend time tricking out the words, but correction of spelling or capitalization and insertion of punctuation were almost automatic operations which most compositors regarded as their responsibility.

Usually printer and author corrected proof. Much greater care

[86] Evans 27104, 29426.   [87] Letter, Sept. 3, 1806, in Thomas Papers.
[88] Letter, July 2, 1802, in Thomas Papers.   [89] *Mem. U. Crocker*, p. 33.
[90] David Kaser, *Messrs. Carey & Lea of Philadelphia* (Philadelphia, [1957]), p. 75.

was taken for important editions of the Bible. Isaac Collins is said to have had the proof for his quarto Bible (1791) read "eleven times, the last time by his daughter, who was a very skillful reader."[91] Ten years later Mathew Carey used the Collins edition to check the proof of his quarto:

> I had eighteen various editions to collate in the reading of the proof sheets,—four London, three Cambridge, three Oxford, six Edinburgh, and two American,—those of Isaac Collins and Isaiah Thomas,—and found a most extraordinary number of discrepancies, some of which are incredible.[92]

For such projects the printers recruited special help.

From time to time short texts marking special occasions received a more elaborate presentation by being printed on silk. Among the broadsides on silk may be found carriers' addresses of Salem, Massachusetts, newspapers (1797, 1802), Charles Caldwell's *An Elegiac Poem* on Washington's death (1800), Jefferson's inaugural speech (1801), and a poem in memory of Stephen Decatur (1820).[93] Although this manner of printing was never very extensive, it deserves at least a historical survey to place it in proper perspective.

Another variation of established practice, hot-pressing, appeared in this country after its introduction in England by John Baskerville. In 1795 Manning & Loring of Boston printed Samuel Rogers' *The Pleasures of Memory* in a hot-pressed edition.[94] One year later John Thompson and Abraham Small of Philadelphia advertised the publication of their Bible in a manner which implies that they had been influenced at least a little by Baskerville, whose text they used for their edition:

> It claims patronage as being wholly American; the paper, by far the best ever used here, in printing, is made within a few miles of Philadelphia; the types, which are truly beautiful, are also American, and the whole apparatus for hot-pressing has been procured from different parts of the Union. It is also the cheapest hot-pressed Bible ever printed in any country.[95]

[91] *Am. Dict. Print.*, p. 101.

[92] "Autobiography of Mathew Carey," *New-England Mag.*, VI (1834), 230.

[93] Tapley, pp. 365, 385; *American Bibliography . . . for 1801*, pp. 78–79; *Sacred to the Memory of the Late Commodore Stephen Decatur* (Washington City, 1820).

[94] Evans 29426.   [95] Evans 30066.

Thompson also printed a hot-pressed edition of William L. Smith's *A Comparative View* during the same year, and this fashion spread to other cities.[96] In 1798 David Longworth of New York announced a book in which the "hot press is done on a plan entirely new."[97] As hot-pressed editions continued to come from the presses, a lively monologue, probably by William Cobbett, found them unbearably ridiculous:

> All books of all kinds are now advertised to be printed on a *wire-wove paper* and *hot-pressed*, with *cuts*, down to the *Philosophical* Transactions, (the uniformity of which work is destroyed by this folly unworthy of such a society) and Major *Rennell's* learned Memoir on Hindostan; as if the intention were, that they should be looked at and not read. . . . As to these *wire weavers* or drawers of *paper* and *hot-pressers*, must we say to the public, in the indignant words of Apuleius, "Quousque frustra pascetis *ignigenos* istos?" Surely this foolery must soon cease.

.   .   .   .   .

> While this note was printing, I was informed that *Coke upon Littleton, with Hargrave's notes* is advertising to be published on a *wire-wove paper* and *hot-pressed*. This folly, by such a proceeding, must surely sign its own death-warrant. I wish, to be sure, some of our *statutes at large* could be a little *wire-drawn* and *hot-pressed* by a committee of *parliamentary* Printers and Compositors.[98]

The craze for hot-pressing abated as its deficiencies (paper changed from white to beige, ink ran or spread) became better known. But cold-pressing, wrote a biographer of David Bruce, did become a function of the printing office soon after the firm of D. & G. Bruce began in 1806:

> In those days the pressing of the sheets was left to the book-binder, no standing presses being used in the business of printing. To render their work more acceptable, a standing press was ordered of Mr. Adam Ramage, of Philadelphia; and they received severe denunciation from the craft for making what was deemed an unwarrantable innovation upon the established order of things in printing offices.[99]

Nevertheless the craft adopted this procedure, and the 1815 price list of the master printers of New York includes an extra charge for pressing sheets.[100]

---

[96] Evans 31209.   [97] New York *Daily Advertiser*, Jan. 1, 1798.
[98] "Hot-Pressed Books," *Porcupine's Gazette*, Jan. 29, 1798.
[99] "Mr. David Bruce," *Typographic Messenger*, II (1867), 33.
[100] Van Winkle, p. 213.

None of these processes led to a radical advance in printing technique. Until the time of heavy investment in power presses and cylinder presses, printed matter was produced in much the same manner as always, albeit more efficiently with presses of iron instead of wood. Work was done in the traditional way, but American shops retained very few of the ancient customs described by Moxon because "they have seemed foolish to American workmen, and without good reason for their existence."[101]

In 1818 *The Printers' Guide* by Cornelius S. Van Winkle was published in New York. For the first time American printers had their own manual with descriptions of American presses, specimens of American typefounders, price lists for printing, and information on supplies. While some parts of the manual, as Wroth has demonstrated, derive from Stower, it was prepared by an American printer for the use of American printers.[102] In one sense, American printing may be said to have come of age with the publication of Van Winkle.

[101] *Am. Dict. Print.*, p. 308.
[102] Lawrence C. Wroth, "Corpus Typographicum: A Review of English and American Printers' Manuals," *The Dolphin*, No. 2 (1935), 166–67.

CHAPTER 4

PRINTER AND AUTHOR

IN THE early years of the Republic when the function of publishing had not yet been separated from that of printing, the
American author usually contracted directly with the printer for publication of his work. Each contract differed, with the amount of royalties, if any, dependent on profitable sales. Educational texts and
works of reference for American use sold well, usually paying their
authors a fee, but novels and poems often brought them nothing.
The imaginative writer was at the mercy of printers, who, as the
result of freedom from any international copyright law, could reprint English authors without payments of any kind. Novelists and
poets wrote in a society which regarded them as cheap labor and
saw no need to give them decent treatment. Printed authors were of
necessity amateurs with some dependable income. In 1790 Benjamin Rush, warning "Europeans Who Are Disposed to Migrate,"
advised that "literary men who have no professional pursuits will
often languish in America from the want of society. Our authors and
scholars are generally men of business and make their literary pursuits subservient to their interests."[1] There were other reasons, too,
why an author found it necessary to have other sources of income. In
a bitter letter to Noah Webster in 1806 David Ramsay accused his
booksellers of being uncivil and probably larcenous:

Readers are increasing in these states, and I trust the day is not
far distant when the sale of two thousand copies of an original work

---

[1] *Letters of Benjamin Rush*, ed. L. H. Butterfield (Princeton, N.J., 1951), I,
549–50.

might be counted upon. This would make it worth while to write books. All that I have ever done in that way, has not cleared actual expenses. Many booksellers never accounted at all for the books put into their hands for sale.[2]

Often an author considered publication a sufficient reward, and he risked his own funds to achieve it. If he found himself losing money on the publication, he looked for possibilities of recapturing his investment in one way or another. Jedidiah Morse, in 1790, offered Isaiah Thomas copies of his geography at a reduced price in order to settle the bill for printing.[3] Back in 1788 Joel Barlow tried to extricate himself by offering Mathew Carey republication rights for *The Vision of Columbus:*

I have part of the second edition on hand in sheets, which I wish to dispose of, that I may not lose money by the work—for I expect not to make any. One hundred of the copies I designed for Philadelphia and its neighborhood, by which I mean all the Middle States south of this place. To accommodate us both, I will now send you, by the first vessel, this hundred copies, which if you will receive and account for to Mr. Hazard at three shillings Penn. currency, you have my full consent to publish one impression as numerous as you please, and as soon as you please, besides inserting it in the *Museum.*[4]

But in other instances much of the edition was eventually bound, and unsold copies left in bookstores on consignment, so Joel Barlow's maneuver seems unlikely to have been tried very often. Ramsay could have told Webster more about mercenary booksellers after the publication of *The History of the American Revolution* (1789). One bookseller paid him for eighteen copies but deducted one-third of the amount for advertising; pirated editions were imported from the British Isles. At the end of ten years more than fifty of the sixteen hundred copies printed for Ramsay remained unsold.[5]

If a printer did accept the responsibility of printing a book, he might insist on farming out some of the costs and work of distribution to the author. William Spotswood's proposition to Jeremy Belk-

---

[2] Emily E. F. Skeel, *Notes on the Life of Noah Webster* (New York, 1912), II, 2n.

[3] Letter, April 19, 1790, in Thomas Papers.

[4] Charles B. Todd, *Life and Letters of Joel Barlow, LL. D.* (New York, 1886), pp. 63–64.

[5] Robert L. Brunhouse, "David Ramsay's Publication Problems, 1784–1808," *PBSA*, XXXIX (1945), 64–66.

THE

HOLY BIBLE,

CONTAINING THE

OLD AND NEW

TESTAMENTS:

TRANSLATED OUT OF THE

ORIGINAL TONGUES:

AND WITH THE FORMER

TRANSLATIONS

Diligently compared and revifed.

TRENTON:

PRINTED AND SOLD BY ISAAC COLLINS.

M.DCC.XCI.

XIII. The Isaac Collins Edition of *The Holy Bible* (Trenton, N.J., 1791). (Reduced from 8⅛ x 11⅜)

Before CHRIST 1451.

C H A P. XXXVI.

1 *The inconvenience of the inheritance of daughters* 5 *is remedied by marrying in their own tribes,* 7 *left the inheritance should be removed from the tribe.* 10 *The daughters of Zelophehad marry their father's brothers sons.*

AND the chief fathers of the families of the children of Gilead, the son of Machir, the son of Manasseh, of the families of the sons of Joseph, came near, and spake before Moses, and before the princes, the chief fathers of the children of Israel :

a Chap. 27 1
Josh. 17 3

2 And they said, ª The LORD commanded my lord to give the land for an inheritance by lot to the children of Israel : and my lord was commanded by the LORD to give the inheritance of Zelophehad our brother unto his daughters.

3 And if they be married to any of the sons of the *other* tribes of the children of Israel, then shall their inheritance be taken from the inheritance of our fathers, and shall be put to † Heb. unto whom they shall be. the inheritance of the tribe † whereunto they are received : so shall it be taken from the lot of our inheritance.

4 And when the jubile of the children of Israel shall be, then shall their inheritance be put unto the inheritance of the tribe whereunto they are received : so shall their inheritance be taken away from the inheritance of the tribe of our fathers.

5 And Moses commanded the children of Israel according to the word of the LORD,

saying, The tribe of the sons of Joseph hath said well.

6 This *is* the thing which the LORD doth command concerning the daughters of Zelophehad, saying, Let them † marry to whom they think best ; ᵇ only to the family of the tribe of their father shall they marry.

† Heb. be wives.
b Tob. 1 9

7 So shall not the inheritance of the children of Israel remove from tribe to tribe : for every one of the children of Israel shall † keep himself to the inheritance of the tribe of his fathers.

† Heb. cleave to the, &c.

8 And every daughter, that possesseth an inheritance in any tribe of the children of Israel, shall be wife unto one of the family of the tribe of her father, that the children of Israel may enjoy every man the inheritance of his fathers.

9 Neither shall the inheritance remove from *one* tribe to another tribe ; but every one of the tribes of the children of Israel shall keep himself to his own inheritance.

10 ¶ Even as the LORD commanded Moses, so did the daughters of Zelophehad :

11 ᶜ For Mahlah, Tirzah, and Hoglah, and Milcah, and Noah, the daughters of Zelophehad, were married unto their father's brothers sons :

c Chap. 27 1

12 *And* they were married † into the families of the sons of Manasseh the son of Joseph, and their inheritance remained in the tribe of the family of their father.

† Heb. to some that were of the families.

13 These *are* the commandments and the judgments, which the LORD commanded by the hand of Moses unto the children of Israel in the plains of Moab by Jordan *near* Jericho.

¶ The Fifth Book of MOSES, called DEUTERONOMY.

1490.

C H A P. I.

1 *Moses' speech in the end of the fortieth year, briefly rehearsing the story* 6 *of God's promise,* 13 *of giving them officers,* 19 *of sending the spies to search the land,* 34 *of God's anger for their incredulity,* 41 *and disobedience.*

‖ Or, Zuph.

THESE *be* the words which Moses spake unto all Israel on this side Jordan in the wilderness, in the plain over against ‖ the Red *sea*, between Paran, and Tophel, and Laban, and Hazeroth, and Dizahab.

2 (*There are* eleven days *journey* from Horeb by the way of mount Seir unto Kadesh-barnea.)

1451.

3 And it came to pass in the fortieth year, in the eleventh month, on the first *day* of the month, *that* Moses spake unto the children of Israel, according unto all that the LORD had given him in commandment unto them ;

a Numb. 21 24

4 ª After he had slain Sihon the king of the Amorites, which dwelt in Heshbon, and Og the king of Bashan, which dwelt at Astaroth in Edrei :

5 On this side Jordan, in the land of Moab, began Moses to declare this law, saying,

6 The LORD our God spake unto us in

Horeb, saying, Ye have dwelt long enough in this mount :

7 Turn you, and take your journey, and go to the mount of the Amorites, and unto † all the places nigh thereunto, in the plain, in the hills, and in the vale, and in the south, and by the sea-side, to the land of the Canaanites, and unto Lebanon, unto the great river, the river Euphrates.

† Heb. all his neighbours.

8 Behold, I have † set the land before you : go in and possess the land which the LORD sware unto your fathers, ᵇ Abraham, Isaac, and Jacob, to give unto them and to their seed after them.

† Heb. given.
b Gen. 15 18
& 17 7 8

9 ¶ And I spake unto you at that time, saying, I am not able to bear you myself alone :

10 The LORD your God hath multiplied you, and behold, ye *are* this day as the stars of heaven for multitude.

11 (The LORD God of your fathers make you a thousand times so many more as ye *are*, and bless you, as he hath promised you !)

12 How can I myself alone bear your cumbrance, and your burden, and your strife ?

13 † Take ye wise men, and understanding, and known among your tribes, and I will make them rulers over you.

† Heb. Give.

14 And ye answered me, and said, The thing

XIV. The Isaac Collins Edition of *The Holy Bible* (Trenton, N.J., 1791). (Reduced from 8⅛ x 11⅜)

XV. Frontispiece of *The Self-Interpreting Bible* (New York, 1792). (Reduced from 9½ x 16⅜)

AN

ADDRESS

TO THE

PEOPLE

OF THE

UNITED STATES.

From GEORGE WASHINGTON, President.

NEW-CASTLE:

PRINTED BY SAMUEL & JOHN ADAMS.

1796.

XVI. George Washington, *An Address to the People of the United States*
(New Castle, Dela., 1796). (Reduced from 4⅝ x 8)

nap in 1789 for publishing *The Foresters* was to "advance paper, printing, and binding, and the profits on the sales to be mutually divided, each of us to make the necessary exertions to promote its circulation, the expences to be paid for out of the first sales." Belknap refused Spotswood's offer, contracting instead with Thomas & Andrews, although his own son, Joseph, and Alexander Young had just opened a printing office in Boston. His reasons were practical and conclusive: "I prefer having T. & A. for proprietors, for two reasons: First, they have extensive connections, and can push a sale. Secondly, there will probably be no suspicion who the author is, which would infallibly be the case if my son were to stand as proprietor; and I wish to remain *concealed*, if possible."[6] Under date of December 28, 1791, his contract with Thomas & Andrews disposed of the copyright, for which Belknap, his heirs, and assigns would receive one-third of the copies in sheets, or the full value of the sheets at wholesale price, of every edition

to be paid as fast as the Books shall be sold. Provided that the s[d] Belknap, his heirs & assigns shall not receive any part of his third part of the first Edition of said Book (excepting six copies only if called for) until there shall be so many copies of s[d] Book sold as will pay the amount of the paper on which said first Edition is printed—and if at the Expiration of two years from the first publication of said first Edition, there should not be so many copies sold as will pay the amount of the paper aforesaid, then the s[d] Belknap, his heirs & assigns shall pay to the s[d] Thomas & Andrews, their heirs & assigns one half the value of the s[d] paper, and the said Thomas & Andrews their heirs & assigns shall deliver to s[d] Belknap his heirs & assigns one third part of the printed copies which shall then remain unsold in sheets.[7]

Another clause defined the wholesale price of the book in sheets as equal to half the price of the same book bound.[8] The author therefore received a number of his own books equal in value to one-sixth of a bound edition. In this instance he assumed a slight risk but was still saddled with part of the distribution. Belknap's outrage at the extortionate price his nerves and pocketbook paid for the profession of authorship is summarized in a letter about the second and third

[6] Massachusetts Historical Society, *Collections* (Boston, 1877), 5th ser., III, 135–36, 278.

[7] Rollo G. Silver, "Three Eighteenth-Century American Book Contracts," *PBSA*, XLVII (1953), 384.

[8] *Ibid.*, p. 385.

volumes of his history of New Hampshire, published in 1791 and 1792:

I would also beg leave to observe, that the several classes of tradesmen whom I employ in this work do not run any risque at all. The paper-maker is paid by the rheam; the printer by the sheet; the bookbinder by the volume; and the engraver at a stipulated price. I expect to be the bookseller myself, & I am the only person concerned whose expense is certain & whose profit is uncertain. I must pay them for their work, whether the books are sold or not. If they are sold I shall be a gainer, & if not a loser. This is precisely the state of the case, & I am the more particular on this head, lest it should be suggested that the advantage arising from the sale of the books would belong to the printers & booksellers, rather than to the author.[9]

Under optimum conditions (popular treatment of a popular subject, shrewd negotiations with the printer), a book could be profitable for its creator. In her autobiography America's first professional woman author, Hannah Adams, told with satisfaction how, under the watchful eye of a minister, she arranged for the publication of the second edition (1791) of her dictionary of religions:

I now applied to a large number of printers to know on what terms they would publish my work. But, though I wrote nearly the same letter to all, consisting of a few direct questions, their answers were generally various, prolix, and ambiguous.

I at length concluded to accept the terms of one of the printers to whom I applied, who offered me one hundred dollars in books, for an edition of one thousand copies. When I went to Boston for this purpose, a friend of mine introduced me to the Rev. Mr Freeman, whom I had only once before seen: but I was well apprised of his benevolent character, which I found more than realized the ideas which I had formed of it from report. I shall ever recollect the generous interest he took in my affairs, with the most lively gratitude. He removed my perplexity, by transacting the business with the printer. By his advice, a subscription paper was published; and I soon found the benefit of his patronage, in procuring a large number of subscribers, and concluding an advantageous bargain for me with Mr Folsom, the printer.[10]

According to the contract, Folsom agreed to print one thousand copies for twelve dollars a sheet on paper costing the author eight-

[9] Mass. Hist. Soc., *Coll.*, 6th ser., IV, 502.
[10] *A Memoir of Miss Hannah Adams, Written by Herself* (Boston, 1832), pp. 20–21.

een shillings a ream. It also specified that Folsom would sell copies to the subscribers until his bill had been paid, at which time he would deliver the remaining copies to the author. It has been estimated that, with a total production cost of about $510, the edition would have been paid for when approximately half was sold.[11] That this transaction actually made a profit is confirmed by Hannah Adams' statement that "the emolument I derived from it not only placed me in a comfortable situation, but enabled me to pay the debts I had contracted during mine and my sister's illness, and to put out a small sum upon interest."[12] Here, again, the author participated in the distribution.

The Reverend Mr. Freeman with his "large number of subscribers" was invaluable; a long subscription list, an indication of sales potential, enabled an author to induce the best possible terms from the printer. If the book appeared a lively prospect for success, an author with foresight, like Hannah Adams, retained the copyright and sold the right to print only a specified number of copies. Authors of less promising books sold the copyright with a provision for payment for future editions. Belknap did this with *The Foresters*, as Peter Whitney did with his history of Worcester County:

Memorandum of An Agreement made this fifteenth day of August, one thousand, Seven hundred & Ninety three between Peter Whitney of Northborough, in the County of Worcester & Commonwealth of Massachusetts, Clerk, on the one part; & Isaiah Thomas of Worcester, in s⁰ County & Commonwealth, Printer, on the other part, witnesseth that the s⁰ Whitney hereby sells & relinquishes to the s⁰ Thomas the Copy-Right of a Book, whereof he is the Author entitled "A history of the County of Worcester, in the Commonwealth of Massachusetts: with a particular account of every Town from its first Settlement to the present time, &c. together with a Map of the County at large, from actual Survey,"—for the Consideration that the said Thomas give him the said Whitney Ninety four Copies of said Book, when published, bound and lettered, Six Copies bound lettered and gilt, and Fifty Copies in Sheets (said Thomas to bind said Fifty Copies for said Whitney, he paying said Thomas therefor the sum of Two Shillings for each copy); and further to give said Whitney one hundred Copies, bound and lettered, of all future Editions of said Book provided said Whitney revise, correct and add to the same whatever may by said Thomas be deemed necessary, and also by said Whitney.[13]

[11] Silver, *PBSA*, XLVII, 382–383.   [12] Adams, p. 21.
[13] Thomas Papers (box).

When Belknap compiled *American Biography* (1794–98), a book likely to succeed, Thomas & Andrews gave him relatively better terms, limiting their contract to one edition, assuming all risks, giving Belknap twenty-five copies in sheets and royalties equal to one-sixth of all copies bound, in addition to endorsing a hundred-pound note for the author. In order to obtain these terms, Belknap evidently dangled a subscription list as bait. This may be surmised because the contract shows that proposals had been printed previously: "The said Thomas & Andrews engage to fulfil to all subscribers the Conditions of the proposal, a printed Copy of which is hereto annexed." It should be remembered that a subscription list itself was subject to agreement between printer and author. Hannah Adams, in her contract with Folsom, authorized him to sell copies to subscribers; Belknap's contract for *American Biography* allowed him to keep advance payments from subscribers as part payment of royalties.[14]

Because royalty payments were not stabilized, they could be easily adjusted to the work at hand. The following contract provides a low, but probably fair, royalty:

This certifies that I, Maria Winchester, of Walpole, in Newhampshire, have given to Thomas & Thomas, of said Walpole, permission to print and vend an edition of, "A course of Lectures, written by Elhanan Winchester;" the edition to consist of any number not exceeding one thousand; and that I will not sell the copyright of the said Lectures, or the privilege of printing an edition of them to any other person, without restricting the purchaser of the said work, or privilege before mentioned, not to print or vend any, till the edition, which Thomas & Thomas shall print, may be sold.

For the consideration of fifty sets of the work, bound and lettered, I have bound myself to the above. The copy of the work to be found by Mrs. Winchester.

Maria Winchester

Walpole, July 1799[15]

At least Maria Winchester did not have to finance the costs of publication, a gruesome experience, particularly if the author had already sacrificed health and funds in his thankless profession. Even if he had money, and even if he were lucky enough to have the printer sell his books, it did not necessarily mean that he would promptly receive the money collected, as Robert Proud found to his

---

[14] Silver, *PBSA*, XLVII, 385–387.   [15] Thomas Papers.

sorrow after he advanced $915 for publication of *The History of Pennsylvania in North America* (1797–98). One accounting from Poulson, the printer, is dated 1806.[16] If the author was poor, then he was almost entirely helpless; Hannah Adams remembered her sufferings during the time she issued her *Summary History of New England* (1799):

Before my eyes failed, I had sent out a subscription paper; but afterward, the idea that I never should be able to complete the compilation, induced me to drop it; and I was obliged to publish the work almost entirely at my own expense. The printers were in low circumstances, and required payment before I could dispose of the books. I was therefore obliged to borrow a sum of money to defray the expenses of the work, which, as it was printed on very good paper, were large, and I derived but little profit from my labor.[17]

Unable to tolerate such misery, she again asked the Reverend Mr. Freeman to bargain with the printers. That canny man arranged for her to receive a total of five hundred dollars in yearly payments for the two thousand copies of the 1801 edition of her dictionary of religions.[18]

Most printers were not necessarily hoggish nor unfeeling; the exigencies of their business kept their own chances for survival very low. A printer with a manuscript before him knew that his business depended on his keeping a staff at work, his costs at a minimum, and his profits as high as possible. The financial condition of his business at each particular time determined the acceptance or rejection of a manuscript, rate of royalty, and the amount of expenses shared with the author. The variables which cropped up when least expected, often smashing well-laid plans, they could not control; and being often on the verge of disaster themselves, they became seemingly indifferent to the plight of their authors. In this letter of November 29, 1802, from Alexander Thomas to Isaiah Thomas, the writer regretfully explains his own small profit in comparison to the author's getting "his rather too easy:"

Have begun "Foster's Candid examination &c" making perhaps 300 pages 8vo.—Print it on paper at 19/. He gives us up all the subscribers perhaps 3 or 400 or more. We give him 500 in sheets— We take 500 ourselves, we find paper & print it at our expense—At

[16] Lathrop C. Harper, Inc., *Catalogue No. 1* (New York, 1953), p. 76.
[17] Adams, pp. 26–27.   [18] *Ibid.*, p. 27.

the end of a year if our 500 are not all sold he obligates himself to take them at 5/6 in sheets. Therefore suppose we sell 300 it will be

$$450 \text{ dol.}$$
$$\text{dedt. bindg.} \quad \underline{75}$$
$$\overline{375.}$$
$$200 \text{ to be returned @ 5/6} \quad \underline{166}$$
$$\overline{541} \text{ the sum we}$$

shall probably receive for the whole work—I engaged it when we had little work on hand. We shall make in this view perhaps two hundred dollars. He however gets his rather too easy as you will perceive.[19]

Many authors did not get theirs "rather too easy," but at least they were encouraged to continue. Thus when English books appeared free of royalty, John Davis was paid for *The Farmer of New Jersey* (1800): "The emoluments I had derived from the publication of my little Novel, induced me to undertake another, which I was resolved to make more voluminous."[20] And in Salem, Massachusetts, Bernard Macanulty paid Joseph Story at least two hundred dollars for the copyright of his poem, *The Power of Solitude* (1804).[21] It is to be hoped that the detailed analyses of the royalties paid to American authors prepared by the late Professor William Charvat will eventually be published. His lifetime study would undoubtedly clarify many aspects of the subject.

The legal right to reprint any foreign work at any time was gradually restrained by the "courtesies of the trade." These unwritten laws of the book trade upheld the prior rights of the person who first advertised a specific foreign work in press and forbade this work to be "printed upon." The laws made taboo the issuance of another edition until the advertised one was exhausted or the claim to it relinquished. If a firm printed one work of a foreign author, it was understood in the trade that it had the right to print his other works unless the author or his foreign publisher committed themselves elsewhere. Violators of this code could not, of course, be legally punished but were subjected instead to reprisals, which included the possibility of being "printed upon" and ostracism from their peers, on whom they were dependent for exchange of publications and information.[22]

[19] Thomas Papers.

[20] John Davis, *Travels of Four Years and a Half* (New York, 1909), pp. 179–80.

[21] Tapley, opp. p. 191.   [22] Kaser, *Carey & Lea*, pp. 143–45.

Authors and editors of educational texts fared better than writers of novels or poetry because of greater popular success. As is happening today, the printing trade at the end of the eighteenth century did a larger volume of business in textbooks than in "trade books." Moreover, most of the textbooks, intended for American use and written by Americans, could be copyrighted. Printers tried to strengthen the wall against competition in textbooks by sometimes inserting a clause in the contract which prohibited the author from writing a competitive book within a stated period. Ebenezer T. Andrews wrote to Isaiah Thomas about one such incident in 1793:

Have looked up your letter respecting Alexander's Grammar— you therein say "Finally he agreed to take £40—half books and half money—books on demand— 10£ of the money in 6 months and the remainder in 12 months."—If he will not take less, think we must give him this sum—but would specify in the agreement that he should not make or compile any other English Grammar during the period of 14 years, otherwise he will have another copyright to sell in the course of a few months.[23]

As the expiration of copyright of a successful book approached, printer and author prepared for a revised edition. Most authors revised the text themselves, but a busy author could hire somebody to do the chore. Jedidiah Morse employed Joseph T. Buckingham for one revision, which Buckingham looked back upon with regret:

The copy-right of the Doctor's "Geography made easy," was about expiring in 1808, and, in order to prevent the publication of it by others, it was necessary that some changes should be made in the matter, while the title should be secured by a new patent. This was a labor, which he forsaw, would conflict with some other project he had in view, and, at his request, I undertook to do it for him. Matter might be taken from any of his geographical works, with or without alteration, as I might judge proper. Much of it, however, was re-written, and the whole was sent to him, for inspection. It was returned with a certificate of his entire approbation. The work was limited, by contract with the publishers, to three hundred and sixty pages; and, consequently, some times an excision or an expansion was necessary to reduce the various parts to their proper proportions. This was my first and only attempt at book-making *to order*. I was *silly* enough to offer to do it for *fifty cents a page*, and he was *prudent* enough to hold me to the bargain.[24]

[23] Letter, July 21[?], 1793, in Thomas Papers.
[24] "Croaker, No. XXVI," Boston *Courier*, Sept. 22, 1849.

Royalties for elementary texts, inexpensive and printed in large editions, were usually calculated by the size of the edition and its popularity. In 1803 Thomas & Thomas published an edition of *The Child's Companion* which paid Caleb Bingham ten dollars a thousand.[25] In the following year John Hubbard earned thirty dollars a thousand for *The American Reader*. However, it was not unique for an entire copyright to be sold for a specific price or for texts to be sold on a percentage basis, especially if their popularity was doubtful. In 1804 Alexander Thomas, who had ensured himself from loss by a percentage deal, told Isaiah Thomas about it: "I have engaged to print, as you will see by our notice of it in the paper, Tully de Oratore, with English notes and a life of the Author by Professor Smith. We are to give him 20 p. Ct. on all that are sold, *more or less*. I think the work will sell pretty well."[26] If sales were assumed, royalties increased and the textbook writer's life became less despairing. It is interesting that although Ebenezer T. Andrews rubbed his hands with glee when he wrote to Isaiah Thomas of his hard bargain with Jedidiah Morse, signed about 1801, he made a contract for payment to the author of fifteen hundred dollars, a good amount of money for that period: "We gave Dr. Morse only 1500 Dolls. for his Abridgment, and Elements, when they had 8 years to run."[27] Even texts written for a tiny fraction of the population brought a sizable amount, so that in 1805 Benjamin Rush could write to John Adams: "Even my pen has lately added to my resources. I am to receive 1000 dollars for the copyright of the new edition of my medical works which will be published in a week or ten days."[28]

The transformation of the printer-bookseller into the publisher who deliberately sought out qualified authors and enthusiastically marketed their books was gradual and continuous throughout the first three decades of the nineteenth century. The transition was finally made when publishing books was no longer ancillary to the major function of a printing firm but was its major source of income. As the publisher superseded the printer and bookseller in importance to the author, it was he who conducted the perilous and delicate negotiations in their relationship.

[25] Contract, Jan. 21, 1803, in Thomas Papers.
[26] Letter from Alexander Thomas to Isaiah Thomas, Feb. 6, 1804, in Thomas Papers.
[27] Letter, May 20, 1804, in Thomas Papers.
[28] *Letters of Benjamin Rush*, II, 909.

The printer-author relationship, particularly complex in agreements for educational texts and different from the later publisher-author relationship, is disclosed in the voluminous papers and correspondence of Noah Webster. Webster's speller, grammar, and reader, all issued as parts of *The Grammatical Institute*, had a phenomenally large sale, estimated as high as twenty million copies before 1829. Skeel and Carpenter's excellent bibliography of Webster states that the first edition of the first part, five thousand copies, was printed in Hartford by Hudson & Goodwin in 1783, with the printers accepting "Webster's note for the printing bill, in return for sole printing rights 'for a term of years.'" In 1786 the contract was renegotiated with Hudson & Goodwin retaining a part of the monopoly but allowing Webster to make his own arrangements elsewhere. He proceeded to do so, contracting with William Young of Philadelphia in 1787 for "the exclusive right to print and sell all three parts of the *Grammatical Institute* in Pennsylvania, Delaware, Maryland, and Virginia for a period of three years."[29] About the same time he signed a five-year contract with Samuel Campbell of New York granting "unlimited rights for selling in New York, New Jersey, North Carolina, South Carolina, and Georgia" for £80 New York money or $200 cash.[30] Unfortunately, Webster did not foresee the possible consequences of this transaction. Campbell violated the contract by sending copies to the Hartford market and, worse, printed at least fifty thousand copies just before the contract terminated.[31] Webster could do little about this excess when he planned another Philadelphia edition. He decided to issue it himself and asked Timothy Pickering to secure a printer for it. Pickering reported back in a letter, December 8, 1791:

I called several times on some of the printers named by you—or rather at their houses,—without meeting them: others took time to answer: and my own business occasioned some delays. I now inclose the terms proposed by Mr. Cist & Mr. Bache. Mr. Crukshanks has too much other work on hand to engage in yours. Mr. Fenno in the same condition. Mr. Bailey could not undertake on terms as low as Mr. Cists. Mr. Young imagined that a man who had printed for him might do it: but was disappointed.
　　Mr. Young thinks it would be cheaper for you to get the books printed in New England. Mr. Bailey says that Gain of N. York

[29] *Bibliog. of N. Webster*, pp. xix, 6, 9–11.
[30] Harry R. Warfel, *Noah Webster* (New York, 1936), p. 71.
[31] Skeel, I, 308; Warfel, p. 71.

sends his testaments to Boston & other places in Massachusetts, & gets them bound for 5d. each; when in Philadelphia the price would be 9d.

There is so much printing now done in this city, that paper is dearer by 10 P cent or more than it was but a year or two ago.

Mr. Young told me that your printers in New York, just as their contract was expiring, struck off 50,000 copies. Perhaps he may have mentioned it to you. He spoke of it as a very disingenuous thing.[32]

Webster's reply from Hartford included a reference to his plan to neutralize Campbell's edition:

The price of printing is so much higher in Philadelphia than here, that at present I shall relinquish the plan of getting work done in Philadelphia. I *can* get the Spelling book printed here for *four* pence, *Pennsylvania* Currency, paper included; and any of our printers would do it for less than *five* pence. I should however be under no apprehension of not selling the book at a profit even giving *six* pence, were it not for Campbell whose conduct, in striking off 50,000 at the close of his term, I was before apprized of, and which *deserves*, and may hereafter *receive*, serious notice. On this subject however it is necessary to observe silence. But he may push thousands into the Philadelphia market at a very *low* price, he almost certainly will, altho he has no more right, than any of the New England Printers, so to do. However I have an additional half sheet for the work, which will contain what I call "A Moral Catechism, or Lessons for Saturday." This I think will be a valuable addition to the work, and give my impression a decided preference in market. As Campbell cannot print this little pamphlet to add to the Spelling book, I hope to obtain in part that sale for my impression which his integrity would not give me in the Philadelphia market, which is now wholly my right.[33]

Webster was the model of the businessman who is an operator. His spelling book which sold in the millions was a brilliant idea in a land hungry for education and should have started him on a fortune, but he could not be satisfied with a sound business practice. If he had sold his books on a royalty basis according to copies printed, instead of selling the right to print in specific areas, he would not have been so often on the verge of bankruptcy. If he could have maintained a stable scale of prices everywhere instead of undercutting prices in different areas as a trick to sell more, he would not have done business with a cheat who worsted him at his own game.

[32] Skeel, I, 307.   [33] *Ibid.*, p. 308.

As it was, some of his contemporaries thought him low class. John Carter, writing to Isaiah Thomas, expressed contempt, which other printers must have shared:

By the Controversy between Messieurs Webster and Campbell, I find the latter purchased a Copy-Right much lower than it was offered to me, and perhaps lower than you gave.—Printers should beware of being duped by Authors, especially when they assume that Character, and are only mere Compilers.—You might have employed a judicious Person to revise all the Spelling-Books extant, and compiled a Copy, for perhaps less than 100 Dollars.[34]

The sale of the right to print a revised edition copyrighted in 1804 became even more difficult because printers continued to issue the first version in competition. Under the agreements he had made, Webster failed to secure the compensation he deserved, although he thought a new copyright would solve his problem. In 1793 he was powerless: "If I survive 11 years, & the copy-right of my Institute returns to me again, as it will, the present sale of it, *without increase*, will render it worth to me at least £2000—but nothing can be drawn from this resource at present."[35]

During the interval a few sharp printers issued the spelling book without licenses, sometimes renting the forms from unscrupulous license holders.[36] Licenses to print were also sold at auction.[37] When negotiating new contracts about 1804, Webster specified prices, wholesale and retail, and agreed to a royalty on every thousand copies printed. But as the years passed, his need for funds caused him to sell the rights for the remaining years of at least one of these contracts. "Thus," said his biographer, "necessity drove Webster time and again to take a fraction of the income he might have had."[38]

The printer-author relationship had one by-product which disappeared with the growth of publishing: the author, acting as his own publisher, commixed with book production. Webster's knowledge extended to making his own specifications for Timothy Pickering in 1792:

Enclosed with this I send you a Copy of the Prompter, which I will thank you to get printed in Philadelphia. Experiment proves it will sell. One impression here is gone, another at Albany is selling rapidly. I am willing to take the risk of an impression of

[34] Letter, Nov. 15, 1792, in Thomas Papers.　　[35] Skeel, II, 427.
[36] Warfel, p. 301.　　[37] *Bibliog. of N. Webster*, p. 26.　　[38] Warfel, p. 302.

1500 or 2000 in Philadelphia. Please to get it done in the cheapest and best manner, but on a smaller letter and in a less size. My opinion is that it should be done in *sixteens* and on a *small pica*. In that manner it will make about the same number of pages, or *three sheets*. A ream of paper to ½ a sheet will make about 900 complete copies. Six reams then will make that number of books. I believe it will be safe to print *two* reams in a *half* sheet; so that 12 reams will complete 1800 books. If it is necessary to advance money for the paper, please to draw on me for it at a short sight. I wish the paper to be very good and the letter also. The binding I wish to be in *marble paper*, but as they may be bound as they are called for, little money need be advanced for that; indeed they may be sold in sheets, at a price we can fix, when the expense of the paper and printing is ascertained.[39]

Authors could not avoid acquiring some knowledge of printing during negotiations. Evidence of this appears in various places. Ezra Stiles, to cite one example, recorded prices in his diary for October 9, 1793: "Price of Print at Warren by Phillips Eight Doll. a sheet 16 pages 8ᵛᵒ, 1500, 1800 or 2000 Lett. a page. Price Paper 12 to 15/ a Rheam. Eight Doll. per sheet for 300 Copies, after which half price per hundred."[40] To cite another, a contract was signed by Samuel Hall in 1792:

I the subscriber promise to Mʳ Jeremy Belknap that I will print five hundred Copies of his Sermon on 1 Corinthians 3.11. on Crown paper & with a pica type & will deliver them to his order stitched in blue paper covers at three pence three farthings each Copy, provided the said Sermon can be comprehended in two sheets—& at four pence each Copy provided it do not exceed two sheets & a quarter.[41]

Many ministers became familiar with printing techniques while arranging for publication of their sermons. These small pamphlets, discussing topics ranging from theology to current events, increased the prestige of the author and sometimes provided him with extra money. Many were joint financial ventures on the part of printer and author. But probably because the author was a minister, the etiquette of publication differed from the usual procedure: neither printer nor author circulated proposals before the sermon was delivered. William Bentley remembered this when he attended a Congregational convention in 1801:

[39] Skeel, I, 309–10.   [40] *Lit. Diary of E. Stiles*, III, 508.
[41] Contract, June 1, 1792, in Massachusetts Historical Society.

For the first time that ever I saw it, printed proposals were left in the pews before the sermon was delivered. In the present manners of our Country, this was felt as a great indelicacy. They tell such things of Dr. Cotton Mather, as of delivering Sermons for the press before the delivery, but this is the first of a Subscription prepared for the purpose by a Printer.[42]

Nor was it proper for a minister to sell his own publications. When Isaiah Thomas printed Samuel Deane's *The New-England Farmer*, Deane wrote to Thomas about distribution to subscribers: "Is there nobody in Portland that has done such kind of business for you? If I were not a clergyman, I wd. offer you my service, without fee. But in my situation, I cannot be collector of the money."[43]

Undoubtedly authors were delighted when the growth of the function of publishing relieved them of the onerous tasks of learning about and arranging for production. Publishers were equally delighted to accept the responsibility because they realized that few authors knew trade conditions well enough to obtain the best possible prices for printing. During the transitional period some publishers paid more than necessary for printing that had been contracted for by the author. Carey & Lea purchased the first edition of *The Last of the Mohicans* (1826) only to discover that the printer overcharged by more than three hundred dollars, whereupon they notified James Fenimore Cooper that they were penalized by his "want of knowledge of bookselling and manufacturing."[44]

After 1790 the printer-author relationship was primarily based upon the federal copyright law. This legal recognition of literary property gave authors and printers of American works a degree of protection they had not had before and enabled them to maintain control over the domestic reprinting of their publications. A campaign led by Noah Webster had induced all states except Delaware to pass copyright laws between 1783 and 1786, but these were of varying potency. Some states insisted that protection should not extend to citizens of any other state until that state had passed a similar law. Other states provided that their acts should not take effect until every state had passed a similar law.[45] Under such circumstances, authors at best possessed local copyrights, which, since

[42] *Diary of W. Bentley*, II, 374.
[43] Letter, May 29, 1790, in Thomas Papers.   [44] Kaser, *Cary & Lea*, p. 79.
[45] *Copyright Enactments of the United States, 1783–1906*, comp. Thorvald Solberg (Washington, 1906), pp. 11–31.

they did not extend to all states, lacked sufficient strength. The need for federal action in this, as in other situations, was obvious to the statesmen who drafted the Constitution. Their response is clearly stated in the eighth section of the first article wherein Congress is given the power to "promote the progress of science and useful arts, by securing, for limited times, to authors and inventors, the exclusive right to their respective writings and discoveries." The first session of the first Congress met on March 4, 1789. On April 15 the House received a petition from David Ramsay requesting copyrights for his *The History of the Revolution of South-Carolina* and his *The History of the American Revolution.* The committee considering this petition reported favorably and the House ordered the preparation of a general copyright law. While the Congress worked on the law, other authors also submitted petitions for copyrights. These were either referred to the committee or tabled. The committee's bill was presented on June 23, but action was delayed and finally postponed until the second session, when a copyright bill was passed and sent to the President, who signed it on May 31, 1790.[46]

The first federal copyright act provided for copyrighting maps, charts, and books already copyrighted as well as those not yet printed or published. The privilege of copyright was limited to citizens or residents. After the first term of fourteen years a copyright could be renewed for another term of the same length if the author was still living and a citizen or resident. No person could obtain a copyright unless a printed copy of the title was deposited "in the clerk's office of the district court where the author or proprietor shall reside" and "such author or proprietor shall, within two months from the date thereof, cause a copy of the said record to be published in one or more of the newspapers printed in the United States, for the space of four weeks." Within six months after publication the author or proprietor had to deliver a copy of the work to the Secretary of State, "to be preserved in his office."[47] These provisos created very unreliable records of publication: many of the printed titles never appeared as publications and many of the publications were never delivered to the Secretary of State.[48]

[46] *Copyright in Congress, 1789–1904*, prep. Thorvald Solberg (Washington, 1905), pp. 112–114, 123.

[47] *Copyright Enactments*, pp. 32–34.

[48] Frederick R. Goff, "The First Decade of the Federal Act for Copyright, 1790–1800," in *Essays Honoring Lawrence C. Wroth* (Portland, Me., 1951), p. 102.

In 1802 a supplementary act required that a copy of the copyright record "be inserted at full length in the title-page or in the page immediately following the title." Maps and charts would also bear a copyright notice. Other clauses added prints to the classes of works allowed for copyright and established a penalty for illegally printing a copyright notice in a publication. Another act, in 1819, extended the jurisdiction of the circuit courts to copyright and patent cases.[49]

At the beginning comparatively few items received copyright protection. Between 1790 and 1800 a total of 556 titles, some of which were never issued, were copyrighted in Pennsylvania, Massachusetts, New York, Virginia, and Maine.[50] And it has been estimated that "less than one-tenth of the works printed in Massachusetts between 1800 and 1809 were copyrighted."[51] American authors had not yet grown in numbers nor popularity sufficiently to compete with the influx of literature from across the ocean. Until they did, printers, for the most part, appropriated the foreign texts without the necessity of procuring the right to print. As the popularity of American authors increased in the nineteenth century, it was the publisher, not the printer, who learned how to work with an author, help him and at times finance him, edit his work with him, publicize him, and maintain a relationship of mutual trust and respect.

[49] *Copyright Enactments*, pp. 35–37.   [50] Goff, "First Decade," p. 101.
[51] Ruth S. Leonard, "Bibliographical Importance of Copyright Records," *Coll. and Res. Lib.*, VII (1946), 37.

CHAPTER 5

EXPANSION OF THE PRESS

AFTER the Revolution the new democratic beliefs that all citizens should have the opportunity to partake equally of available knowledge, that all citizens were equally capable of mastering profitable knowledge, and that knowledge was power began their relentless pressures on the public consciousness. These deepest of American vanities were reinforced by the thrust of social and economic forces: a rising population, the rapid and sustained increase in manufacturing, and the pervasive appeal of migration. The play of these influences on the supply and demand for printed information led to the building of new and enlarged printing offices alongside the new factories and new stores in the cities and towns. When the pioneers moved west from the older settlements, they were the veterans of a battle for economic, religious, and political freedoms, with minds formed by the Bible and ·the newspaper; they knew at first hand the value of the printing press as a means of communication in any kind of a struggle. In this precapitalist period of the economy the press expanded vertically in the urban centers, and at random horizontally into the new territories. Between 1787 and 1825 the first presses began in Kentucky, the District of Columbia, the area of present-day West Virginia, Tennessee, Ohio, Michigan, Mississippi, Indiana, Alabama, Missouri, Illinois, Texas, and Arkansas.

The hunters of game and the hunters of land who had passed through the Cumberland Gap and settled down in the District of

Virginia known as Kentucky officially asserted their personal feelings about the significance of the press at their first convention to consider separate statehood. At Danville, on December 30, 1784, they resolved "that the freedom of the Press is highly subserviant to Civil Liberty and therefor such measures ought to be taken as may be most likely to encourage the introduction of a Printer into the District."[1] The following year, at their second convention, they passed a similar resolution and appointed a committee to find a printer who could be induced to locate in the District.[2] But printers were far too cautious to emigrate without a guaranteed salary; even though a search was made as far away as Philadelphia, no printer could be found willing to take the risk. Finally, after a two years' search, John Bradford of Cane Run volunteered to set up a press if he was assured of public patronage.[3] His proposal was accepted and in July, 1787, the Trustees of the town of Lexington decreed

that a part of In lot No. 43, containing two poles in front on Main Street and six poles back adjoining No. 44, be granted to Mr. Bradford on condition that the printing press be established in the town of Lexington, in consideration of which Mr. Bradford shall be entitled to the sole use of said lot as long as the press continues in the town.[4]

Bradford, who was born in Prince William County, Virginia, in 1749, took up land near Lexington about 1780, bringing his family to settle there about five years later. Once a surveyor and militiaman, he seems at that time to have been primarily interested in land claims. He admitted that he knew nothing about printing, but he did possess "a confidence in my own mechanical talents . . . together with a belief that I could execute the business on a small scale until I should be able to instruct my sons (of which I had five), added to the prospect of future advantages to them and myself."[5]

He was certain of himself, and practical. He ordered press and type from Philadelphia, probably shipped by way of Pittsburgh, where they were forwarded by John Scull of the *Pittsburgh Gazette.*

[1] Thomas P. Abernethy, "Journal of the First Kentucky Convention," *Jour. South. Hist.*, I (1935), 73.

[2] Perrin, p. 9.

[3] J. Winston Coleman, Jr., *John Bradford, Esq.* (Lexington, Ky., 1950), p. 5.

[4] *Ibid.*, p. 6.

[5] Samuel M. Wilson, "The 'Kentucky Gazette' and John Bradford Its Founder," *PBSA*, XXXI (1937), 110–14.

(From Pittsburgh they would have had to be sent down the Ohio River to Limestone [Maysville], thence by packhorses along the dangerous trail.) He brought in paper. He probably sent his younger brother, Fielding, to learn how to print in John Scull's Pittsburgh shop.[6] By the summer of 1787 his shop was equipped, and he had learned the rudiments of his new profession. On August 11 he issued the first number of the *Kentucke Gazette*. It was a small, rough sheet, without a heading, containing two short articles, one advertisement, and this apology:

My customers will excuse this, my first publication, as I am much hurried to get an impression by the time appointed. A great part of the types fell into pi in the carriage of them from Limestone to this office, and my partner, which is the only assistant I have, through an indisposition of the body, has been incapable of rendering the smallest assistance for ten days past.[7]

Shortly after the first issue, the Bradfords hired Thomas Parvin, a journeyman printer, as assistant; Fielding left the firm in June, 1788, but John Bradford held on to success.[8] This self-possessed man could split his talents in many ways: he served on the boards of Transylvania University, the town of Lexington, the Transylvania Library, and the Fayette Hospital, as well as holding various public offices and building the largest printing shop in Kentucky.[9] He died in 1830. This "Caxton of Kentucky" was commended by Wilson for his rational, many-sided life:

By some he was called "Old Wisdom;" by others, "the Kentucky Franklin." Like Franklin, he was a printer, an almanac-maker, an author, a dispenser of homely philosophy, and an active and intelligent participant in all the current affairs of his day. While, in his earlier years, he was inclined to be litigious, he was of an amiable and equable temperament. He was a Jeffersonian Republican in politics, and a member of the Democratic Society of Lexington . . . but he seems never to have been a violent partisan and was remarkably impartial in admitting the writings of controversialists to his paper.[10]

Bradford hoped to improve the health of the book trade by promoting greater contact among printers and booksellers through lit-

[6] *Ibid.*, pp. 116, 123.   [7] *Ibid.*, p. 117.
[8] Coleman, p. 10; Brigham, I, 163.   [9] Wilson, *PBSA*, XXXI, 112.
[10] *Ibid.*, p. 132. Reprinted by permission of the Bibliographical Society of America.

erary fairs "similar to the Literary Fair in the Atlantic States, thereby to facilitate the publication and interchange of works of merit." At a meeting of Ohio and Kentucky printers and booksellers held at Lexington in 1805, he was elected president of the association which planned to conduct the fairs. Apparently support languished as no record of subsequent meetings has been found.[11]

As the first "Printer to the Commonwealth" Bradford produced official publications. Among his other imprints are a series of Kentucky almanacs beginning in 1787, books, pamphlets, broadsides, and legal blanks, all of which were obviously necessary in a newly populated region. In his shop his sons Daniel, Benjamin, and James received the instruction Bradford had planned and they, too, became printers.[12]

At the end of the first ten years of printing in Kentucky Bradford's shop was the largest, but others had been set up. Bradford, in his application to the legislature in 1798 for public printing, enumerated three:

The number and names of all the artists in the printing business in the state, as far as has come to my knowledge, and which I believe is correct, is as follows: In the office of messrs. Hunter & Beaumont, Thomas Field; in the office of mr. Moffatt, William Longfield; in the office of mr. Stewart, James Winnard and Joseph Collins; and in my office, Benj. J. Bradford, Daniel Bradford, James M. Bradford, Elisha Elam, and Elihu Stout; and mr. Thomas Parvin who considers himself engaged to assist me whenever called on, is at present in no office. There are several boys who have been a few months at the business in mr. Stewart's and my office, and perhaps in the other offices also, who cannot be considered as artists, and who are incapable of rendering any considerable services. There are in the state six printing presses; three of which are in mine, and one a piece in each of the other offices. As to the quantatity [*sic*] of types I have no knowledge, except of those in my own office, which is in quantity sufficient for the three presses. I have on hand at present about 50 ream of paper; I know of no other stock in the state, and the paper mill I believe does not work.[13]

By 1821 probably over a thousand books, pamphlets, and broadsides had been printed by the presses in at least seventeen Kentucky settlements. More than eight hundred publications have been identi-

[11] *Ibid.*, pp. 121–22.   [12] *Ibid.*, p. 118.
[13] *Journal of the Senate at the Second Session of the Sixth General Assembly of Kentucky* (Frankfort, Ky., 1798), pp. 15–16.

fied: a little less than one-third about religion—hymn books, sermons, propaganda, controversy; about one-quarter on government and politics—journals, laws, documents, legal works.[14] There were books of fiction, verse, economics, schoolbooks, and Masonic titles.[15] These publications, used by local persons with little money, were not very lucrative and few printers achieved financial security. It must have taken exceptional bravery to start printing in Kentucky. Before 1821, of the 88 newspapers established in twenty-five places in that state 73 had expired.[16]

One year after Bradford established his press in Kentucky, Maryland ceded the land for the new national capital to the federal government, thus setting into motion the trek of printers who hoped to make a fortune out of their proximity to the government. After the site had been donated but before it had been accepted, the first press appeared in Georgetown, already a busy port with a tobacco trade and a college founded by the Jesuits. The wheels of government are historically slow: Congress, on accepting the land and creating the District of Columbia in 1790, declared that the government would be established there in 1800. Thus long before the government arrived, printing began. On February 12, 1789, the partnership of Charles Fierer and Christian Kramer issued the first number of the *Times and the Patowmack Packet* in Georgetown.[17] Soon the partnership ended. Fierer continued publication, admitting Thomas U. Fosdick into partnership the next year.[18] Fierer, "a printer soldier of fortune," first arrived on this continent as "Ensign Führer" in a Hessian regiment. Captured at Trenton in 1776 and taken to Dumfries, Virginia, he was released in 1778 and deserted to join Washington's army. After seeing active service in the Southern Campaign, he became incapacitated in 1781 and returned to Europe but was back in America in 1788.[19] He and Fosdick

---

[14] Douglas C. McMurtrie, *Check List of Kentucky Imprints, 1787–1810* (Louisville, Ky., 1939), pp. xiii, xvii–xix; Douglas C. McMurtrie, *Check List of Kentucky Imprints, 1811–1820* (Louisville, Ky., 1939), pp. vii–ix.

[15] McMurtrie, *Kentucky Imp., 1811–1820*, p. ix.

[16] Harry B. Weiss, *A Graphic Summary of the Growth of Newspapers in New York and Other States, 1704–1820* (New York, 1948), pp. 3, 9–10.

[17] Brigham, I, 95.

[18] Alice H. Lerch, "A Printer Soldier of Fortune," *PBSA*, XXX (1936), 96; Frederick R. Goff, "Early Printing in Georgetown (Potomack), 1789–1800," *Proc. Am. Ant. Soc.*, LXVIII (1958), 111.

[19] Lerch, *PBSA*, XXX, 93–96.

published their newspaper in Georgetown until the summer of 1791, when they left to start another newspaper in Dumfries.[20]

More printers, dreaming of wealth in the future capital, soon followed Fierer and Fosdick to Georgetown, but they had come too early. There were no consolations; the government was absent so business was poor; whatever business existed they lost to competition from printers in the larger cities nearby. Goff, in his study of the early Georgetown press, found the situation regrettably harsh:

The conclusions to be drawn from this early period of Georgetown printing are few and hardly startling. Twenty-six titles, including nine newspapers, comprise the output of the press from 1789 to 1801. The early printers obviously were not successful. One newspaper floundered after another, each editor believing he would succeed where his predecessor had failed. Job printing seems to have been negligible. Local almanacs, that stock in trade of all printers of that period, likewise did not flourish, and as Parson Weems' statement was doubtless true, "nothing can keep afloat but Almanacs," one cannot help but express compassion for that dauntless group of pioneer printers whose only successful publications appeared to be Catholic devotional tracts which the College and local Catholic citizens supported. And even in this limited field of publication, the local printers could hardly compete successfully with Mathew Carey's output in Philadelphia.[21]

And the village of Washington was like a graveyard to a few printers who settled there. To quote McMurtrie, "All attempts at printing in Washington had ended in failure; after March, 1798, there was no printing done there for two and a half years. And of the adventurers in Georgetown, Green & English were the only survivors at the beginning of 1800."[22]

At last the government bustled into Washington in the summer of 1800 bringing in its wake the Philadelphia printers who had already been receiving government work. Printing offices began to burst out in the muddy streets as printers from other cities began to pile in; soon eight or nine offices were functioning.[23] This section of the economic invasion of Washington in 1800 deserves the investigation suggested by Powell, who has referred to it as "an important episode in the annals of the printing craft in America."[24] The compe-

---

[20] Douglas C. McMurtrie, *A History of Printing in the United States* (New York, 1936), II, 256.

[21] *Proc. Am. Ant. Soc.*, LXVIII, 119–20.   [22] *Hist. of Print.*, II, 264.

[23] *Ibid.*, p. 265.   [24] P. 110.

tition was like a fever, decimating the printers who lacked the vitality to hold on while waiting for supplies, who could not wheedle orders or beg for loans. Samuel Harrison Smith's Republican *National Intelligencer* and William Alexander Rind's *Washington Federalist* became the two leading newspapers. Charles Cist, Way & Groff, and Rapine, Conrad & Company were among the leading printers of books and pamphlets in those early days. Official printing jobs, not yet restricted to specified government printers, were distributed; for example, Smith, William Duane, and Way & Groff all issued government documents.[25] Powell, in *The Books of a New Nation*, has described the complexities involved in official printing during the organization of the government.[26] It must have been turmoil: the rootless population from which steady labor must be hired, the atmosphere of jealousies and politics, the demand from members of the government for rapid, careful work to be delivered on time. The secretary of the Senate and the clerk of the House continued to contract for printing until 1819, when Congress established fixed rates for the printer elected in each chamber and the rates remained unchanged until 1846.[27] In the first twenty-five years of its existence the printing trade in the District of Columbia fought the exhaustion of its vitality in the variable political climate by being expedient and courageous, by compromise and independence as the occasion demanded. Then the entrance of the British in 1814 forced it to begin all over again.

Inland and across the Alleghenies the pioneer printer continued his headway. His goal was to establish a newspaper in a county seat or well-settled community. The incurable American esteem for culture he had in full measure; in the jumble of printing offices established during the first forty years of printing in what is now West Virginia, all except four issued a newspaper. Printing there began in the Eastern Panhandle in the fall of 1790 when Nathaniel Willis moved to Shepherdstown. He was a true Yankee, a member of the Boston Tea Party, a printer who learned his trade in the Boston shop of Green & Russell. In the period between 1776 and 1786 he published newspapers in Boston. Then restlessness overtook him; he seems to have rarely stopped moving about. First in

---

[25] McMurtrie, *Hist. of Print.*, II, 269–72.   [26] Pp. 123–32.
[27] *Ibid.*, p. 85; *100 GPO Years*, pp. 14–16.

March, 1790, he issued a newspaper at Winchester, Virginia, which he closed within seven or eight months. He had heard of a local movement to make Shepherdstown the national capital. On investigation he judged the town to be little affected by competition. There was no newspaper and there was a chance of his getting the legal advertisements for the county. Willis established the *Potowmac Guardian and Berkeley Advertiser* at Shepherdstown in November, 1790, but about one year later moved his shop to Martinsburg, the county seat. There he printed his newspaper until 1799; he moved to Ohio in the spring of 1800.[28]

While at Shepherdstown and Martinsburg, Willis produced several pamphlets and broadsides. Bookwork was evidently not needed; the few books wanted could be obtained from larger cities. In fact, the first book known to have been printed in what is now West Virginia did not appear until 1797. As would be expected, it was a theological work, containing Richard Watson's *Christian Panoply*, his *An Address to Scoffers at Religion*, and William Paley's *A Brief View of the Historical Evidences of Christianity*. This volume of 332 pages came from the Shepherdstown press of Philip Rootes and Charles Blagrove, owners of the second West Virginia newspaper, the *Impartial Observer*, founded in 1797.[29]

The early printers in the Eastern Panhandle did not venture into other sections of the state. Printing was introduced into the Monongahela Valley in 1804 and extended by men, mostly from Pennsylvania, who followed the settlements up the Monongahela River. These men, too, frequently moved from place to place, but remained in their own section. Similarly, the Northern Panhandle after 1807 contained printers who circulated within the Panhandle, northeastern Ohio, and southwestern Pennsylvania. The less-populated southern section of West Virginia lacked any facilities for printing until about 1818.[30]

West Virginia printing of the period, as analyzed by Rice, comprised "newspapers, religious books and pamphlets, educational materials, almanacs, periodicals of a religious and literary nature, legal printing, and job printing, such as handbills and broadsides."

[28] Rice, *W.Va. Hist.*, XIV, 299–303.
[29] *Ibid.*, pp. 303–4; *West Virginia Imprints, 1790–1863*, comp. Delf Norona and Charles Shetler (Moundsville, W.Va., 1958), p. 163.
[30] Rice, *W.Va. Hist.*, XIV, 312, 319, 331.

Rice also found that "perhaps more than any other single area, the Northern Panhandle, through its leadership in the publishing field, contributed to a raising of the cultural level of early nineteenth century West Virginia."[31]

Close upon North Carolina's cession of part of its area to the national government in 1790, Congress established the "Territory south of the River Ohio," now known as Tennessee.[32] Within eighteen months after appointment as its first governor, William Blount planned the organization of the territory and arranged to have a printer, George Roulstone, settle in the capital.[33] Roulstone, a Bostonian by birth, had published a newspaper for a short time in Salem, Massachusetts, in 1786 before going to Fayetteville, North Carolina, where he printed for newspaper publishers. He is placed in Fayetteville from 1789 until 1791, probably the year in which he received the invitation from Governor Blount.[34] By climbing the Blue Ridge Mountains and going down the Holston River by flatboat, Roulstone arrived in the new territory before the construction of Knoxville, the capital, was completed. He set up temporary quarters at Hawkins Court House, now Rogersville, and in partnership with Robert Ferguson, a printer from Hillsboro, North Carolina, issued the first number of the *Knoxville Gazette* on November 5, 1791. In the next year the shop was moved to Knoxville.[35] After Ferguson resigned from the partnership in 1793, Roulstone remained accessible in anticipation of government work. In 1794 the territorial legislature established the office of public printer, the appointment and a six-hundred-dollar appropriation going to Roulstone, and on the admission of Tennessee to statehood in 1796 he became "Printer to the State."[36]

Roulstone seldom veered from the original purpose of his move to Tennessee. Except for two sermons in 1794, he restricted himself to printing the *Knoxville Gazette* and official publications.[37] The

[31] *Ibid.*, pp. 298, 330.   [32] McMurtrie, *Early Print. in Tenn.*, p. 17.
[33] American Imprints Inventory, *A Check List of Tennessee Imprints, 1793–1840* (Chicago, 1942), p. xii.
[34] McMurtrie, *Early Print. in Tenn.*, p. 19.
[35] Joseph H. Sears, *Tennessee Printers, 1791–1945* (Kingsport, Tenn., n.d.), p. 5; McMurtrie, *Early Print. in Tenn.*, pp. 19–20.
[36] McMurtrie, *Early Print. in Tenn.*, p. 20; Am. Imp. Inv., *Check List Tenn. Imp.*, p. 19.
[37] Am. Imp. Inv., *Check List Tenn. Imp.*, pp. 15–24.

Knoxville Gazette was succeeded by the *Knoxville Register*, published by George Roulstone and John R. Parrington in 1798. In the following year Roulstone again issued the *Knoxville Gazette*, which, between August, 1799, and November, 1800, was combined with the *Impartial Observer* and published in partnership with George Wilson.[38] Roulstone's major printed book, the 344-page *Laws of the State of Tennessee*, a compilation of all the acts to that time, appeared in 1803. He was public-spirited: "The present undertaking has been very laborious and expensive to the editor—the stock for carrying on which, being brought many hundred miles at great expence—If he has performed an acceptable service to the public by the production of the present edition, his main wish will be gratified."[39] Before his death in 1804 the first printer in Tennessee had served as clerk of the Territorial Council (1794–95), clerk of the first State Senate (1796), and postmaster in 1797.[40]

In Nashville printing began in 1799; in Jonesboro in 1801, ceasing temporarily in 1804, thus leaving Knoxville and Nashville the only cities in Tennessee with presses until Carthage in 1808.[41] Knoxville and Nashville printers shot ahead of others in the state by producing about three hundred items (books, pamphlets, broadsides) before 1826.[42] In 1810 Nashville became the leader, outstripping Knoxville. Newspaper mortality was a characteristic of the pioneer press: of the 42 newspapers established in fourteen Tennessee places before 1821, 33 expired before that year.[43]

In the young country the printers moved about as unconcernedly as the people moved. Their fixation was on the pot of gold just ahead. William Maxwell started a shop in Lexington, Kentucky, in 1793, but after printing at least two items in the domain of John Bradford's newspaper with its control of public printing, he left before a year was over.[44] He transported his equipment to Cincinnati, becoming the first printer in Ohio. In the first issue of the *Centinel of the North-Western Territory*, November 9, 1793, he announced his mission: "Having arrived at *Cincinnati*, he has ap-

---

[38] McMurtrie, *Early Print. in Tenn.*, pp. 22–23; Brigham, II, 1059.
[39] *Laws of the State of Tennessee* (Knoxville, 1803), p. iii.
[40] McMurtrie, *Early Print. in Tenn.*, pp. 22–23.   [41] *Ibid.*, pp. 24, 28.
[42] Am. Imp. Inv., *Check List Tenn. Imp.*, pp. 245–48.
[43] Weiss, pp. 3, 9–10.
[44] Douglas C. McMurtrie, *Antecedent Experience in Kentucky of William Maxwell* (Louisville, Ky., 1932), pp. 8–11.

plied himself to that which has been the principal object of his removal to this country, the Publication of a *News-Paper*."[45]

Maxwell, from New York, had fought in the Revolution and had lived for a time in New Jersey before going west about 1790.[46] Fewer than two hundred people inhabited the wilderness of Cincinnati when he arrived, but he confidently expected to print for the whole territory. He evidently knew where he stood, for he was appointed printer by the territorial legislature whose laws were previously printed in Philadelphia.[47] For the legislature he produced the first book printed in Ohio, *Laws of the Territory of the United States North-West of the Ohio* (1796) and sold the 225-page volume for eighty-six cents a copy, unbound.[48] But he was still uneasy; the postmastership of Cincinnati in 1795 was no consolation. He finally sold his shop to Samuel Freeman & Son in June, 1796, and apparently renounced printing to move himself and his wife to Dayton, Ohio, where he directed the building of a road. He became a farmer in Greene County and something of a politician. Before his death in 1809 he held many offices in the state: representative, associate judge, sheriff, and officer in the state militia.[49]

Cincinnati became the printing and publishing center for the Northwest Territory after it was opened by the Ordinance of 1787. Two paper mills erected on the Little Miami River in 1811 reduced somewhat the expensive importation of paper from Pennsylvania and Kentucky.[50] By 1815, it will be remembered, each of Cincinnati's two newspaper offices had bought an extra press for bookwork. Sutton's admirable study, *The Western Book Trade*, describes in detail the increasing production of printed matter which made Cincinnati the "Literary Emporium of the West" during the nineteenth century.[51]

Chillicothe, the second Ohio town to own a press (1800), was a rival of Cincinnati in the printing business for the next twenty years.[52] With the two towns supplying the major portion of needed

[45] Thwaites, *Proc. Am. Ant. Soc.*, n.s., XIX, opp. p. 338.

[46] Douglas C. McMurtrie, *Pioneer Printing in Ohio* (Cincinnati, 1943), p. 3.

[47] Sutton, p. 10; Evans 24633, 27428.

[48] Thomas W. Streeter, *Americana—Beginnings* (Morristown, N.J., 1952), p. 57.

[49] McMurtrie, *Pioneer Print. in Ohio*, pp. 5–6.

[50] Hunter, *Papermaking*, p. 104; Sutton, p. 11.   [51] Pp. 3–67.

[52] American Imprints Inventory, *A Check List of Ohio Imprints, 1796–1820* (Columbus, Ohio, 1941), p. 169.

printing, the progress of the printer slowed. Eventually he reached Columbus in 1814 and Cleveland in 1818.[53] Of approximately six hundred Ohio imprints before 1821 (other than newspapers and periodicals) which have been identified, almost one-third constituted items about religion, one-fifth were official territorial or state publications, slightly less than one-fifth related to political and civil affairs, and approximately one-tenth could be classified under literature and the arts. The remainder included almanacs and titles concerned with geography, travel, education, history, biography, medicine.[54] It must not be forgotten that these imprints were, as usual, supplemented by shipments from the East.

The characteristic way in which printing expanded from Kentucky northward changes at the borders of Michigan. McMurtrie said that printing in Michigan "had a unique and independent development, influenced very little by the surrounding territory."[55] In our knowledge of the beginning of printing in Michigan we are in a cul-de-sac. Little is known. One John M'Call printed a pamphlet, *An Act Passed at the First Session of the Fourth Congress of the United States of America*, at Detroit in 1796, and some legal forms, printed by him or his unnamed successor, apparently continued to appear until 1805. A merchant's journal of 1796 refers to M'Call as a printer, but the source of his equipment has not been definitely established, although the press he used may have been the one imported by Alexander and William Macomb, who, according to present evidence, never used it.[56] The contents of his shop and additional data on M'Call probably burned in the fire which destroyed the village of Detroit in 1805.

From the devastated village there went east Father Gabriel Richard, priest of St. Anne's Church and a supplicant for money to rebuild school and church. The unworldly, scholarly Sulpician who devoted his life to his parishioners was an impeccable realist; he went to the heart of the matter. He returned with a press and type and, of course, had also arranged to bring a printer, James M. Miller, from Utica, New York. Father Richard directed that a shop

[53] McMurtrie, *Pioneer Print. in Ohio*, p. 10.

[54] Am. Imp. Inv., *Check List of Ohio Imp.*, pp. 8–9.

[55] Douglas C. McMurtrie, *Pioneer Printing in Michigan* (Springfield, Ill., 1933), p. 1.

[56] Douglas C. McMurtrie, *Early Printing in Michigan* (Chicago, 1931), pp. 17–23.

be set up at Bellefontaine, three miles below Detroit, and installed Miller, who began printing about August, 1809.[57] Miller soon produced, among the first items, a twelve-page pamphlet entitled *The Child's Spelling Book*, some political broadsides, and the first issue of the first Michigan newspaper, the *Michigan Essay*, dated August 31, 1809.[58] In 1810 Aaron Coxshaw succeeded Miller as printer. Two years later, the year in which the press was moved to Detroit, Father Richard hired Theophilus Mettez, a printer of French-Canadian extraction trained by Miller, as successor to Coxshaw.[59] Much of the work was printed in French; all three printers extemporized by substituting apostrophes when fonts lacked acute accents.[60] Proclamations, pamphlets, forms, and at least nine books, eight of them school texts, came from the press.[61] The ninth, *Some of the Acts of the Territory of Michigan* (1816), is known as the "Cass Code."[62] About 1816 Father Richard closed the press; the freight wagons were now periodically visiting Detroit from the big cities to deliver his orders for books and school equipment. He cannily stored the "printing press with 800 pounds of types or letters" and then in 1832, the year of his death, offered it to a priests' college at Detroit.[63]

Local printing was done by John P. Sheldon and Ebenezer Read, publishers of the first long-lived Michigan newspaper, the *Detroit Gazette*, beginning in 1817. Sheldon & Read became the official printers to the territory and later, in 1824, official printers to the city of Detroit. In addition, they produced a few regional items (Masonic addresses, sermons, a poem extolling Michigan, pamphlets about the Indians) as well as an unsuccessful French newspaper.[64] The next printing office in Detroit was established in 1825 by Henry Chipman and Joseph Seymour as publishers of the *Michigan Herald*. In the same year Edward D. Ellis, using equipment brought

[57] Norman E. Clarke, *The Richard Press, 1809–1823* (Detroit, 1951), p. 2; McMurtrie, *Early Print. in Mich.*, pp. 25, 35–36.
[58] American Imprints Inventory, *Preliminary Check List of Michigan Imprints, 1796–1850* (Detroit, 1942), pp. 22–24; McMurtrie, *Early Print. in Mich.*, p. 36.
[59] McMurtrie, *Early Print. in Mich.*, pp. 44–49; Clarke, p. 3.
[60] McMurtrie, *Early Print. in Mich.*, p. 42.
[61] Albert H. Greenly, *A Selective Bibliography of . . . Michigan History* (Lunenburg, Vt., 1958), p. 80; Clarke, pp. 7–25; Albert H. Greenly, *A Bibliography of Father Richard's Press in Detroit* (Ann Arbor, Mich., 1955), pp. 3–48.
[62] Greenly, *Select. Bib.*, pp. 77–78.
[63] McMurtrie, *Early Print. in Mich.*, pp. 62–64.
[64] *Ibid.*, pp. 65–75; Am. Imp. Inv., *Pre. Check List Mich. Imp.*, pp. 33–41.

from Buffalo, started to print the *Michigan Sentinel* at Monroe, thirty-five miles from Detroit. Not until 1829 did another Michigan place have a press at work. That place was Ann Arbor.[65]

The Territory of Mississippi was created by Congress in 1798. In August of that year, Winthrop Sargent, the first governor, wrote to the Secretary of State that "we have no printing office in this country" and that a small traveling press "would be a blessing to the people of the Territory." Quite remarkably, before the end of the year a man with a press had been discovered in the territory and Governor Sargent had spirited him off to Natchez to print the territorial laws. The man was Lieutenant Andrew Marschalk, stationed in Fort McHenry at Walnut Hills. He had been born in New York in 1767 and is thought to have been a soldier in the Revolution before sailing to England in the late 1780's. He is known to have escaped from impressment into the British Navy and to have returned to America in 1790. Evidently he had been in the printing trade in Britain, for when he escaped he carried with him a small mahogany press.[66] For a short period he was a bookseller in New York.[67] Then he enlisted in the United States Army in 1791, either lending or selling his press to someone. As an ensign he fought Indians in the Northwest and by 1794 became a captain. Two years later, with the army now reduced to peacetime numbers, his rank was reduced to lieutenant. About that time he retrieved his press, which he then transported with about thirty pounds of type to Walnut Hills, a small post on the Mississippi River. He probably arrived at the fort in the spring of 1798, and soon after used his little press to strike off a ballad, "The Galley Slave."[68] Word was sent to the governor of the existence of the press and Marschalk was quickly transferred to Natchez. Optimistically he constructed a larger press, produced a 53-page pamphlet, John Henderson's *Paine Detected* (1799), and began to print the laws of Mississippi.[69] But soon politics showed its head: Marschalk incurred Governor Sar-

---

[65] McMurtrie, *Early Print. in Mich.*, pp. 75–83.

[66] Mary Ann Welsh, *Andrew Marschalk* (ACRL Microcard ser., no. 112; Rochester, N.Y., 1959), pp. 2–6.

[67] *A Register of Artists, . . . Printers & Publishers in New York City, 1633–1820*, Comp. George L. McKay (New York, 1942), p. 48.

[68] Welsh, pp. 6–8; Douglas C. McMurtrie, *A Bibliography of Mississippi Imprints, 1798–1830* (Beauvoir Community, Miss., 1945), p. 19.

[69] Welsh, p. 11; McMurtrie, *Bib. Miss. Imp.*, pp. 20–22; William B. Hamilton, "The Printing of the 1799 Laws of the Mississippi Territory," *Jour. Miss. Hist.*, II (1940), 89.

gent's displeasure and a superior officer insisted that Marschalk return to duty at Walnut Hills or go on furlough.[70] Realizing that "my prospects of an establishment in this country appear to be entirely frustrated," Marschalk loaded his equipment for the journey back to Walnut Hills, where he resumed duty about August, 1799.[71] An ailing wife and a shortage of leather for inking delayed his work, but by October he completed printing the *Laws of the Missisippi [sic] Territory.*[72] In December, when he was ready to apply for leave of absence to go north with his dying wife, he wrote to Governor Sargent:

> The Bearer is a Mr. Stokes, a Printer, from Pittsburgh—he comes forward, as an adventurer towards establishing a Press in the Mississippi Territory—he informs me that he has sufficient materials at Cincinnati—I have offered him the use of my press—to try the experiment—and am in Hopes he will succeed—as I knew Mr. Stokes at Pittsburgh.[73]

The "experiment" succeeded well enough for Marschalk, on leaving Walnut Hills, to sell his press to Benjamin M. Stokes. In 1801, still only thirty-four years of age, he remarried, and the next year he returned from Philadelphia to Natchez after having received an honorable discharge from the army. This adventurer, whose peregrinations had been so typical of the energetic, unsettled, fortune-seeking members of his trade, banked down in the Natchez community as printer and contentious politican. Marschalk, whose physical appearance resembled Benjamin Franklin's, had other associations with the history of printing. He was all these: the first printer in the Territory of Mississippi, the first public printer in that territory, the first public printer in the state, and the founder of the first long-lived newspaper in Mississippi.[74]

Benjamin M. Stokes was the casualty behind Marschalk's adventure. The introduction to Governor Sargent led to Stokes's publication of the first Mississippi newspaper, the *Mississippi Gazette*, at

[70] Hamilton, *Jour. Miss. Hist.*, II, 93; Charles S. Sydnor, "The Beginning of Printing in Mississippi," *Jour. South. Hist.*, I (1935), 51–52.

[71] Hamilton, *Jour. Miss. Hist.*, II, 94; Welsh, p. 29.

[72] Hamilton, *Jour. Miss. Hist.*, II, 95–96; McMurtrie, *Bib. Miss. Imp.*, pp. 22–23.

[73] Hamilton, *Jour. Miss. Hist.*, II, 98–99.

[74] Welsh, pp. 41–65; *Encyclopedia of Mississippi History* (Madison, Wis., 1907), II, 169–70.

Natchez late in 1799. Stokes was in trouble almost as soon as he began; the scarcity of extant copies of the newspaper indicates that he may have been forced to suspend publication for an interval. For about seven months in 1801 R. T. Sackett was his partner. A month after the partnership dissolved, Stokes sold the *Gazette* to Sackett & Wallace, who soon discontinued it. His failure was the perennial failure of the businessman on the scene either too early or too late. His newspaper was hardly begun when James Green established *Green's Impartial Observer* in May, 1800. The two newspapers swallowed each other up, and Green's ceased in 1801.[75] The feverish, impatient town of Natchez, growing to a population of about 7,500 in 1800, was not the environment for a newspaper, let alone two newspapers.[76]

Marschalk emerges once more as the dogged tempter of fortune. He founded the *Missisippi* [*sic*] *Herald* at Natchez in 1802 and was able to maintain it for six years, the first two years without first-rate competition.[77]

By 1826 at least six more places had presses turning out, at one time or another, newspapers and local matter. The total of 202 books, pamphlets, and broadsides identified as Mississippi imprints before 1826 included a large group of public documents and lesser groups classified under religion, political affairs, almanacs, and Masonic items.[78]

John Bradford's account of the Kentucky printing offices in 1798, quoted above, listed Elihu Stout among his employees. Stout at that time was probably being trained by Bradford, for he was still young, having been born in New Jersey in 1782 and brought to Lexington with his family about 1793. Sometime between 1799 and 1803 he left Bradford's employ, perhaps going to Nashville to work for Benjamin Bradford. It has been said that Stout went to Vincennes in 1803 and that after General William Henry Harrison, governor of the Indiana Territory, promised him the territorial printing, he returned to Kentucky or Tennessee to procure equipment.[79] Be that as it may, Stout certainly set up shop in Vincennes in

[75] Brigham, I, 424–26.   [76] Sydnor, *Jour. South. Hist.*, I, 51.
[77] Brigham, I, 426–27.
[78] McMurtrie, *Bib. Miss. Imp.*, pp. 19–110, 149–52.
[79] Valerie C. H. Knerr, *Elihu Stout* (ACRL Microcard ser., no. 48; Rochester, N.Y., 1955), pp. 3–12.

the summer of 1804. On July 31 he issued the first number of the *Indiana Gazette*, the first newspaper in what is now Indiana.[80] The love for the romantic and grandiose in the pioneer printer is displayed in his "Address to the Public," a public which, Miss Walker reminds us, "consisted mostly of French, half-breed Indians, and a straggling number of trappers and traders." All his geese were indeed swans:

At length, after great trouble and much expense the Public is presented with the Indiana Gazette. Without deviation from the general rule of newspaper printers, the Editor addresses the Public, and lays down the principles which shall govern the publication. His object shall be to collect and publish such information as will give a correct account of the productions and natural advantages of the Territory, to give the latest foreign and domestic intelligence; original essays, political, moral, literary, agricultural and on domestic economics; to select such fugitive literary productions as will tend to raise "the genius or mend the heart" etc., will be the second. The political complexion of the paper shall be truly republican; but it never shall be prostituted to party. Essays of any political complexion couched in decent language shall find a ready insertion; but the editor pledges himself that the columns of the Gazette shall never be tarnished with matter that can offend the eye of decency, or raise a blush upon the cheek of modesty and virtue.

With this outline the Indiana Gazette is submitted for patronage, to a generous and enlightened public; and the editor feels confident of encouragement equal to his merit; and though it is not always in our power to command success, yet he will ever "endeavor to deserve it."[81]

Governor Harrison, who had the first Indiana laws printed in Frankfort, Kentucky, immediately assigned the territorial printing to Stout.[82] Before the year ended, Stout had produced the first book printed in the territory, the 89-page *Laws Adopted by the Governor and Judges of the Indiana Territory*, as well as the 137-page *Laws for the Government of the District of Louisiana*.[83] The destruction of his shop by fire in April, 1806, forced him to suspend until new equipment arrived. In July, 1807, he recommenced his newspaper under a new title, the *Western Sun*, and published it alone or in

[80] Brigham, I, 144.
[81] Mary Alden Walker, *The Beginnings of Printing in the State of Indiana* (Crawfordsville, Ind., 1934), p. 13.
[82] *American Bibliography . . . for 1802*, p. 82.
[83] Cecil K. Byrd and Howard H. Peckham, *A Bibliography of Indiana Imprints, 1804–1853* (Indianapolis, 1955), p. 1.

partnership until he became postmaster of Vincennes in 1845. The postmastership was only one of many public, social, and religious positions he occupied during a career that ended in 1860.[84] Byrd and Peckham, in their *Bibliography of Indiana Imprints*, emphasize that "even after other printers arrived and Vincennes lost the capitol and was outstripped in growth by newer towns, Stout remained the most significant printer. His name recurs year after year through 1840."[85]

Stout's total production consisted of his newspaper, the official territorial printing which he did until 1814, and a few separate items annually. He had no competition in Vincennes until 1817. In the meantime printing began in a second town in the territory when Seth M. Levenworth and William Hendricks started the *Western Eagle* at Madison in 1813.[86] By 1821 twenty newspapers had been printed, at one time or another, in eleven Indiana places.[87] The nature of the other items printed by early Indiana printers caused Byrd and Peckham to recall "the observation of Abraham Lincoln's cousin, Dennis Hanks, about their residence in southern Indiana: 'We lived the same as Indians 'cepting we took an interest in politics and religion.'" Public documents, political propaganda, and religious, particularly Baptist, matters prevailed as subjects for print. The first book of poetry, Joel Barlow's *The Vision of Columbus*, did not appear until 1824; it was preceded by only one other literary work, a life of Bonaparte (1818).[88]

A pioneer printer, still an itinerant, who had advanced to the outer border of the frontier struck off the first item in what is now the state of Alabama. On board ship at Wakefield on the lower Tombigbee, this man whose name is not known printed *The Declaration of the American Citizens, on the Mobile, with Relation to British Aggressions* in September, 1807. The five-page pamphlet, prepared "in consequence of the attack by the British ship of war Leopard, on the United States frigate Chesapeake," bore a note on the last page: "Printed on the Mobile. The printer apologizes for the execution of his work; his types are old and much worn: and the situation of the country does not justify his purchasing new ones."[89]

At that time the area that is now Alabama belonged to Missis-

---

[84] Knerr, pp. 22, 36–37. [85] P. ix. [86] Brigham, I, 141–42.
[87] Weiss, pp. 3, 10. [88] Pp. viii, 18, 42.
[89] Ellison, p. 4n.; American Imprints Inventory, *Check List of Alabama Imprints, 1807–1840* (Birmingham, Ala., 1939), p. 1.

sippi Territory except for the section still held by the Spanish. Four years later, when it seemed that Mobile was about to be occupied, two newspapermen prepared themselves to move in as soon as possible.

Samuel Miller and John B. Hood were among a crowd of prospective lot-buyers who hovered along the Mobile River just above the thirty-first degree of northern latitude, waiting for the evacuation of the Spanish. They had provided themselves with a printing outfit and with it had journeyed by land from Chattanooga to Mims' Ferry on the Alabama River, thence by boat south to Fort Stoddert, the United States military and customs port near Wakefield, just above the Spanish line. Here, while they waited impatiently to enter Mobile in the wake of the invading army, they edited and printed the first newspaper in what is now Alabama, the *Mobile Sentinel*.[90]

In the first issue, May 23, 1811, they told of their plan:

The original intention of the editors was to have issued their paper from the town of Mobile; but they cannot yet congratulate their fellow-citizens on the possession of that spot, to this country so important. . . . Other persons can, perhaps, give better reasons why we have it not in possession. Until they can announce this desirable intelligence, their paper will be printed at this place.[91]

The last issue extant, January 29, 1812, also has a Fort Stoddert imprint.[92] Not until 1813 was Mobile opened to Americans.

Both men had printed newspapers before the *Centinel* (or *Sentinel*): Hood in Camden, South Carolina (1803), and Knoxville, Tennessee (1805–10); Miller in Carthage, Tennessee, (1808–9). It is easy to imagine the cursing of these two formidable men as they faced the delay in getting into Mobile. Hood did not wait. By the middle of 1812 he returned to Tennessee as a partner in the *Carthage Gazette*.[93] At Hood's departure, the *Mobile Centinel* probably terminated.

In the northern Tennessee Valley another venturesome printer was starting the second Alabama newspaper. Sometime in May or June, 1812, the *Madison Gazette* of Huntsville first appeared. Because the earliest extant issue, October 19, 1813, names the firm of T. G. Bradford & Co. as publisher, it has been suggested that Bradford founded the newspaper in partnership with William W.

---

[90] Ellison, pp. 7–8.   [91] *Ibid.*, p. 8.   [92] Brigham, I, 4.
[93] *Ibid.*, II, 1054–55, 1432.

Parnham, who later published it alone.[94] In fact, Thomas G. Bradford, at that time a leading publisher in Nashville, may have regarded the Huntsville paper as a subsidiary, with Parnham in complete charge from the beginning. Alabama's third newspaper was
the realization of the project envisioned but not accomplished by
Hood and Miller, a Mobile newspaper. Founded in 1813, the *Mobile
Gazette* was published in that year by James Lyon although God-
win B. Cotten claimed to have established it. One of the most
peripatetic printers of his time, Lyon issued at least fifteen newspapers in thirteen places from Vermont to Louisiana between 1793
and 1821. Cotten's ownership of the *Mobile Gazette* in 1818 implies
that Lyon, as usual, had moved on.[95] The mobility of pioneer printers made it possible for a new community to have a press soon after
the need for it became apparent. This was certainly true in Alabama. In her detailed study of early Alabama publications Miss
Ellison reports that "within two decades after printing had been
introduced within the region, it had spread through all the log-cabin
settlements that could afford a press and had become a potent force
in the politics and culture of the frontier."[96]

Of the seventy-five Alabama imprints (other than newspapers
and periodicals) before 1826 which Miss Ellison lists, approximately one-half are government documents. The next largest group,
about one-seventh, are Baptist publications, closely followed in
quantity by Masonic items. A scattering of almanacs and political
material (including a poem attacking a local demagogue) are the
only other significant classes.[97] Such publications are in the tradition
of the frontier people who clung to religion and politics while they
endured the rugged life of the backwoods.

Not every territorial governor had the luck of Governor Sargent
to discover a press within his own jurisdiction. General James Wilkinson, governor of the Missouri Territory, appealed to Secretary of
State James Madison on September 7, 1805:

We are exceedingly embarrased for the want of a Printing Press
and our population will not support a public paper; we have two

[94] *Ibid.*, I, 5; F. Wilbur Helmbold, "Early Alabama Newspapermen,
1810–1820," *Ala. Rev.*, XII (1959), 55; Douglas C. McMurtrie, *A Brief History
of the First Printing in the State of Alabama* (Birmingham, Ala., 1931), p. 5.
[95] Brigham, I, 6, II, 1447.   [96] Ellison, p. 7.
[97] *A Check List of Alabama Imprints, 1807–1870* (University, Ala., 1946), pp.
27–32.

good compositors in the Territory, who have offered their services to print the Laws &c; and as we are destitute of Funds, we must implore the aid of Government; for at present no Law can be generally promulgated, before it had been sent to Kentucky, there printed and returned—Should it be consistent for the government to send forward a small Font of Types, with Paper Ink and apparatus, it would relieve our difficulties and if required, the Territory will doubtless reimburse the expense.[98]

There is no record of an answer, but on September 24 the *Kentucky Gazette* advertised the intention of Francis Peniston to publish a newspaper in St. Louis. His plan, for reasons unknown, failed. Three years later, Meriwether Lewis, a succeeding governor still anxious for a press, disposed of the problem by offering Joseph Charless, a Kentucky printer, financial aid to move his shop to the territory. Charless had been selling books and publishing the *Louisville Gazette*, not too successfully, for less than a year. His biography, ably written by David Kaser, portrays a roving and crowded life which began in Ireland, where he worked in Dublin as a printer. Charless moved to the United States about 1795, immediately thereafter journeying to Kentucky, moving again to settle in Pennsylvania as printer and bookseller. In 1802 he returned to Kentucky and lived by the same trade. At Lexington his newspaper, the *Independent Gazetteer*, was disposed of six months after it began. He then leased his press for newspaper work, retained the book and job work, and also did itinerant bookselling. Unable to resist the gamble of publishing another newspaper and addicted to change of place, he moved to Louisville in 1807.[99]

To bring Charless to St. Louis, Governor Lewis floated a one-year loan among the citizens for two hundred and twenty-five dollars. Charless, accompanied by Jacob Hinkle, a compositor, arrived in St. Louis in the summer of 1808 and almost at once distributed a prospectus for the *Missouri Gazette*. It bore the statement that the "first Number of the Gazette, will appear as soon as possible, the Types being ready at Louisville, Ky. and the press expected in the course of a month, from Pennsylvania." The press, most likely a Ramage, was set up in a two-room house on Main Street. On July 12 Joseph Charless, "Printer to the Territory," issued the first number of the *Missouri Gazette*, the first trans-Mississippi newspaper.[100]

[98] Kaser, *Joseph Charless*, p. 58.   [99] *Ibid.*, pp. 13–56, 59.
[100] *Ibid.*, pp. 63–65.

His shop seems to have been a public meeting place without class divisions. John Bradbury who visited St. Louis about 1810 witnessed the scene:

I frequented the printing-office of Mr. Joseph Charless, when at St. Louis, to read the papers from the United States, when it often happened that the Indians at that place on business came into the office and sat down. Mr. Charless, out of pleasantry, would hand to each a newspaper, which, out of respect for the custom of the whites, they examined with as much attention as if they could read it, turning it over at the same time that they saw me turn that with which I was engaged.[101]

In the *Gazette* Charless heroically "assumed the role of the public conscience and pursued it impervious to implied threats of bodily harm and less-veiled efforts at economic harassment." After 1814 the "attacks upon him became overt rather than concealed." The opposition organized a competitive paper, the *Western Journal* in the following year. And when Thomas Hart Benton edited the new opposition newspaper in 1818, the editorial battles increased in virulence. In the midst of his fulminations against dueling, cheating, and mismanagement in banks, Charless conducted his printing office and other businesses: money lending, real estate, sale of drugs and patent medicines, slave trading. After he relinquished the shop in 1820, he became a hosteler and apothecary.[102]

As "Printer to the Territory," he printed, about December, 1808, *An Act Regulating the Fiscal Concerns of the Territory*, which, according to Kaser's investigation, was probably the first imprint west of the Mississippi. He retained the territorial printing until 1819 even though the opposition tried to take it away. Aside from the newspaper and public documents, the output of his St. Louis shop was small: a few books, pamphlets, and broadsides.[103]

As the 1820's approached, printing started to spread through what is now the state of Missouri; it began at Franklin and Jackson in 1819, at St. Charles in 1820, and at St. Genevieve in 1821.[104] These shops, primarily newspaper offices, did little book and job work. The seventy-seven identified Missouri imprints before 1826 conform to the frontier pattern of a greater number of public docu-

---

[101] *Ibid.*, p. 79.   [102] *Ibid.*, pp. 93, 101–35.   [103] *Ibid.*, pp. 74, 120.
[104] Douglas C. McMurtrie, *Early Missouri Book and Pamphlet Imprints, 1808–1830* (Chicago, 1937), p. 3.

ments, lesser numbers of religious, Masonic, and political items, as well as almanacs and a few works of literature and education.[105]

Ninian Edwards, governor of the Territory of Illinois, needing a printer for the laws passed in the first session of his legislature, sent copy to a friend who published a newspaper in their little home town of Russellville, Kentucky. The order came just in time for Matthew Duncan, who was at a low point in his business, his newspaper, the *Farmer's Friend*, about to close or already closed and few prospects in sight. Duncan printed the Illinois laws in 1813 and, induced by Governor Edwards, moved to Kaskaskia, where he was assured of patronage and hoped for financial assistance.[106] At Kaskaskia he established the first Illinois newspaper, the *Illinois Herald*, in May, 1814.[107] By the end of the year he had also printed, in addition to at least one other item, the earliest Illinois pamphlet now extant, the 24-page *Governor Edwards's Communication to Both Houses of Illinois Legislature*. In June, 1815, he issued the first volume of the first Illinois book, Nathaniel Pope's *Laws of the Territory of Illinois*. But the next year he sold his newspaper and shop to Daniel Pope Cook & Co. His later career had its ups and downs: county recorder, justice of the peace, real estate agent, five years as an officer in the rangers and dragoons, a dealer in anything he could buy or sell.[108]

Cook and a printer, Robert Blackwell, under the firm name of Daniel P. Cook & Co., used Duncan's equipment to publish the *Western Intelligencer*, a newspaper which continued at Kaskaskia, with changes of partnership and name, until moved in 1820 to Vandalia, the new capital.[109] Before 1826 printing began in two more Illinois towns. The law of 1814 allowing a second newspaper to print United States laws if ordered by the Secretary of State, "*Provided*, In his opinion, it shall become necessary and expedient," enabled Peter Kimmel of Pittsburgh to apply for authorization to print the laws in Illinois.[110] When the authorization came through, with its assurance of a steady income, Kimmel's son, Allen W., and

[105] American Imprints Inventory, *A Preliminary Check List of Missouri Imprints, 1808–1850* (Washington, D.C., 1937), pp. 5–31, 219.
[106] Cecil K. Byrd, *A Bibliography of Illinois Imprints, 1814–58* (Chicago, [1966]), pp. 3–4.
[107] Brigham, I, 135.   [108] Byrd, pp. 3–5.   [109] Brigham, I, 135–37.
[110] Douglas C. McMurtrie, "The First Printers of Illinois," *Jour. Ill. State Hist. Soc.*, XXVI (1933), 210.

Henry Eddy, a lawyer, left Pittsburgh to settle in Shawneetown. From their press came the first number of the *Illinois Emigrant* in May, 1818.[111] A year later Hooper Warren founded the first anti-slavery newspaper in Illinois, the *Edwardsville Spectator*, at Edwardsville.[112]

The stamp of the pioneer character is on the fifty-seven identified pre-1826 imprints. Most of them are legal documents and religious and Masonic tracts. Under the eagerness for religious and political freedom is the pioneer ideal, material progress. The incredible energy is centered on a position in life but redeems itself in a desire for culture and refinement. An 1819 broadside, the catalogue of the Edwardsville Library, has an astonishing list of over eighty titles available to members: history, biography, poetry, fiction, and essays.[113]

There are sharp historical divisions in the prelude to the permanent establishment of printing in Texas, each one splashed with color and violence. In his masterly bibliography Thomas W. Streeter outlines the events before the stabilization of printing in 1829:

The first stage, which ended in 1823, might be called that of the transient press, with presses brought into Texas by the expeditions of Toledo in 1813, Mina in 1817, and Long in 1819, and by the Provincial government in 1823. All these presses were carried out of Texas soon after they were brought in, the first apparently without having produced an imprint.[114]

Though it may not have produced an imprint, the first press narrowly escaped doing so. Indeed, type had been set. José Alvarez de Toledo and William Shaler, United States special agent to Cuba and Mexico, brought a press and printer (Aaron Mower of Philadelphia) into Texas in 1813, intending to issue a newspaper "to further their side of a political quarrel."[115] They ended up escaping with their lives: "Shaler reported to Secretary of State Monroe on June 12, 1813, that they had established a press at Nacogdoches, in Texas, had set the type for the issue of May 25, and then had been

[111] Brigham, I, 136–37.
[112] *Ibid.*, p. 135; [Douglas C. McMurtrie], *The Contribution of the Pioneer Printers to Illinois History* (Springfield, Ill., 1939), pp. 9–10.
[113] Byrd, pp. 3–22.
[114] *Bibliography of Texas, 1795–1845* (Cambridge, Mass., 1955), I, xxxi.
[115] *Ibid.*, p. 3; Brigham, II, 1069.

forced to flee from Texas to Natchitoches in Louisiana, where the paper was finally issued early in June."[116]

The second press arrived in the baggage of the expedition led by General Xavier Mina to help the revolutionists in Mexico. Mina had brought the portable press from England when he left in 1816.[117] When he landed at Galveston Island, he ordered the press set up and a proclamation struck off. The proclamation is dated February 22, 1817, but, according to Streeter, it probably was printed after March 16, 1817. Evidence indicates that the printers were John J. McLaran and Samuel Bangs, a nineteen-year-old from Boston who joined the expedition in Baltimore.[118] Bangs, a picaresque figure, is the subject of a recent biography.[119] No copy of the original *Proclama del General Mina* has been found nor is there any copy of the *Compañeros de armas* printed by McLaran and Bangs in the same year. This address by Mina to his companions in arms in April, 1817, creates several bibliographical problems because at that time the expedition lay anchored off the mouth of the Rio Grande where the bar was shoal and the water rough. Streeter's analysis is logical:

It is highly improbable that a printing press would have been lugged ashore amidst all these difficulties to strike off a fifteen-line proclamation, and I agree with Robles (*La Primera Imprenta en las Provincias Internas de Oriente*, Mexico, 1939, p. 41) that it was printed on board ship, probably while the fleet was anchored at the mouth of the river. We do not know whether the ship was anchored off the Texas or the Mexican shore. If, as is quite likely, it was off the Texas shore, the address becomes the second Texas imprint of which we have knowledge.[120]

It is possible that other early, perhaps earlier, imprints existed. Spell, citing an undated manuscript, said that Bangs printed daily orders of the camp as well as decisions of the prize court.[121]

The Mina expedition proceeded to Mexico, leaving Texas without a known press until the arrival of the Long expedition in 1819. Its press belonged to one of the members, Eli Harris, a native of North Carolina and formerly of Lexington, Kentucky. At Nacogdoches on

---

[116] Brigham, II, 1069.

[117] Douglas C. McMurtrie, *Pioneer Printing in Texas* (Austin, Tex., 1932), p. 7.

[118] Streeter, *Bib. Texas*, I, xxxiv, 6.

[119] Lota M. Spell, *Pioneer Printer* (Austin, Tex., [1963]).

[120] Streeter, *Bib. Texas*, I, 5.   [121] P. 16.

August 14, 1819, he issued the first number of the *Texas Republican*, which continued into September and perhaps beyond.[122] Then nothing more is known about a Texas press until 1823 when one operated for a few months at San Antonio de Bexar. Early in the year it arrived there in a shipment imported from the United States by José Felix Trespalacios, governor of Texas. Its first known imprint, a broadside *Prospecto* for the *Correo de Texas*, dated April 9, 1823, proposed the publication of a newspaper in Spanish and English. However, the existence of the newspaper itself cannot be proved because copies have not been found. There is evidence of one more imprint, its subject the "Constitution," dated before Trespalacios resigned as governor on April 17. Although he went to Monterrey, the press continued, producing at least four more items, three of which are listed in the bill Trespalacios sent the *junta gubernativa* for the costs of printing. The name of the printer, Asbridge, appears on some of these imprints, and Streeter suggests that this may have been the George Asbridge who published a weekly in New York in 1812.[123] After Luciano Garcia took office as governor of Texas on July 8, 1823, the press followed Trespalacios to Monterrey, as Streeter recounts:

On July 9 Garcia wrote to Felipe de la Garza, the new Commandant General at Monterrey, that the press would be forwarded to him at Monterrey as soon as transportation became available and that the printer, that is Asbridge, and his assistant had been reluctant to turn over the press as the greater part of their salaries as agreed upon with Trespalacios was still unpaid. It appears that the press was finally shipped on July 17 by pack mule "in seven loads, well packed and wrapped by Adbrig [Asbridge], the printer," and that the press and its equipment were sold by Trespalacios "to the Most Excellent Deputation of [Monterrey] . . . [for] the sum of 3500 pesos.[124]

During this period the Territory of Arkansas began to form, and John McArthur of St. Genevieve, Missouri Territory, applied in June, 1819, for the privilege of printing the federal laws in the new territory. In four weeks or so he arrived at Arkansas Post, where he issued proposals for the publication in October of the *Arkansas*

---

[122] Streeter, *Bib. Texas*, I, xxxv; Brigham, II, 1069.

[123] Streeter, *Bib. Texas*, I, xxxv–xxxvii, 8–9.

[124] *Ibid.*, p. xxxvi. Copyright 1955, by Thomas W. Streeter. Reprinted by permission of the publisher, Harvard University Press.

Herald, but by August, his plans apparently obstructed, he quit the territory.[125]

About the same time another man, William E. Woodruff, was on his way to Arkansas and success. He was to be productive, sagacious, and long-lived, representative of the best in the pioneer printer. He had served his apprenticeship with Alden Spooner at Sag Harbor, Long Island, New York, had next worked in West Virginia and Kentucky, and had then begun his preposterous travels to get to Arkansas. He bought press and type in Franklin, Tennessee, and transported them down the Cumberland River to the Ohio; he crossed the Ohio with his equipment to the Mississippi; he went down the Mississippi with his cargo to White River; he then carried it to the Arkansas River and paddled it up to Arkansas Post. He arrived, accompanied by two helpers, on October 30, 1819. There he built a two-room log cabin and on November 20 issued the first number of his *Arkansas Gazette.*[126] His luck was as prodigious as his health; the territory needed his newspaper—he had the gift of knowing the right moment for an undertaking—and the legislature elected him "Printer to the Territory," the desideratum of his profession. In 1821 Woodruff printed the first book in what is now the state of Arkansas, the 152-page *Laws of the Territory of Arkansas.*[127] At the end of the year he moved to Little Rock, where he continued printing the *Gazette* as well as public documents and added to his income by doing job work. Of eight Arkansas imprints before 1826 (all printed by Woodruff), five are territorial documents, two are the minutes of the Little Rock Association of Regular Baptists, and one is the broadside appeal of a candidate for Congress.[128] Woodruff was on top of his work, no matter what it might be; he understood politics and the counting house as thoroughly as printing and he served as postmaster of Little Rock, treasurer of Arkansas, and president of the state bank. His temperament seems to have been the familiar one of the Western pioneer who had no fear of the future because he was in control of his own

---

[125] Jessie Ryon Lucke, "Correspondence concerning the Establishment of the First Arkansas Press," *Ark. Hist. Quart.,* XIV (1955), 161–66.

[126] Oswald, pp. 388–90; Lucke, *Ark. Hist. Quart.,* XIV, 162.

[127] Oswald, p. 390; *Arkansas Imprints, 1821–1876,* ed. Albert H. Allen (New York, 1947), p. 1.

[128] Lucke, *Ark. Hist. Quart.,* XIV, 162; *Ark. Imp.,* pp. 1–3.

future. He had few misfortunes and died in 1885 at the age of ninety.[129]

In those states where printing had been established before 1787 the number of presses increased and printing production mounted according to the requirements of the population. In 1791 the Secretary of the Treasury, Alexander Hamilton, reported to the House of Representatives that "the great number of presses disseminated throughout the Union, seem to afford an assurance that there is no need of being indebted to foreign countries for the printing of the books which are used in the United States."[130] Aided by duties on imported books, the book trade gained strength. By 1810 the United States printing industry was becoming assertedly self-sufficient and was no longer so vulnerable to the competition of importation. Albert Gallatin in his report, "American Manufactures," thought that the printing industry had become secure at last:

Printing is carried on to an extent commensurate with the demand. Exclusively of the numerous newspapers, which alone form a considerable item in value, all the books for which there is an adequate number of purchasers, are printed in the United States. But sufficient data have not been obtained to form an estimate of the annual aggregate value of the paper made, and of the printing and book binding executed in the United States, other than what may be inferred from the population.[131]

By 1820, with the national population in excess of nine million, the volume of book production alone, according to Goodrich's estimate, totaled two and a half million dollars.[132]

In New York City the approximate numbers of printers were 26 in 1790, 56 in 1800, 95 in 1810, and 164 in 1820.[133] In these thirty years the expansion of printing in the state followed commerce in the Hudson Valley, on the Mohawk, along the Susquehanna, and in the region of the Finger Lakes. In his detailed analysis Hamilton concludes that "by 1820 most sections of the state were served by local printers."[134]

[129] Oswald, p. 390.
[130] *The Debates and Proceedings in the Congress of the United States . . . Second Congress* (Washington, D.C., 1849), col. 1031.
[131] *The Debates and Proceedings in the Congress of the United States . . . Eleventh Congress* (Washington, D.C., 1853), col. 2231.
[132] S. G. Goodrich, *Recollections of a Lifetime* (New York, 1856), II, 380.
[133] Harry B. Weiss, *The Number of Persons and Firms Connected with the Graphic Arts in New York City, 1633–1820* (New York, 1946), p. 8.
[134] *Country Printer*, p. 89.

For Philadelphia, the rate of increase in the approximate numbers of printers was not as rapid as that of New York: 53 in 1791, 81 in 1800, 168 in 1810, 207 in 1820.[135] But New York's population was about 33,000 in 1790 and about 124,000 in 1820 compared with Philadelphia's population of about 28,000 in 1790 and about 64,000 in 1820.[136] The greater number of printers in Philadelphia at a time when it had about half the population of New York manifests Philadelphia's position as the center of the book trade.

Overshadowing the expansion of the press in eastern Pennsylvania (Reading in 1789, Harrisburg in 1791, Wilkes Barre in 1795) were the printing offices on the other side of the Alleghenies which began when Hugh Henry Brackenridge brought two young Philadelphia printers, John Scull and Joseph Hall, to the little river port of Pittsburgh in 1786.[137] In that village of less than forty log houses Scull and Hall, on July 29, issued the first number of the *Pittsburgh Gazette*, the first newspaper west of the Alleghenies.[138] After the death of Hall in November, Scull formed a partnership with John Boyd, which terminated in 1788. Thereafter Scull continued alone until 1816, when his son assumed control of the *Gazette*.[139] Scull, of course, endured all the hardships of the pioneer printer. (It will be recalled that when paper did not arrive from the East, he borrowed cartridge paper from the commander of Fort Fayette.) His subscribers in the early years lived mostly east and southeast of Pittsburgh to escape the Indian war west and northwest. There was, obviously, little time for the production of anything but his newspaper. The few early imprints include a Fourth of July oration in 1786, a children's book and an almanac in 1787, the third volume of the first part of Brackenridge's *Modern Chivalry* in 1793. As a newspaper printer he ingeniously, for six months, printed the federal laws imposed on the final two pages so that they could be folded into an eight-page pamphlet.[140]

[135] Harry B. Weiss, "The Growth of the Graphic Arts in Philadelphia, 1663–1820," *Bull. N.Y. Pub. Lib.*, LVI (1952), 82–83.

[136] John F. Watson, *Annals and Occurrences of New York City and State* (Philadelphia, 1846), p. 189; *Hazard's Register of Pennsylvania*, July 30, 1831.

[137] *Am. Dict. Print.*, p. 431; McMurtrie, *Hist. of Print.*, II, 88.

[138] Thwaites, *Proc. Am. Ant. Soc.*, n.s., XIX, 310; Brigham, II, 965.

[139] McMurtrie, *Hist. of Print.*, II, 90–91.

[140] Thwaites, *Proc. Am. Ant. Soc.*, n.s., XIX, 312; McMurtrie, *Hist. of Print.*, II, 88–92; *BAL*, I, 264.

The most important of the other early Pittsburgh printers, Zadok Cramer, sold books there in 1800 after serving a printing and bookbinding apprenticeship in Washington, Pennsylvania. Until he bought his own press in 1805, he published items printed outside. His long series of almanacs began with one for 1802. A series of guides, the *Navigator*, beginning about 1801, served thousands of pioneers as a guide to the rivers and surrounding country. The edition of John Brown's *A Dictionary of the Holy Bible* (1807) printed by Cramer may have been the first illustrated book issued west of the Alleghenies. Conducted first by Cramer alone and later in partnerships with John Spear and William Eichbaum, Jr., his firm made Pittsburgh a publishing nucleus in the early decades of the nineteenth century. From his shop various assortments of books reached Maryland, Virginia, Kentucky, and Ohio as well as the western Pennsylvania area.[141]

Printing began at a second point in western Pennsylvania with the publication of the *Western Telegraphe* by Colerick, Hunter & Beaumont at Washington in 1795.[142] This firm also produced almanacs, pamphlets, and bookwork.[143] Eventually, as people filled the western Pennsylvania settlements, the printer and the press followed as surely as the church and the school.

Expansion of the press as described for New York and Pennsylvania occurred, in varying degrees, in other states and territories where printing had been introduced before 1787. In some territories, as in Florida, the press revived after years of interruption. Florida's first press operated in 1783 and 1784 at St. Augustine, which was under British sovereignty in 1783. That press ceased in 1784 after Florida was ceded to Spain by Great Britain in 1783, and no more printing occurred in Florida until the ratification in 1821 of the treaty ceding Florida to the United States. In July of that year Richard W. Edes & Company issued the first number of the *Florida Gazette* at St. Augustine; in August Nicholas & Tunstall began the *Floridian* at Pensacola; four years later the *Florida Intelligencer* appeared in Tallahassee. By 1825 these later presses had produced little but newspapers and several public documents.[144] In Louisiana

[141] McMurtrie, *Hist. of Print.*, II, 92–94.   [142] Brigham, II, 981.
[143] McMurtrie, *Hist. of Print.*, II, 95.
[144] Douglas C. McMurtrie, *The First Printing in Florida* (Atlanta, 1931), pp. 9–16.

printing was revived by Louis Duclot in 1794 after a twelve-year hiatus. His press turned out few items other than a French newspaper, the *Moniteur de la Louisiane*. Duclot's name disappeared from New Orleans printing after 1796, but the *Moniteur* continued under the control of the Spanish government. McMurtrie's inability to find any publications other than the newspaper between 1799 and 1803 led him to conclude that "the contemporary Spanish governors did nothing to encourage the activities of printers in New Orleans, if and when there were any."[145] Not until after knowledge of the cession of Louisiana to the French Republic became general in 1803, the same year in which Louisiana was ceded to the United States, did printing become permanently established in what is now the state of Louisiana.

Charless, Stout, Marschalk, and the others, known and unknown, tramped in mud or snow on the forest trails, ached with fever in the steaming swamps, crossed swollen rivers, and fought the wild animals of the brutal American landscape, all to reach some tattered settlement where they could not be certain of anything, even a living. They kept coming for more than thirty years and did the printing of the frontier when it had to be done. The city printers, living and working in a coarse, dirty, hard-drinking environment, sustained their craft until it grew to an industry of respectability and power. These men supplied the means of communication needed for the country to survive and in addition, made life tolerable for thousands of people isolated from European culture and isolated from each other in the new rootless communities in an America on the verge of industrialization.

[145] Douglas C. McMurtrie, *Early Printing in New Orleans, 1764–1810* (New Orleans, 1929), pp. 53–60.

CHAPTER 6

TYPOGRAPHY AND
ILLUSTRATION

ALTHOUGH the number of people in the printing craft increased in the period before 1825, the quality of production remained liable to opportunity. Locked in the struggle to find satisfactory equipment, decent paper, and ink anywhere he could, short of money, time, and competent help, the printer, like the small businessman, always tried to be ready for the worst. If he had the love of turning out an artistic piece of printing, he could do so only rarely. But on that fortuitous occasion he showed that he had skill and taste.

In a country dedicated to manufactures and commerce, only just emerging from the British occupation, any writing on typography was, of course, also rare. But Francis Hopkinson, a rich Philadelphia lawyer, close in thought to his English aristocratic ancestry, could afford this luxury; he composed a little music, painted a bit, and wrote essays with gaiety. In an essay printed in 1787, "Plan for the Improvement of the Art of Paper War," he proposed "an improvement in the art of printing, so as to make it expressive not only of an author's narrative, opinions, or arguments, but also of the peculiarities of his temper, and the vivacity of his feelings." This would be accomplished by having "the degree of vociferation, such as pianissimo, piano, forte, fortissimo, with all the intermediate gradations, designated by the size of the letters which compose the emphatic words." Pearl to five-line pica, he suggested, afforded the printer an ample scale. Mathew Carey printed the essay with each type size displayed when Hopkinson referred to it: a description of a newspaper quarrel begins in long primer, the reply to follow in pica, the next argument in great primer, the retort in double pica, and so on, concluding with five-line pica, "which, indeed, is as far as the art of printing, or a modern quarrel can well go" (Plate V).[1] Hopkinson had built up a reputation as a society wit, but here, under the foolery and fancies, is a hard understanding of the variety of sensations type can convey to the reader.

Conservative printers naturally rejected any departure from conservative typographical style. The dread of change from the bread-and-butter pattern of his printing career hit Benjamin Franklin hard in his old age. Once able to appreciate the quality of Baskerville, he now resented upgrading as a threat to the salability of printing. He seemed to regard printing from a shopkeeper's point of view and complained garrulously to Noah Webster in 1789:

If therefore we would have the benefit of seeing our language more generally known among mankind, we should endeavour to remove all the difficulties, however small, that discourage the learning it. But I am sorry to observe, that, of late years, those difficulties, instead of being diminished, have been augmented. In examining the English books that were printed between the restoration and the accession of George the 2d. we may observe, that all substantives were begun with a capital, in which we imitated our mother tongue, the German. This was more particularly useful to those who were not well acquainted with the English, there being such a prodigious number of our words, that are both verbs and substantives, and spelt in the same manner, tho' often accented differently in pronunciation. This method has, by the fancy of printers, of late years, been laid aside; from an idea, that suppressing the capitals shews the character to greater advantage; those letters, prominent above the line, disturbing its even, regular appearance. The effect of this change is so considerable that a learned man of France, who used to read our Books, tho' not perfectly acquainted with our language, in conversation with me on the subject of our authors, attributed the greater obscurity he found in our modern books, compared with those of the period abovementioned, to a change of style, for the worse, in our writers; of which mistake I convinced him by marking for him each substantive with a capital, in a paragraph, which he then easily understood, tho' before he could not comprehend it. This shews the inconvenience of that pretended improvement.

[1] "Plan for the Improvement of the Art of Paper War," *American Museum*, I (1787), 437–44.

stamped with wisdom and virtue; that, in fine, the happiness of the people of these states, under the auspices of liberty, may be made complete, by so careful a preservation, and so prudent a use of this blessing, as will acquire to them the glory of recommending it to the applause, the affection, and the adoption of every nation which is yet a stranger to it.

Here, perhaps, I ought to stop: but a solicitude for your welfare, which cannot end but with my life, and the apprehension of danger, natural to that solicitude, urge me, on an occasion like the present, to offer to your solemn contemplation, and to recommend to your frequent review, some sentiments, which are the result of much reflection, of no inconsiderable observation, and which appear to me all important to the permanency of your felicity as a people. These will be offered to you with the more freedom, as you can only see in them the disinterested warnings of a parting friend, who can possibly have no

personal motive to bias his counsel: nor can I forget, as an encouragement to it, your indulgent reception of my sentiments on a former and not dissimilar occasion.

Interwoven as is the love of liberty with every ligament of your hearts, no recommendation of mine is necessary to fortify or confirm the attachment.

The unity of government, which constitutes you one people, is also now dear to you. It is justly so; for it is a main pillar in the edifice of your real independence; the support of your tranquility at home, your peace abroad; of your safety; of your prosperity; of that very liberty which you so highly prize. But as it is easy to foresee, that, from different causes and from different quarters, much pains will be taken, many artifices employed, to weaken, in your minds, the conviction of this truth; as this is the point in your political fortress against which the batteries of internal and external enemies will be most constantly and actively

XVII. *George Washington to the People of the United States* (Philadelphia, 1800). (Reduced from 6¾ x 11)

RULES of DISCIPLINE

A N D

CHRISTIAN ADVICES

O F T H E

YEARLY MEETING

O F

F R I E N D S

F O R

PENNSYLVANIA and NEW JERSEY,

FIRST HELD AT BURLINGTON IN THE YEAR 1681, AND FROM 1685 TO 1760,
INCLUSIVE, ALTERNATELY IN BURLINGTON AND PHILADELPHIA:
AND SINCE AT PHILADELPHIA.

Alphabetically digefted and Printed by direction of the faid
Meeting.

———————————

PHILADELPHIA:

PRINTED BY SAMUEL SANSOM, Jun.

1797.

XVIII. *Rules of Discipline and Christian Advices of the Yearly Meeting of Friends for Pennsylvania and New Jersey* (Philadelphia, 1797). (Reduced from 7½ x 9½)

WAR, AND TAXES THEREFOR.

Carefully to act up to our peaceable Principles. ADVISED, that Friends be careful to keep up to the peaceable principles professed by us as a People, and no way unite with such who make warlike preparations, offensive or defensive, but upon all occasions to demean themselves in a Christian and peaceable manner, thereby demonstrating to the World, that when put to the trial, we are uniform in Practice and principle. 1739.

Certificates not to be given to excuse from Militia Fines. It appearing that a Militia Law is lately passed in the lower Counties, by which Friends are to be excused from some part of the penalties inflicted, on producing Certificates from the Monthly Meetings to which they respectively belong, of their being Members; which being considered, it is the sense of this Meeting, that the granting of such Certificates may be attended with inconvenience, and therefore adviseth against them. 1742.

Privateering or going with Letters of Mart cause of Disownment. It having been represented and complained of, that notwithstanding we as a People have looked upon ourselves, as the primitive Christians also did, included in that notable Prophecy, " They " shall beat their Swords into Ploughshares and their Spears into " Pruning hooks, and learn War no more." Isa. II. Agreeable to which is the Doctrine of our Blessed Lord and Saviour Jesus Christ and his Apostles; whereto our antient Friends abundantly bore testimony, both in Doctrine and Practice, and suffered deeply for; which hath been confirmed by several of our Yearly Meetings, by their express declarations and testimonies against carrying of Guns for defending our Ships, Persons, and Goods; being under many strong obligations to observe the same; nevertheless, some professing to be of our Society have slighted and neglected this our antient and Christian Testimony to that degree as to be concerned in Privateering, or as Owners of Ships going with Letters of Mart, which is a flagrant and lamentable departure from our peaceable principle, which hath always been to confide in the protection and Providence of Almighty God, and not in weapons of war. And as these practices are attended with injustice, barbarity, and blood-

XIX. *Rules of Discipline and Christian Advices of the Yearly Meeting of Friends for Pennsylvania and New Jersey* (Philadelphia, 1797). (Reduced from 7½ x 9½)

38 P O E M S.

To Mrs. BINGHAM,

With the History of the Count de St. Julian.

To Anna these lines I addrefs,
  With ftory of fanciful woe;
For fancy muft form the diftrefs,
  That Anna is deftin'd to know.

The Gods have ordain'd that our day,
  Some tint of dejection fhall wear,
And fo for their favourites raife,
  In others misfortunes a fhare.

To Anna, fo bleft, they impart,
  To chequer her beautiful hours,
The throbs of a bountiful heart,
  And fweet fenfibility's powers.—

Go on, lovely fair, ftill to pay
  To others hard fortunes the figh,
While thine ever pleafing and gay,
  No caufe for complaining fupply.

Smooth then and harmonious fhall glide,
  Thy life's ever peaceable courfe,
While angels watch over the tide,
  And conduct it, like theirs, to its fource.

P O E M S. 39

To Miss BRODEAU,

With a Bunch of Flowers.

'Tis Flora fends thefe beauteous flowers,
  On Anna's breaft to bloom;
She'd add to Anna's magic powers,
  But love has left no room.

P O E M S

O N

SEVERAL OCCASIONS.

JOHN SWANWICK, Esq.

One of the Reprefentatives in the Congrefs of the
United States, from the State of Pennfylvania.

PHILADELPHIA:

PRINTED BY F. AND R. BAILEY, AT YOR-
ICK's HEAD, NO. 116, HIGH-STREET.

MDCCXCVII.

XXa. John Swanwick, *Poems on Several Occasions* (Philadelphia, 1797)

XXb. John Swanwick, *Poems on Several Occasions* (Philadelphia, 1797)

From the same fondness for an even and uniform appearance of characters in the line, the Printers have of late banished also the Italic Types, in which words of importance to be attended to in the sense of the sentence, and words on which an emphasis should be put in reading, used to be printed. And lately another fancy has induced some Printers to use the short round *s* instead of the long one, which formerly served well to distinguish a word readily by its varied appearance. Certainly the omitting this prominent letter makes the line appear more even; but renders it less immediately legible; as the paring all Mens' Noses might smooth and level their Faces, but would render their Physiognomies less distinguishable. Add to all these improvements backwards, another modern fancy, that *grey* printing is more beautiful than *black;* hence the English new Books are printed in so dim a character as to be read with difficulty by old Eyes, unless in a very strong light and with good Glasses. Whoever compares a Volume of the Gentleman's Magazine printed between the years 1731 and 1740 with one of those printed in the last 10 years, will be convinced of the much greater degree of perspicuity given by black Ink than by grey. Lord Chesterfield pleasantly remarked this difference to Faulkener, the Printer of the Dublin Journal, who was vainly making encomiums on his own Paper, as the most complete of any in the World; "but, Mr. Faulkener," says my Lord, "don't you think it might be still farther improved, by using Paper and Ink not quite so near of a colour." For all these reasons I cannot but wish that our American Printers would in their Editions avoid these fancied improvements, and thereby render their works more agreeable to Foreigners in Europe, to the great advantage of our Bookselling Commerce.

Two improvements were suggested by Franklin:

This leads me to mention an old error in our mode of printing. We are sensible that when a Question is met with in reading, there is a proper variation to be used in the management of the Voice. We have therefore a point, called an Interrogation, affix'd to the Question in order to distinguish it. But this is absurdly placed at its end, so that the reader does not discover it 'till he finds he has wrongly modulated his voice and is therefore obliged to begin again the Sentence. To prevent this, the Spanish Printers, more sensibly, place an Interrogation at the Beginning as well as at the End of a Question. We have another error of the same kind in printing Plays, where something often occurs that is marked as spoken *aside.* But the word *aside* is placed at the end of the Speech, when it ought to precede it, as a direction to the reader that he may govern his Voice accordingly. The practice of our Ladies in meeting five or six together to form little busy parties, where each is employed in some useful work, while one reads to them, is so commendable in itself, that it deserves the attention of Authors and Printers to make it as pleasing as possible, both to the Reader and Hearers.[2]

[2] *Am. Mercury,* May 10 and 17, 1790.

Franklin was now outside the path which printing was to follow: capitalized substantives and the long *s* soon disappeared; of his two improvements, one, the placement of *aside*, was adopted by other printers.

In contrast to this mercantile approach to typography, there were occasional cheerful signs of the aesthetic: John Mycall of Newburyport, Massachusetts, tried to please the eye and dress up his work. As early a 1789 he used three colors to produce a pamphlet containing a red woodcut and blue initial on the first page of the text.[3] He was also fond of composing decorations of printers' flowers arranged in patterns which were, in a later day, characteristic of Bruce Rogers.[4]

Mycall was exceptional among his American contemporaries because he probably owed his ideas to France and not to England.[5] Most American printers, like the writers and architects of the period, tried to better their work by studying and copying English models. In the letters of Ebenezer T. Andrews to Isaiah Thomas there is an example of the influence of John Bell, himself in debt to French typography.[6] The letters are indicative of the latent pull of aristocratic English taste in the land of equality. On October 4, 1791, Andrews wrote:

I have thoughts of publishing Proposals for an edition of Charlotte Smith's Sonnets and Della Crusca's Poems, both late works of great merit, the latter printed by Bell in his stile of printing, adorned with an elegant frontispiece to each volume—the former is handsomely printed, with 3 elegant copperplates. My wish is to do them in every respect equal to the copy, and they being works of taste, think I can get a few of the principal literary gentlemen in town to patronise and aid the work. Should the subscription succeed, and I think it likely and the work be executed as well as I think we can do it with care and attention, it will gain us reputation at least, as they will circulate among persons of the first fashion, and those it is I wish to convince that we can work as well here as anywhere, if properly encouraged.—Bemis thinks he can make the paper, and that some way may be found to polish it after it is printed, in the way Bell does his work. . . .

[3] E. Harold Hugo, "Three-Color Printing before 1789?," *PaGA*, V (1957), 16.
[4] Harold Hugo, "Mycall: An 18th-century BR?," *PaGA*, VIII (1960), 18.
[5] Richard S. Wormser, "John Mycall's Materials and Decorative Printing," *PaGA*, VIII (1960), 47.
[6] Stanley Morison, *On Type Designs*, new ed. (London, 1962), p. 55.

I don't know but you will think I am vain to attempt the imitation of such an excellent piece of work—but if it is vanity, it a laudable one.[7]

Five days later:

I am almost discouraged about attempting to execute Della Crusca in imitation of Bell's Edition. Suppose we should issue Proposals for Miss Smith's Sonnets first, and in the Proposal for that work mention we have in contemplation an edition of Della Crusca also, if encouragement offers. By our success in the execution of the Sonnets we might be enabled to judge how we could succeed with Della Crusca—and we might try the experiment of polishing the paper of the Sonnets.[8]

On November 23, Andrews had doubts about the type, "Have [you] not sent for some new Burgeois to come out in the Spring? I ask because I wish to know respecting Della Crusca—I do not think our Burgeois good enough to do it as handsomely as we wish." Three days later, he was willing to compromise: "Della Crusca is done on Burgeois, and Smith's Sonnets on Long Primer—but they may both be done on Long Primer if it is not convenient to have the Burgeois."[9] The fact that no copies of Della Crusca printed by Andrews can be found leads to the assumption that he abandoned the project. His partner, Isaiah Thomas, eventually printed Charlotte Smith's *Elegiac Sonnets* in Worcester in 1795, and Della Crusca's poems were printed in Boston by two other admirers of Bell. These two, Joseph Belknap and Thomas Hall, made no secret of the ancestry of their inspiration. They called their press the Apollo Press and on November 23, 1792, announced the proposed publication of *The British Album* containing the poems of Della Crusca, Anna Matilda, and others. It would "be printed page for page, and as nearly as possible resemble *Bell*'s London edition."[10] Belknap & Hall assured their patrons that "no expense or exertion shall be wanting on their part to render the work an honour to *American Typography*."[11] The honor is questionable because the edition is merely Bell's reproduced. When Stanley Morison compared them, he found that

the Belknap style of display, of title-page, text, and format, is identical with that of Bell; not only so, but the Bell device . . . was

[7] Thomas Papers.   [8] *Ibid.*   [9] *Ibid.*
[10] Stanley Morison, *John Bell, 1745–1831* (Cambridge, 1930), p. 130; *Am. Apollo*, Nov. 23, 1792.
[11] *American Apollo*, Nov. 23, 1792.

exactly copied. Nor did plagiarism stop at the typography, . . . the whole of the text of *The British Album* was reprinted from John Bell's original edition of 1789. The variation in the typography is that while Bell's title line BRITISH ALBUM is set in paragon roman capitals of his own founding, Belknap and Hall's is in Fry's; the body of both works is set in a small size of Fry's or Caslon's roman.[12]

Editions of classical and European authors were sometimes linked to the continent. A direct influence was openly admitted by Joshua Cushing of Salem, Massachusetts, in the prospectus for his 1805 edition of Sallust. The text of the edition was not a page-for-page copy, having been "carefully revised and collated with three of the best editions of this author," but "with respect to the typographical execution the Elzevir editons of the Classics have been made the model as to the arrangement of the page and size of the characters" (Plate VI).[13] The influence of French typography is less easy to determine because it may have arrived via French-style specimens issued by Caslon and Fry. There are some instances, particularly the books printed by Moreau de St. Méry at the end of the eighteenth century, where it is probable that the style stemmed directly from the French, though the type may have been English (Plate VII).[14] The English influence predominated, however, and in Philadelphia, according to Hyder, "German printing assimilated English styles."[15]

In reprinting imported books, printers were automatically influenced by the typography of the book they used for copy, but they sometimes committed themselves to improvement, seemingly for aesthetic reasons, with careful attention to detail in manufacture and exactness in proofreading. An anonoymous review of an American edition of Lavoisier's *Elements of Chemistry* (1799) found the book the result of the freedom of a new society and worthy of it:

Republications of valuable European works in America have become frequent, and we are pleased with their appearance on several accounts. They indicate a taste for reading and study well becoming

[12] *John Bell*, p. 133. Examples of the use of Bell type in America are noted in Silver, *Typefounding*, p. 121.

[13] Tapley, pp. 182–83.

[14] Lawrence C. Wroth, *The John Carter Brown Library: Report to the Corporation of Brown University, July 1, 1957* (Providence, 1957), pp. 57–58; Henry W. Kent, "Chez Moreau de Saint-Méry, Philadelphie," in *Bibliographical Essays: A Tribute to Wilberforce Eames* (n.p., 1924), p. 73.

[15] Darrell Hyder, "Philadelphia Fine Printing 1780–1820," *PaGA*, IX (1961), 92.

a free and intelligent people; and they evince a skill in manufacture, and an application of labour, highly agreeable to the patriotic mind. Indeed, from several specimens of American typography which have lately appeared, we judge that, in the manufacture of paper, correctness of execution in printing, preparation of leather for covers, and neatness of binding and decoration, distinguished excellence is already attained. In another respect, to us poor Reviewers, the American editions are preferable to the British: they are generally cheaper, and, in the present extravagant price of books, cost the reader oftentimes less than a third of the money demanded for a London edition of the same work.

The volume before us is a confirmation of these remarks. The publisher has, in every respect that we can discern, equalled, to say no more, the original performance. In one particular this edition has a preference, inasmuch as certain typographical mistakes are here corrected. Indeed, in regard to paper, type, engraving and binding, this book will bear a comparison with any one intended for common use. As to its contents, it is merely a re-impression of Kerr's translation of Lavoisier's celebrated work on the Elements of Chemistry.[16]

In 1804 booksellers encouraged improvement in typography by offering prizes:

NEW-YORK, June 30.

PRIZE MEDALS.—The fourth meeting of the American Company of Booksellers was held in this city last week. We understand that several specimens of elegant printing were exhibited, in consequence of a resolution adopted by the company at their last meeting, offering prize medals for three samples. The works displayed, we hesitate not to say, would vie with the most celebrated London productions, and are a flattering demonstration of the rapid improvement in the art. The Medals were adjudged as follows:

First Medal to Robert Carr, of Philadelphia, on an octavo edition of the Bible, printed for Benjamin Johnson: second medal, to Hopkins and Seymour, of this city, on an edition of the Emperor Charles 5th; third medal, to Isaac Collins & Son, on an edition of the French Reader.[17]

The judges, whoever they were, chose three able printers: Robert Carr later printed Alexander Wilson's *American Ornithology;* George F. Hopkins "justly boasted that his edition of Robertson's Charles V. was the most accurately printed work of the time. He was fastidious almost to a fault in typographical neatness"; the

---

16 "Foreign Works Republished," *Am. Rev.*, I (1801), 96–97.
17 *American Daily Advertiser*, July 2, 1804.

Collins family is still mentioned for the accuracy of its Biblical texts.[18]

On another occasion typography seems to have received a blue ribbon along with the jellies and jams:

1819.—At the Hartford, Ct., cattle show and fair, Messrs. Lincoln & Stone, printers of that city, left with the committee a superb specimen of Goldsmith's Poems, which they had printed. The committee reported that in point of typographical elegance, they had seen nothing of American workmanship which equaled it.[19]

At present our knowledge of the use of printer's marks by American printers is restricted to fugitive references. Morison, in the quotation above, notes that Bell's mark was exactly copied by Belknap & Hall, and Hamilton cites the names of other printers who placed a device on their books.[20] The practice was not extensive. Perhaps many printers thought that, inasmuch as the country was still in political and social revolt from class structures, a device with its connotation of aristocracy would seem virtually immoral on an American book.

There were artists capable of designing devices and their talents were used for illustration. When particular attention was devoted to the typography as well as when pictures would clarify the text, illustrations were considered necessary. Therefore any discussion of the typography of the period must include illustrations as well. The extensive use of illustrations, it may be added, enabled artists to maintain themselves until their work became more acceptable. The art produced was on a fairly low level and of secondary importance, as was realized by Joseph Hopkinson in 1810: "But when independence and peace were obtained, and when, by the adoption of a regular and free government, that independence and peace were secured, the arts began to show themselves like the verdure of the spring, spare and feeble, but full of health and promise."[21]

An artist could render on request an original portrait of an American, a picture of an American building or scene, or a map to illus-

[18] John W. Francis, "Reminiscences of Printers, Authors, and Booksellers in New-York," *Int. Mag.*, V (1852), 263; *Eng. Bible in Am.*, p. 7.

[19] Munsell, *Typ. Misc.*, p. 142.

[20] Sinclair Hamilton, *Early American Book Illustrators and Wood Engravers, 1670–1870* (Princeton, N.J., 1958), pp. 42–43.

[21] *Annual Discourse* (Philadelphia, 1810), p. 15.

trate a pamphlet, book, or periodical article. Most illustrators copied illustrations from imported books. In the cheaper publications the text was printed with woodcuts, wood engravings, or type metal cuts; some expensive works were dandified with separately printed engravings on copper, later also on steel. Griffin's statement was accurate: "For a good part of the nineteenth century there was just as much piracy of illustration as there was piracy of text, and English models set the standards and the pace."[22] Isaiah Thomas frankly advertised his copies of children's books as being done "exactly in the English Method, and it is supposed the paper, printing, cuts and binding are every way equal to those imported from England."[23]

The point at which American engraving began to grow is distinctly marked by the appearance of the *Encyclopaedia* printed by Thomas Dobson in Philadelphia. Each of the eighteen volumes, issued between 1790 and 1797, contained approximately eight hundred pages and thirty plates. The text, taken from the third edition of the *Encyclopaedia Britannica* but revised in places, was printed on paper manufactured in Pennsylvania.[24] For the first ten volumes the type was specially cast by John Baine & Grandson in Philadelphia.[25] Throughout the work Dobson's excellent typography presented the massive amount of information clearly and with dignity. To provide the more than five hundred plates, Dobson employed practically all the engravers in the Philadelphia area (Plate VIII). Work on the *Encyclopaedia* kept them so fully occupied that when Jeremy Belknap wished to have a map engraved in 1791, Ebenezer Hazard could not help him: "I have made some enquiry about the map, but cannot yet find a good engraver who is disengaged. Dobson keeps them hard at work, and I cannot get them to say what they *suppose* such a plate will cost."[26] Almost half the engravings were made by Robert Scot, James Thackara, and John Vallance, with the remainder supplied by other artists including James Akin, William Barker, Joseph Bowes, Francis Shallus, and Henry W. Weston.[27]

[22] Gillett G. Griffin, "The Development of Woodcut Printing in America," *Princeton Univ. Lib. Chron.*, XX (1958), 8.

[23] Shipton, p. 58. [24] Wroth, *Col. Printer*, pp. 293–94; Evans 22486.

[25] Hyder, *PaGA*, IX, 72. [26] Mass. Hist. Soc., *Coll.*, 5th ser., III, 250.

[27] Georgia C. Haugh, "The Beginnings of American Book Illustration," in *Essays on Book Illustration*, ed. Frances J. Brewer (Berlin, 1963), p. 38.

Dobson's magnificent achievement in the production of the *Encyclopaedia* signified, as Wroth says, "the end of printing in America as a household craft and the beginning of its factory stage of development."[28] It also proved that a market existed for expensive publications. Dobson began with 246 subscribers but found that his printing of one thousand copies of the first volume was too small. He doubled the printing for the second volume and later reprinted the first.[29]

American engravings of the period were executed by unsophisticated men, badly taught or self-taught, whose main business was initialing household effects, with engraving pictures a side line. Their crude plates often had an unintentionally comic look, even as their foreign counterparts were mostly skilled and accurate (Plates VIII and IX). Hopkinson's comment on the spirit of nascence in the craft is amplified by Alexander Lawson, who found his fellow craftsmen pompous and naïve:

Thackara and Vallance were partners when I came to Philadelphia. I engraved with them two years. They thought themselves artists, and that they knew every part of the art; and yet their art consisted in copying, in a dry, stiff manner with the graver, the plates for the Encyclopedia, all their attempts at etching having miscarried. The rest of their time, and that of all others at this period, was employed to engrave card plates, with a festoon of wretched flowers and bad writing—then there was engraving on type metal—silver plate—watches—door plates—dog collars and silver buttons, with an attempt at seal cutting. Such was the state of engraving in 1794.[30]

At the same time that Dobson was planning and printing the first volume of the *Encyclopaedia*, Isaiah Thomas undertook a remarkable project—his folio Bible of 1791 (Plate X). Thomas had seriously printed many small, inexpensive, illustrated children's books, including *A Curious Hieroglyphick Bible* (1788), which contained almost five hundred cuts, but never anything as majestic as this Bible. To establish the text of this, the first folio Bible in English printed in America, Thomas said that he used nearly thirty editions and that "every sheet of the Text, before its commitment to the Press, was carefully examined by the Clergymen of Worcester, and

[28] Wroth, *Col. Printer*, p. 294.   [29] Hopkinson, *Ann. Discourse*, pp. 16–17.
[30] William Dunlap, *A History of the Rise and Progress of the Arts of Design in the United States*, new ed. (Boston, 1918), II, 123–24.

by other capable persons—and compared by not less than eight different Copies."[31] Three relief cuts and fifty engravings illustrated the text.[32] The engravings were made by four artists: Amos Doolittle, John Norman, Joseph Seymour, and Samuel Hill. Hill also cut the title and at least one of the relief cuts.[33] In the prefatory address Thomas referred to his efforts to make this a significant publication: "No cost, care or labor hath he spared to render the Editions correct, neat and elegant."[34] For those who preferred a smaller size, the Bible was also available in royal quarto. The publication of the Thomas Bible, following so closely upon the *Encyclopaedia*, shows that Dobson's pursuit of excellence was not unique. Their contemporaries also produced commendable work in a smaller way: Hyder says that the title page of Thomas Lang's pamphlet, *Of Commerce and Luxury* (1791), "shows the best Fry typography in the country at that time"; Evans called Michael Billmeyer's 791-page quarto, *Christliche Betrachtungen* (1791), "a very creditable piece of bookmaking" (Plates XI and XII).[35] In the same year Isaac Collins printed an excellent quarto Bible in a restrained style typical of his Quaker affiliation (Plates XIII and XIV).[36]

The antithesis to the classical spirit was the lofty, romantic pride in state and country as shown in *The Self-Interpreting Bible* printed between 1790 and 1792 by Hodge & Campbell. Besides eighteen engravings by other artists there was a frontispiece especially designed by William Dunlap asserting and enshrining the dignity of America as she accepted religion (Plate XV):

America, with the "Constitution" in her hand, receiving the Bible; The Goddess of Liberty on one side; behind America a Pedestal with the Names of Washington, Montgomery, Greene, Franklin, Warren, Adams, Mercer, Putnam, Jay, Clinton, Gates, Morris and Fayette inscribed thereon. The whole surmounted by the arms of the State of New York.[37]

A similar interpolation of patriotism occurred in George H. Maynard's *The Whole Genuine and Complete Works of Flavius Josephus*, printed by William Durell between 1792 and 1794. This is a

[31] John Wright, *Early Bibles of America* (New York, 1894), p. 83.
[32] O'Callaghan, pp. 39–40.
[33] *Ibid.*, p. 39; Sinclair H. Hitchings, "Samuel Hill's Relief Engraving," *PaGA*, VIII (1960), 12–17.
[34] Wright, p. 83.   [35] Hyder, *PaGA*, IX, 73; Evans 23975.
[36] *Eng. Bible in Am.*, p. 7.   [37] O'Callaghan, p. 44.

page-for-page reprint of the London edition but printed in larger type and with additional decoration. At the beginning of each "Book," Durell inserted a decorative cut of an eagle centered and sitting on a medallion on which is the statement: "The American *Edition* of Josephus 1792." The number of its engravings, approximately sixty, stirred Hamilton to regard the volume as "perhaps the most important illustrated work published in New York up to that time."[38] Both the London and New York title pages declared the engravings to be "taken from original Drawings of Messrs. Metz, Stothard, and Corbould, Members of the Royal Academy" and the London title page added "and other eminent Artists." For the American edition the engravings were copied, some in reverse, by American artists including Joel Allen, Alexander Anderson, Amos Doolittle, William Rollinson, Benjamin Tanner, Cornelius Tiebout, and Elkanah Tisdale. When both editions are compared, it is obvious that Durell wanted to prove, with all the patriotic fervor of the New World mind, that American printers could be superior typographically to London printers. By adding the decorated border and rules to the title page, by using a larger and more spacious format as well as adding cuts to the text, he made a more luxurious and individual book.

When Durell was searching for the engravers for his edition of Josephus, he found a talented seventeen-year-old, Alexander Anderson, who had taught himself the art at the age of twelve, manufacturing his own tools and press after reading a how-to-do-it article in an encyclopedia. In a few years he was making and selling relief cuts to newspapers. At his father's wish he studied medicine and practiced in New York, but he never left his avocation. He finally abandoned medicine for engraving in 1798. Since he had been engraving for Durell and other printers throughout his medical career, he continued to sell his illustrations on copperplate, wood, or type metal as if he had never been interrupted.[39] At that time woodcuts began increasingly to appear in the cheaper books despite a resistance to the trend by some printers who liked type metal cuts which did not warp or crack. In 1793, after Anderson saw the work of Thomas and John Bewick, he began to copy it, experimenting about

[38] Hamilton, *Early Am. Book Illustrators*, p. xxxi.
[39] W. J. Linton, *The History of Wood-Engraving in America* (Boston, 1882), pp. 2–6.

a year with the graver on boxwood. Finally he felt able to reproduce the Bewick white-line style, and on September 25, 1794, he brought Durell the first engraved block for the illustrations of *The Looking-Glass for the Mind*, printed by Durell in 1795. Whether or not this book contains the first American white-line wood engravings remains to be determined: an edition of the same title printed by Carter & Wilkinson the year before had cuts in the white-line style, but these may have been on metal rather than wood; Jonathan Fisher also had been engraving on boxwood.[40] Nonetheless, Anderson's reputation as the father of American wood engraving was secure after the publication of Durell's edition. At the time of his death in 1870 at the age of ninety-five, Anderson had provided almost ten thousand illustrations (after 1812 chiefly on wood) for about six hundred books and pamphlets.[41] Some of his more important earlier work may be seen in the New York editions of *The Vicar of Wakefield* (1803), *A General History of Quadrupeds* (1804), and *The Fables of Flora* (1804). Only occasionally did he prepare an original design, being primarily an engraver, and he seldom departed from the Bewick style after he found it. Unquestionably his influence in America was great, but posterity does not rank him among the engravers of genius. Linton, who regrets that Anderson was a lesser artist than he should have been, does not entirely blame him:

Had his work been original, like Bewick's, it had, indeed, been great; but, practised as he was on metal, and with Bewick's work before him, one thinks that, with his undoubted artistic feeling, conscientious study, and constant industry, he should have done more. . . . It must be owned, however, that we never see him at his best. Bad printing is not favorable to an engraver's reputation, nor does good printing avail on worn blocks.[42]

As information on Anderson and other wood engravers is available in Sinclair Hamilton's *Early American Book Illustrators and Wood Engravers*, 1670–1870, their story need be told only briefly here. It took a quarter-century for wood engravings to become popular enough to be widely used as illustrations in American books. The coming of the new iron presses which could make impressions

[40] Hamilton, *Early Am. Book Illustrators*, pp. xxxi–xxxiii, 38.
[41] Helen M. Knubel, "Alexander Anderson and Early American Book Illustration," *Princeton Univ. Lib. Chron.*, I (1940), 18; *American Encyclopaedia of Printing*, ed. J. Luther Ringwalt (Philadelphia, 1871), pp. 37–38.
[42] P. 9.

superior to those of the wooden presses and of the roller with its improved ink distribution stimulated the ambitions of artists who wanted to become wood engravers. The art began to expand. Some of the engravers were self-taught, but others were taught by Anderson in the early days. One pupil, his first, was Garret Lansing, who started his lessons in 1804 and was, according to Hamilton, the second American wood engraver; other Anderson pupils included John H. Hall, William Morgan, and Anderson's own daughter, Ann. Around 1810 the production of wood engravings began to extend to cities other than New York. In Utica, New York, William Williams engraved the illustrations for James Montgomery's *The Wanderer of Switzerland and Other Poems* (1810). William Mason introduced the art in Philadelphia about the same time. In Boston, Abel Bowen who set up shop as an engraver in 1812, was soon followed by Nathaniel Dearborn. As time elapsed, the apprentices and pupils of these men became proficient, independent artists and this, in turn, developed an environment in which the number of wood engravers could increase more rapidly. Soon there was plenty of work to share. It should be remembered that in general these men were engravers, not designers:

During these early years it cannot be said, so far as wood engraving is concerned, that there was any distinctively American book illustration. However, now and then, when the cuts are not mere copies of foreign originals, the name of the designer will appear as well as that of the engraver. In the beginning the engraver was the significant figure, with the illustrator secondary in importance, but this in course of time was reversed.[43]

Engraving on copperplate in America was not much better than American engraving on boxwood. That American experiments in the medium in the 1790's did not equal the quality of foreign copperplate engravings was known to printers and probably to a few sharp-eyed readers. Isaiah Thomas, who had labored to make his work presentable, ruefully apologized for the five illustrations by Joseph Seymour in Charlotte Smith's *Elegiac Sonnets* (1795). He noted with relief that his book had a "first;" it was made of wove paper, the first manufactured by him:

THE Editor of this (Worcester) Edition, intended to have published it nearly four years since, at which time he had the plates

[43] Hamilton, *Early Am. Book Illustrators*, pp. xxxiii–xxxv, 48, 166.

engraved in his Office in this town. His being employed in printing larger and heavier volumes has prevented these Sonnets appearing from his Press till now.—As the Letter Press has been delayed, he could have wished the Engravings had been also; as in the infancy of engraving in this country, four years' additional experience to the artist would doubtless have produced more delicate work than what is now presented. The lovers of this Art will, however, be enabled, in some measure, to mark the progress of Engraving by a comparison of the Plates *now* executed with these, and the Editor doubts not but a proper allowance will be made for work engraved by an artist who obtained his knowledge in this country, by whom these plates were executed, and that done by European engravers who have settled in the United States.

The making of the particular kind of paper on which these Sonnets are printed, is a new business in America; and but lately introduced into Greatbritain; it is the first manufactured by the Editor.

On the whole, the Editor hopes for the candor of those who wish well to the productions of the Columbian Press—their favorable acceptance of this, and other volumes printed in this country, will doubtless raise an emulation to produce others, better executed, on superior paper, and with more delicate engravings.[44]

Dr. William Bentley echoed Thomas. On receiving a copy of the *Elegiac Sonnets*, he wrote in his diary: "His apology for the plates in the work to an American is satisfactory, as we were, & perhaps now are, behind all the world in the art of engraving, & perhaps also in taste for good executions."[45] Bentley's critical, scholarly mind had led him to compare American reprints with the original editions—he was in a position to see a number of them and was a judge of influences and disparities—therefore his criticism of American engraving was well-grounded.

Few contemporary American writers were distinguished enough to cause a printer to extend himself. Curiously enough, one celebrated text did appear in 1796, the year in which Bentley made his comment; it was Washington's Farewell Address. Among the multiple editions, John Russell advertised his as "Elegantly printed, from new type, on vellum paper."[46] Another 1796 edition, printed by Samuel and John Adams, has been described as "the best example of the Press of the Printers" (Plate XVI).[47] Hugh Maxwell's 1800 edition, in the style of Bulmer and Bensley, exemplifies the best Philadelphia printing of the period (Plate XVII).[48] The personal

[44] Charlotte Smith, *Elegiac Sonnets* (Worcester, Mass., 1795), p. xiii.
[45] *Diary of W. Bentley*, II, 209.   [46] Evans 31530.   [47] Evans 31534.
[48] Hyder, *PaGA*, IX, 81.

glory of Washington, the high patriotism of the subject matter, and its popularity challenged printers to pay unusual attention to standards of typography and some printers stretched themselves to the utmost to make the appearance worthy of the content. If ever a comprehensive study of the typography of all editions of the Farewell Address is made, it would reveal much about the comparative abilities of the printers.

One suspects that in the 1790's the number of printers interested in fine typography was greater than is now supposed. An obscure printer, Samuel Sansom, Jr., showed such an interest in his 1797 edition of the *Rules of Discipline* of the Society of Friends (Plates XVIII and XIX). So did Francis and Robert Bailey when they printed John Swanwick's *Poems on Several Occasions* (1797), "a dainty volume of admirable typography" (Plate XXa and b.).[49] Both books relied on careful, formal typography rather than illustrations to make them handsome. Undoubtedly the skill of more printers will be known if other studies like Hyder's on fine printing in Philadelphia are undertaken.[50]

One notable typographical venture was certainly John Thompson's hot-pressed Bible printed between 1796 and 1798 and imitating John Baskerville. As mentioned in a previous chapter, the advertisement for this Bible suggested the Baskerville influence by its references to fine type and hot-pressing. The book itself contained the text of the Baskerville edition and the wide spacing of its composition.[51] But, unlike Baskerville, Thompson elaborated on the original by adding an engraved frontispiece. He exploited, in the advertisement for the book, the feelings of jealousy and rivalry toward England that were stirring in the country: "to shew, that in America, works CAN be executed, in every respect, equal to the efforts of trans-atlantic genius."[52] Although Thompson's Bible was not equal to its English model, it does denote progress in American quality. It was printed with American type on American paper and was a high point in the early competition with English typographical proficiency.

Two books printed in the final year of the century are indicative of the wakening of American printing as an art. One book consists

---

[49] Evans 32898.   [50] Hyder, *PaGA*, IX, 69–99.   [51] O'Callaghan, p. 54.
[52] Hyder, *PaGA*, IX, 79.

of engravings; the other has text without illustrations. The first, *The City of Philadelphia . . . as It Appeared in the Year 1800*, published on the final day of the eighteenth century, contains twenty-nine prints including a map of the city. Twenty-seven plates, "Drawn & Engraved by W. Birch & Son," picture the homes and businesses, the waterfront and public buildings, of Philadelphia. A title page and map engraved by William Barker and an introduction and list of subscribers are included. When, in his autobiography, William Birch referred to the volume, he described the division of labor, implying that his son, Thomas, prepared the original water colors: "I superintended it, chose the subjects, instructing my Son in the Drawings, and our Friend Mr. [Samuel?] Seymour in the Engravings."[53] Aside from what this book conveys about the habits of the people of Philadelphia and its importance as an architectural record, it is an advance in typographical skill and workmanship. Wroth thinks the book "distinctly a jewel in the product of the American press."[54]

The second book, *Pursuits of Literature* by Thomas J. Mathias, is purely typographic without ornamentation. Hugh Maxwell, the printer, used Bell type on the title page and Binny & Ronaldson's Roman No. 1 for the text (Plates XXI and XXII). Two consonant faces, well-arranged pages, and good presswork appear in this, a fairly ordinary book not intended to be a de luxe edition. It is a measure of the distance that American printing had traveled; the point was now reached where, as Hyder said, "the competent could be thought commonplace."[55]

As the new century began, America expanded, its boundary soon reaching to the Rocky Mountains. Canals were dug and turnpikes opened to the West; there were the influential trading ships and the domination of the factories. A few men feared that the new republic would become the plaything of the moneyed class, that its function as the servant of all the people would diminish; among them was Joel Barlow. He reworked a poem of his early days, *The Vision of Columbus*, into *The Columbiad*, making it into an epic which glorified the republican dream. Encouraged by Robert Fulton, Barlow

[53] Martin P. Snyder, "William Birch: His Philadelphia Views," *Pa. Mag. Hist. Biog.*, LXXIII (1949), 275–77, 298–303.
[54] *Col. Printer*, p. 290.   [55] *PaGA*, IX, 80–81.

decided to issue *The Columbiad* in a de luxe edition with the intent to make it the finest book ever printed in this country. He had Fulton in England superintend the engraving and printing of the illustrations there. Eleven were engravings of paintings (based on sketches by Fulton) commissioned from Robert Smirke. The twelfth plate was a frontispiece portrait of Barlow engraved from a painting by Fulton. In Philadelphia, Barlow arranged for publication of the book by C. & A. Conrad & Co.[56] Fry & Kammerer printed three issues of the edition (432 copies on Amies paper, 384 on Levers paper, 96 on "coarse" paper) at Barlow's request because the poet wanted to reach readers at various economic levels.[57] Production of the book cost Barlow about ten thousand dollars, of which Fulton contributed five thousand.[58] Experts supervised every stage. One unknown historian stated that every sheet was

singly examined by the printer before it was wet down; the type, which was large in size, was made by Binny & Ronaldson, and every letter was scrutinized both by a member of that firm and by Mr. Fry. To insure correctness he offered one hundred dollars for each error found after he had revised it for press. . . . Fry made the ink, to do which properly he studied chemistry, and it still remains of its original blackness.[59]

These particulars may not be entirely correct, but the attention to detail is manifest in the volume itself. *The Columbiad*, published in 1807, is a noble quarto in Bulmer style. Very well printed, its chaste elegance captured the respect of reviewers here and abroad (Plate XXIII). Francis Jeffrey of the *Edinburgh Review* acclaimed it: "The infant republic has already attained to the very summit of perfection in the mechanical part of bookmaking."[60] In his swelling rhetoric was the implicit acknowledgment that Barlow's luxurious book could match the de luxe editions of England and Europe. At last American typography was mature.

But the inferior condition of engraving continued to disconcert printers who, feeling the quickening public interest in better books, wanted to manufacture them. Barlow and Fulton had wisely bypassed native limitations by hiring engravers overseas, but this was too expensive for the average American firm. Reconciling them-

---

[56] James Woodress, *A Yankee's Odyssey* (Philadelphia, [1958]), p. 246.
[57] *BAL*, I, 181.   [58] Woodress, pp. 246–47; *BAL*, I, 181.
[59] *Am. Dict. Print.*, p. 218.   [60] Woodress, p. 247.

PURSUITS OF LITERATURE.

A SATIRICAL POEM

IN FOUR DIALOGUES,

WITH NOTES.

TO WHICH ARE ANNEXED,

A VINDICATION OF THE WORK,

AND

TRANSLATIONS OF ALL THE GREEK, LATIN, ITALIAN, AND

FRENCH QUOTATIONS.

Υμεις, ω παντα εν πᾶσι Φυσει και παιδεια χρηστοι, και
μετριοι, και Φιλανθρωποι, και της Βασιλειας αξιοι, τυτοις τοις
λογοις επινευσατε.
Athenagoræ Atheniensis Legatio Imperatoribus Antonino
et Commodo.—ad fin. Op. Justin. Martyr. Ed. Paris.
1636. pag. 39.

PHILADELPHIA:

PRINTED BY H. MAXWELL, FOR A. DICKINS, BOOKSELLER,
NORTH SECOND STREET OPPOSITE CHRIST-CHURCH.
....
1800.

XXI. Thomas J. Mathias, *Pursuits of Literature* (Philadelphia, 1800)

But while the midwife to Lucina prays,   199
The Gorgon glares, and blasts the critic's bays.
Parr prints *a Paper* [y] well; in all things equal,
Sense, taste, wit, judgment; but pray read *The Sequel:*
Sequel to what? the Doctor only knows;
Morsels of politics, most chosen prose,
Of Nobles, Priestley, Plato, Democrats,
Pitt, Plutarch, Curtis, Burke, and Rous, and Rats;
The scene? 'tis Birmingham, renown'd afar
At once for half-pence, and for Doctor Parr.

OCTAVIUS.

Well if none *read* such works, yet all admire---

AUTHOR.

The paper?

---

y Dr. Parr published at Birmingham what he called a " *Printed* " *Paper;*" and after that, " a Sequel to a *Printed Paper,*" a very large pamphlet, *de omni scibili,* as usual.---N. B. I really think it is impossible to point out any man of learning and ability, (and Dr. Parr has both,) who has *hitherto* wasted his powers and attainments in such a desultory, unmeaning, wild, unconnected, and useless manner, as DR. PARR.----*In nullum reipublicæ usum* ambitiosâ loquelâ *inclaruit.*"*---I have done with him.

    * Tacit. Ann. L. 4. Sect. 20.

OCTAVIUS.

    Yes; ten shillings every quire: [a] 210
The type is Bulmer's, *just like* Boydell's plays:
So Mister Hayley shines in Milton's [b] rays.
In one glaz'd glare tracts, sermons, pamphlets vie,
And hot-press'd nonsense claims a dignity.

AUTHOR.

Nonsense or sense, I'll bear in any shape,
In gown, in lawn, in ermine, or in crape;
What's a fine type, where truth exerts her rule?
Science is science, and a fool's a fool.

---

a Not Dr. Parr's paper or printing, which in some of his works is sometimes scarce legible; but I allude to and condemn the general needlessly expensive manner of publishing most pamphlets and books at this time. See the Pursuits of Literature Dialogue 1. If the present rage of printing on fine, *creamy* wire-wove, *vellum,* hot-pressed paper is not stopped, the injury done to the eye from reading, and the shameful expense of the books, will in no very long time annihilate the desire of reading, and the possibility of purchasing. *No new work whatsoever* should be published in *this* manner, or Literature will destroy itself.

b Mr. Hayley wrote a long life, or rather a sort of defence of Milton, as I think, prefixed to Boydell's grand edition of the poet. I like neither the spirit nor the execution of Mr. H's work.

XXII. Thomas J. Mathias, *Pursuits of Literature* (Philadelphia, 1800). (Reduced from 5⅛ x 8½)

Let other years, by thine example prest,
Call forth their heroes to explore the rest.

    Thro different seas a twofold passage lies
To where sweet India scents a waste of skies.
The circling course, by Madagascar's shores,
Round Afric's cape, bold Gama now explores;
Thy well plann'd path these gleamy straits provide,
Nor long shall rest the daring search untried.   490
This idle frith must open soon to fame,
Here a lost Lusitanian fix his name,
From that new main in furious waves be tost,
And fall neglected on the barbarous coast.

    But lo the Chief! bright Albion bids him rise,
Speed in his pinions, ardor in his eyes!
Hither, O Drake, display thy hastening sails,
Widen ye passes, and awake ye gales,
March thou before him, heaven-revolving sun,
Wind his long course, and teach him where to run;   500
Earth's distant shores, in circling bands unite,
Lands, learn your fame, and oceans, roll in light,
Round all the watery globe his flag be hurl'd,
A new Columbus to the astonish'd world.

XXIII. Joel Barlow, *The Columbiad* (Philadelphia, 1807). (Reduced from 8¾ x 11)

XXIV. Illustration by William S. Leney for *The Holy Bible* (New York, 1807). (Reduced from 5¾ x 7½)

selves to the facts before them, Collins, Perkins & Co., about 1807, tried the scheme of a contest, which they hoped would flush out improved engravings. The printers

with a view of exciting an honorable and useful competition among the engravers of this country, selected several of the most eminent in their profession, gave to each a subject to engrave, and offered a gold medal for the best. When the plates were finished they were submitted to the President and Directors of the American Academy of Fine Arts. The plates were intended for a new and elegant edition of the Bible, and the plan pursued by the publishers produced them a collection of plates much superior to any before executed in America. The successful plate was the *Finding of Moses*, by Leney. The *St Paul*, by Tiebout, the *Providence*, by Fairman, and the *Holy Family* by Maverick, jr. were honorably mentioned, by Col. Trumbull, as president of the society.[91]

The Bible, published in 1807, is a small gallery of American engravings of the early nineteenth century. The gold medal winner, William S. Leney, had been an engraver in London before he emigrated in 1805 (Plate XXIV).[62]

One well-known publication, Alexander Wilson's *American Ornithology* (1808–1814), would have become even more celebrated had the engravings been adequate. The publishers hoped that this book, the first great American ornithological work, would be "an honourable testimony of the state of the Arts in the young and growing Empire."[63] The best available paper, printing, and engraving were ordered. Binny & Ronaldson supplied the type for the nine volumes, which Robert and William Carr printed with excellent Bulmerlike design and good presswork on Amies paper.[64] These features surpass the seventy-six engravings in quality. Granted that Wilson possessed little training as an artist, it is still true that the engravers and colorers, if skilled enough, could have embellished his drawings so as to disguise some of the faults.

Engravings were comparatively expensive for bookwork. The printer paid a negotiated price for the engraving and often additional sums for the plates, polishing, paper, lettering, printing, and coloring. Prices submitted by engravers varied considerably accord-

[61] Munsell, *Typ. Misc.*, pp. 105–6.
[62] George C. Groce and David H. Wallace, *The New-York Historical Society's Dictionary of Artists in America, 1564–1860* (New Haven, 1957), p. 393.
[63] Hyder, *PaGA*, IX, 90.
[64] *Ibid.*; Lawrence C. Wroth, *Typographic Heritage* (n.p., 1949), p. 46.

ing to the amount of work on hand and the engraver's estimate of his own worth. While Dobson was keeping the Philadelphia engravers occupied on his encyclopedia, the Boston engravers were intermittingly employed. Jeremy Belknap wanted a Philadelphia engraver but settled for a Boston engraver: "I have agreed with a Mr. Hill to engrave my map. I am to give him 30 dollars for the plate and the engraving, and 1 dollar per hundred for printing; and I am to find the paper. I was induced to make this bargain by receiving from you an account that all your best engravers were engaged, and could not do it."[65] One year later, in 1792, Ebenezer Andrews and Isaiah Thomas enjoyed a buyer's market for engravings: "Have seen Hill, Norman & Seymour about engraving the map of Maine—Hill asks £9—Norman £3. .12—Seymour £4.10—who had we better get to do it?"[66] The wide spread in the bids implies that engraving was still a precarious profession in Boston.

Many data about Philadelphia prices for engraving appear in bills preserved by Mathew Carey at the American Antiquarian Society. For engraving a map of the world for William Guthrie's *A New System of Modern Geography* (1793), Thackara & Vallance charged Carey 47/17/10 (6,455 letters and 27 days' work) plus 1/6/– for the plate.[67] Here is James Smither's bill for four of the plates in Oliver Goldsmith's *An History of the Earth and Animated Nature:*

[1795]
April 1ˢᵗ To Engraving four Plates
   viz—Land Tortoise &c.   6. .15. .
     Sturgeon &c   6. .
     Salmon &c   5. .12. 6
     Sea Lobster &c   7. . 2. 6[68]

There are additional charges of 2/5/9 for polishing ten plates and of 12*s* for the copper for two plates.[69] The small frontispiece (4¼ × 5⅜) in Carey's *The Porcupiniad* (1799) was engraved by Henry W. Weston for eight dollars. Two larger plates (8¼ × 12¾ and 7⅜ × 9½) for Lavoisier's *Elements of Chemistry*, also issued

[65] Mass. Hist. Soc., *Coll.*, 5th ser., III, 258.
[66] Letter from E. T. Andrews to Isaiah Thomas, Sept. 20, 1792, in Thomas Papers.
[67] Am. Ant. Soc., Mathew Carey Papers, III, 710. [68] *Ibid.*, VIII, 2955.
[69] *Ibid.*

in 1799, were engraved by Cornelius Tiebout for fifteen dollars apiece.[70] Robert Scot's bill for other engravings in the same book was more precise:

```
1799
Nov 11 Engraving Pl. 2ᵈ Elements chemistry         12
    19      Dᵒ    Pl. 4ᵗʰ       Dᵒ                  14
            Polishing 2 Pls. 7 by 9½ & 7 by 8½ = 124
                @ 1½ cen. pʳ In.                    1.24 [sic]
Decʳ    Eng. Pl 3ᵈ Elements chemistry               10
        Polishing Do. 8 by 6¾ = 56 @ 1½ cents pʳ In. 0.84
        Eng. Pl. 1ˢᵗ Elements chemistry             8
        Polishing Dᵒ 6¼ by 7 — 44 @ 1½ cents pʳ In. 0.66[71]
```

Carey invested much larger amounts of money in engravings for his Bibles. Of the thirty engravings in his Bible of 1803, five are in this bill from Tiebout:

```
                                                    $
July 8ᵗʰ Engraving a Plate—The last Supper—       75 . . —
         Do          St. John in Prison—          60 . . —
         Do          Pool of Bethesda—            60 . . —
         Do          Resurection of Lazarus—      60 . . —
         Do          Christ teaching              65 . . —
                                  $
         five pieces of Copper at 2-50            12 . . 50
                                                 ─────────
                                                 332 . . 50[72]
```

Lesser but still impressive amounts were required for scientific books. Tiebout charged $292.00 for sixteen plates for James Ferguson's *Astronomy Explained* (1806) and added about one hundred dollars for the copper. Rising prices caused Carey to pay even more for engravings during the following years. By 1809 Tiebout was receiving twenty dollars each for small frontispieces. A few engravers billed their work in terms of time. In 1813 E. G. Gridley charged three dollars a day; in 1816 John G. Warnicke's rate was seventeen dollars a week.[73]

The Carey archives also contain many bills from coppersmiths for plates delivered to artists. In the 1790's a copperplate cost about 4*s* a pound, planishing or polishing about 1*d* or 1½*d* a square inch.[74] At the beginning of the nineteenth century copperplates were charged at about four cents a square inch and planishing or polishing at

[70] *Ibid.*, XIV, 5401, 5434.   [71] *Ibid.*, XXI, 1033.   [72] *Ibid.*, XVIII, 8101.
[73] *Ibid.*, XX, 117; XXIII, 1507; XXVII, 3221; XXIX, 4660h.
[74] *Ibid.*, V, 1744; VII, 2475.

about a cent and a half a square inch.[75] There are also bills for printing the engravings. Maps for atlases which Carey issued in the early 1790's were printed at 7s 6d or 10s a hundred.[76] In 1800 the price was about $1.33 a hundred for large maps, 67 cents a hundred for small maps, and about $1.50 a hundred for large Bible plates.[77] During the following fifteen years these prices remained fairly stable, with frontispieces and illustrations for trade books costing from about 50 cents to $1.00 a hundred for printing. Bills from those who colored maps show prices of 8s 4d a hundred in the early 1790's and $3.50 a hundred in the early 1800's when large maps were colored.[78] Additional expense might be incurred if plates in constant use, particularly maps and Bibles plates, needed retouching. Fees for this work could be as low as a few dollars or as high as about forty dollars.[79] Given the cost in time and money, it is understandable that printers boasted when they described the engravings in their books, even when they knew that they were outstripped by foreign competition.

A share of the expense of illustration was sometimes recaptured by re-use or by selling engravings and cuts after use. In the manner of the *Nuremberg Chronicle*, the same woodcut was used as a portrait of more than one person in *The History of America*, printed by Wrigley & Berriman in 1795. A woodcut frontispiece in an edition of *Robinson Crusoe* printed at Worcester in 1795 had previously been used as an illustration in a 1791 edition of *The Pilgrim's Progress* printed there by Isaiah Thomas. The same cut reappears in a Boston *The Pilgrim's Progress* of 1817.[80] Engravings in the Isaiah Thomas Bible of 1791 reappeared ten years later in William Durell's publication of Paul Wright's *The New and Complete Life of Our Blessed Lord and Saviour Jesus Christ*. They are also found in a Bible printed by Sage & Clough in 1806. In both books Thomas' name is obliterated on the plates.[81] Writing to Isaiah Thomas in 1805, Ebenezer Andrews told him about a recent purchase from John Conrad of Philadelphia:

Have concluded a bargain with Conrad for the Plates of the Atlas he used for Pinkerton's Geography. Propose to use them for

---

[75] *Ibid.*, XXII, 1147; XXIII, 1466; XXIV, 2279.   [76] *Ibid.*, III, 1067–68.
[77] *Ibid.*, XIV, 4901; XV, 5774.   [78] *Ibid.*, VI, 1986; XXVII, 3271.
[79] *Ibid.*, XXVI, 2820; XVII, 7562.
[80] Hamilton, *Early Am. Book Illustrators*, pp. 39–40.
[81] O'Callaghan, pp. 62, 82.

Morse's Geoy.—. . . . We give 2000 Dolls. for the Plates for the Atlas, one half to be paid in six and the other half in 12 months. The maps will print 2000 or 2500 Atlas, to look well, as only 2500 copies have been taken from them.[82]

A few days later Andrews reminded Thomas of the transaction:

I believe we made a good purchase of the Plates for Pinkerton's Geoy. The Copperplate Printers, who printed the Maps for Conrad, sent us on their opinion, (three different persons) that they would print from 2000 to 2500 impressions—and Conrad has engaged to pay for retouching all such maps as will not print 2500 good impressions.[83]

Woodcuts, type metal cuts, and wood engravings also moved from printer to printer and from city to city. Of many examples a few may be mentioned. Woodcuts in *The Pilgrim's Progress* printed by Isaiah Thomas in 1791 were re-used by Joseph Bumstead in Boston for an edition in 1800. Alexander Anderson's type metal cuts for the edition of *The Pilgrim's Progress* issued by John Tiebout in New York in 1804 were re-used for the same title by Joseph Bumstead in Boston two years later.[84] Anderson's wood engravings for *Emblems of Mortality* (1801), used again in 1810, reappear with one block re-engraved in an edition of 1846.[85] At present the stemmata of illustrations are far from completion.

Further research will also disclose more information about the process of engraving. Undoubtedly many illustrations were produced by etching as well as by engraving but the distinction has not received sufficient attention. Nor has the introduction of steel plates been elucidated. First used for currency, steel plates were probably introduced for bookwork about 1810 when a writing book, illustrated with steel plates, was produced by Jacob Perkins and Gideon Fairman.[86] Perkins, an inventor, later constructed a power press, patented on June 29, 1813, for copperplate printing:

1814.—Aug., It was announced that Jacob Perkins of Newburyport, Mass., had effected an improvement in the copperplate printing

[82] Letter of April 7, 1805, in Thomas Papers.
[83] Letter of April 10, 1805, in Thomas Papers.
[84] David E. Smith, "Illustrations of American Editions of *The Pilgrim's Progress* to 1870," *Princeton Univ. Lib. Chron.*, XXVI (1964), 19.
[85] Hamilton, *Early Am. Book Illustrators*, pp. 51, 54, 63–64.
[86] *DAB*, XIV, 472; David McN. Stauffer, *American Engravers upon Copper and Steel* (New York, 1907), Pt. I, 209.

press, which promised great advantage to that branch of mechanics. It had been patented about a year before, and was now in successful operation. It was so constructed as to be impelled by water or other power. Connected with another improvement by Mr. Perkins, in substituting steel for copperplates, it was thought that the price of copperplate printing would be reduced very nearly to that of letter press. It was claimed that this press would give 4000 impressions in 12 hours; the speed of the old press being 500 in the same time.[87]

The Perkins press was one more device to increase production and, as such, was typical of the chief interest of printers during the War of 1812 and in the following depression. Credit being extended rapidly, the easy terms brought speculation and inflation everywhere. New presses of all kinds were built; machine-made paper appeared on the market in 1817; and efficiency was equated with progress. As the leading printers looked for shortcuts as the way to easier money, printing as an art receded and became almost an afterthought.

The continuing problem of reducing time and expense required for colored illustrations was tackled in different ways. Benjamin Dearborn built "an additional apparatus for my printing-press" about 1812 and was able to send Isaiah Thomas a ship's clearance paper as one of "the earliest examples of typographical colouring in this country."[88] Two other examples were a view of Niagara Falls and a plan of Boston. Dearborn, whose inventions included water wheels and scales, evidently forsook the press for the attraction of running steamcars on rails.[89] Dr. Jacob Bigelow utilized the aquatint process for colored illustrations in his *American Medical Botany* (1817–20). He needed sixty plates and sixty thousand colored engravings for the three volumes:

At that time the state of the arts was low and imperfect in this country, and I soon found that I had greatly overrated the ability of my artists and underrated the time and labor necessary to oversee the proceeding of the work. I experienced a considerable struggle between the pride which forbade the abandonment of the undertaking and the apparent impossibility of carrying it to completion.

[87] *List of Patents*, p. 127; Munsell, *Typ. Misc.*, p. 122.
[88] Letter from Benjamin Dearborn to Isaiah Thomas, May 25, 1812, in American Antiquarian Society, Print Collection; Emma F. Waite, "Benjamin Dearborn," *Old-Time New England*, XLII (1951), 47.
[89] Waite, *Old-Time New Eng.*, XLII, 47.

At that period both lithography and photography were unknown. I came to the conclusion that the only mode of extricating myself from the difficulty was to invent some new mode of printing the impressions at once in colors from the copperplates. After many trials and experiments a tolerably successful mode was discovered, which consisted in engraving the plates in *aqua tinta*, thus producing a continuous surface, to the parts of which separate colors could be applied, and the surplus wiped off in different directions, so as not to interfere with each other. In this way the simple plates, or those with few colors, could be delivered from the press complete, without requiring to be retouched. But those which had small or insulated spots were obliged to be finished with the pencil.[90]

In the next paragraph Bigelow shows how quickly a new invention was adopted in that period of change: "The aquatinting of colors, when duly improved, I have no doubt would have passed into profitable use, had not the invention of lithography soon afterwards superseded its employment."[91]

After Bass Otis had produced the first lithographs in the United States, he returned to portrait painting. Barnet & Doolittle, who had learned the new technique in Paris, opened a studio in New York and lithographed the drawings for the October, 1821, issue of the *American Journal of Science and Arts*. Their first lithographed book illustrations appeared in James E. Smith's *A Grammar of Botany*, published by J. V. Seaman of New York in 1822. In the next year James Lovegrove of Baltimore issued *The Timber Merchant's Guide* containing thirty plates lithographed by Henry Stone of Washington. These were the items which introduced lithography to this country. The art became permanently established in this country with the founding in Boston in 1825 of the firm of William S. and John Pendleton; the latter had been a student lithographer in Paris. Within a few years he resigned from the firm, but William Pendleton continued it so successfully that it was the largest and best lithographic firm in the United States when he sold it in 1836.[92] The publication in 1825 of Cadwallader D. Colden's *Memoir at the Celebration of the Completion of the New York Canals* with

[90] Stanley Epstein, "The Earliest American Color Plates," *PaGA*, IV (1956), 45.

[91] *Ibid.*

[92] Charles H. Taylor, "Some Notes on Early American Lithography," *Proc. Am. Ant. Soc.*, n.s., XXXII (1922), 69–71, 74–76.

some plates lithographed by Anthony Imbert is another indication that, as the second quarter of the century began, lithography was becoming an accepted technique.

As reading increased among the new middle class, the presses of the United States stepped up production and more wood engravings were constantly on order. After the formation of the American Tract Society in 1825, the surge of publications issued from its headquarters contained thousands of engravings. The new generation of artists, included seasoned people already at work in the 1820's, such as the talented Joseph A. Adams. The drift of the population to the towns in the first quarter of the nineteenth century and the arrival of the first mass of immigrants increased the available talent. In the city of New York the number of engravers grew steadily: 5 in 1790, 14 in 1800, 16 in 1810, 24 in 1820.[93] In Philadelphia growth was similar: 13 in 1790, 35 in 1800, 42 in 1810, 78 in 1818.[94] Some of these people had other occupations as well, but all were able to engrave.

In typography and illustration the best American printers made slow but definite progress between 1787 and 1825. After the disruption of the Revolution, they settled back into their former static manner of printing books only to find themselves in the midst of strong competition from abroad. To meet this they had to upgrade quality without either the materials or the experience necessary. After the second war with England they suffered the disintegration of purpose that came with inflation and overextension of credit. Although they rarely attained the objective of making a beautiful book, their work improved as resources and skills improved. The sum total of their efforts was an ameliorating effect on the art of printing in a new materialistic America.

[93] Weiss, *Number of Persons and Firms . . . in New York City*, pp. 4–5.
[94] Weiss, *Bull. N.Y. Pub. Lib.*, LVI, 77–79.

APPENDIX AND INDEX

EXAMPLES OF SIZES OF EDITIONS: FROM THE MATHEW CAREY PAPERS

Year	Author	Title	Number of Copies	Carey Papers
1792	Burke, Edmund	*Reflections*	1,000	VI, 2154
1792		*Christian Economy*	1,000	VI, 2074
1793	Cicero	*De Officiis*	1,000	III, 855
1794		*Am. Acad. of Com-pliments*	2,000	VI, 2159
1794	Defoe, Daniel	*Robinson Crusoe*	1,000	IV, 1466
1794	Wollstonecraft, Mary	*A Vindication*	1,500	I, 195
1794	Plowden, F. P.	*A Short History*	1,000	III, 816
1794 (April)	Rowson, S. H.	*Charlotte*	1,000	VI, 2155
1794 (Nov.)	Rowson, S. H.	*Charlotte*	1,500	I, 252
1794	Rowson, S. H.	*The Inquisitor*	1,500	I, 252
1794	Vaughan, William	*Catechism of Man*	1,000	VI, 2159
1795	Goldsmith, Oliver	*History of the Earth*	3,000	VIII, 2687
1795	Russel, Robert	*Seven Sermons*	3,000	IV, 1456
1796	Bunyan, John	*Divine Emblems*	4,250	VIII, 2745
1796	Carey, Mathew	*Address to the House*	500	XIV, 5314
1796	Coxe, Tench	*The Federalist*	500	VIII, 2658
1796	Rousseau, J. J.	*Letters of an Italian Nun*	1,500	VIII, 2745
1796		*The Vocal Companion*	1,500	VIII, 2745
1796	Webster, Noah, Jr.	*The Prompter*	1,500	VIII, 2745
1799	Caldwell, Charles	*An Eulogium*	500	XIII, 4792
1800	Agnew, James	*An Inaugural Disser-tation*	250	XIV, 5135
1800	Carey, Mathew	*The Child's Guide*	3,000	XVI, 6839
1800		*Cinderella*	1,000	XV, 5939
1800	Coxe, J. R.	*A Short View*	250	XIV, 5136
1800	O'Brien, Matthew	*Charity Sermon*	250	XV, 5976
1800		*The Sailor's Medley*	2,000	XV, 5936
1800		*The Syren*	2,000	XV, 5936

Examples of Sizes of Editions (*cont.*)

Year	Author	Title	Number of Copies	Carey Papers
1800	Washington, George	*Farewell Address*	1,000	XV, 5988
1801	Parker, James	*Conductor Generalis*	750	XVII, 7634
1802	Harrison, Ralph	*Rudiments of . . . Grammar*	4,000	XVI, 6871
1806	Carey, Mathew	*Cursory Reflections*	250	XX, 29
1807	Cherry, Andrew	*The Travellers*	1,000	XXIII, 1552
1807		*The Child's Instructor*	1,000	XXI, 593
1807	Dean, Henry	*Hocus Pocus*, 16th ed.	3,000	XXII, 1280
1808	Bunyan, John	*Divine Emblems*	3,500	XXII, 1114
1808	Goldsmith, Oliver	*The Grecian History*	3,000	XXIII, 1575
1809	Challoner, Richard	*Think Well On't*	2,000	XXV, 2468
1809		*Regulations for . . . Troops*	5,000	XXIII, 1521
1810		*The Criminal Recorder*	3,000	XXV, 2468
1811	Reynolds, Frederic	*The Exile*	1,000	XXIV, 2375
1813	Cullen, Margaret	*Home*	1,250	XXVI, 3062
1813		*Tales of Terror*	750	XXVII, 3546

INDEX

The American Printer, 1787–1825

was composed, printed, and bound by
Kingsport Press, Inc., Kingsport, Tennessee.
The plates were printed by
The Meriden Gravure Co.,
Meriden, Connecticut.
The type is Monticello, with
Scotch Roman for the initials.
The paper is Mohawk Superfine.
Design is by Edward G. Foss.